KURUSU

KURUSU

The Price of Progress in a
Japanese Village, 1951-1975

ROBERT J. SMITH

STANFORD UNIVERSITY PRESS

STANFORD, CALIFORNIA

Stanford University Press
Stanford, California

© 1978 by the Board of Trustees of the
Leland Stanford Junior University
Printed in the United States of America

Cloth ISBN 0-8047-0962-9　　　Paper ISBN 0-8047-1060-0
Original edition 1978

Last figure below indicates year of this printing:
88　87　86　85　84　83　82　81　80　79

Original edition published with the assistance
of the Andrew W. Mellon Foundation

This book is dedicated to
the memory of

TAKAO HŌEN

who would have shared much of my surprise
at what has happened to his community

and to

KAZUKO

who spoke for us both when
words failed me

Eight pages of photographs follow p. 166

Contents

Tables

Foreword

"LIFE IN KURUSU, while it exhibits many traditional features, shows also evidence of striking change"—thus Professor Smith, twenty years ago, judiciously concluding the monograph in which he presented one of the most vivid and perceptive of the accounts of Japanese villages in the early fifties. The changes he had in mind were the effects, slowly emerging over half a century, of public education, increased cash cropping, improved transport, greater mobility: households had become much less self-sufficient; extended family ties had diminished in importance; still-remembered customs had been abandoned. "Striking" changes, yes, but not so definitive that their irreversibility did not have to be argued. "It seems virtually certain" was as far as he would go, for instance, in arguing that Shinto and Buddhism would probably not regain their prewar stature as vital religions in Kurusu.

The changes which he records in his present study of Kurusu revisited are of an altogether different order of magnitude. Most of the hamlet's twenty-odd households still count as "farm households" and still have an average of a little over an acre each, divided into a dozen tiny fields; but some have three or four thousand dollars' worth of equipment to work their holding with, and at the same time farming has chiefly become a matter for old men—who give the impression of "puttering about" at it. The younger generation have gone, or commute to jobs elsewhere. The old live longer, more comfortably, but in greater danger of loneliness. Where once possession of a bicycle was a matter of some pride, many families now have two cars. Thatch has long since disappeared; houses have been rebuilt; color television has long since outshone the gilt and jollity of village festivals. In a quarter of a century the boom has carried the people of Kurusu into *and beyond* consumerism. They are now worried about pollution; their schoolchildren are trained to the simple skills and the simple pleasure of sharpening a pencil with a knife, taught to conserve fossil fuels by eschewing the electric sharpener which had become standard classroom equipment.

The fifties were a time when the Kurusu Youth Club earnestly studied a new middle school text on Democracy. The change of which people spoke was sweeping change in laws, institutions, and ideas; hardly at all in farming techniques or the material conditions of life, which changed only slowly. After twenty years it is the material changes which stand out and of which Professor Smith's informants speak most readily. Sometimes they speak despairingly of wholesale change in social relations too—"the young nowadays have *no conception* of filial piety." But the reality is more graduated and subtle.

How much so Professor Smith documents clearly, vividly, and also with feeling, providing a well-rounded account of a not untypical Japanese village which should appeal to a variety of readers. Professional ethnographers can savor the precision and conscientiousness with which he records, for instance, just what the offerings were and who was present at a roof-raising ceremony. Students of social change can find the evolving structures of economic activity or household composition charted in quantified detail. And the ordinary reader can find a sensitive account of a human community by someone who is not afraid to judge, and whose criteria of judgment reflect a warm concern with the quality of human relationships and the same humane ambivalence about material progress that most of us share. The qualities of his writing reflect the nature of his relations with the people of Kurusu. We lose something, perhaps, from his self-denying resolve not to quote any gossip passed on to him by one Kurusu resident about another. But we learn as much as we do about Kurusu residents precisely because the relationship of trust and understanding which Professor Smith and his wife established with them necessarily entailed such scruples.

Studies of "my village twenty years later" usually carry a faint air of disappointment. Few mature anthropologists can recapture the excitement of their first experience of fieldwork—or prevent themselves from half expecting to be able to do so. One gets occasional glimpses of such disappointment in the present book, but Professor Smith avoids projecting them into an easy romantic nostalgia for the snows of yesteryear. There is no elegy for the loss of quaint simplicities, of the colorful customs and the simpler, purer pleasures of the Kurusu of 1951. He is offended, to be sure, by the spoliation of the Inland Sea, but he is equally offended by those who deny the real increase in popular welfare which that spoliation has brought, particularly the middle-class urban zero-growthers in whose praise of lost simplicities and scorn of vulgar mass-produced pleasures he rightly discerns a certain snobbish contempt for farmers who have got above their proper station. He approves of the greater freedom of the young; at the same time he does not conceal his distaste for the insensitively selfish way that freedom is sometimes used.

Where he does give way to nostalgia, perhaps, is in his saddened discussion of the way Kurusu as a community "came unstuck" in vehement dispute over the rights and wrongs of inviting a broiler fowl enterprise to build its factory in the village. An affair of this kind points up the difficulty of community studies. It is not only that Kurusu is enmeshed in the national economy and polity. Kurusu culture is at once a part of a national Japanese culture, a local version of it, and influenced by it. The cohesive Kurusu of the early fifties still reflected a prewar Japan in which overt protest against authority was outlawed as a manifestation of bad thoughts. Kurusu in the seventies was part of a nation in which the role of the protestor—what Professor Smith refers to at one point as "the new style of open and angry verbal confrontation"—had been accepted and institutionalized (even, as a Marcuse would say, by repressive tolerance contained). Without this availability of the protestor role, and without the national press concern with environmental pollution, one can be sure that his Clover affair would never have attained the proportions that it did. Professor Smith tells us of the posters, the demonstrations, the stone-throwing. No doubt there were also barricades, armbands, sweatbands tied tightly around foreheads—the whole protest idiom.

But conflict on television between cohorts of police and students is one thing; a similar style and intensity of conflict within face-to-face communities like Kurusu is quite another, and it is not too difficult to understand why, as Professor Smith suggests, the people of Kurusu should feel "ashamed" at having let things go so far. But the fact is that they did *and* managed to patch things up again. The new generation of Kurusu residents, one could argue, are not only less "involved" in their community by virtue of their more widely ramifying ties outside the village but also, by some definitions of maturity, more mature. Their repertoire of personal relations no longer consists of the all-or-nothing alternatives of living in each other's laps in total harmony or violently "speaking bitterness." They can, as Americans say, "handle" conflict. Which is, I suppose, a good augury for Japanese society as a whole.

At least it is a good augury as long as people continue to *care* about maintaining friendly relations with their fellow men as well as with putting on their sweatbands to stand up for their rights or for justice. Veblen wrote some sixty years ago about "Japan's opportunity." He meant an opportunity to carve out an empire. Industrialization was gradually increasing Japan's potential strength in military hardware. It was also inexorably breeding individualism and gradually sapping the feudal cohesiveness which was a precondition for invincible military fanaticism. The 1920's, he thought, would see the point of optimum trade-off between the two trends.

Perhaps the present represents an opportunity in another sense. The Japanese economy is capable of delivering an increasing level of material affluence. The trends to selfishness and egotistical self-assertion which Professor Smith discerns in some of the younger generation have still not quite eroded a widespread and responsible concern for community (and for the weaker members of the community) either in Kurusu or in the macro-community of the nation. Perhaps this is the point of optimum trade-off between the rising trend of prosperity and the declining trend of community. Japan now has acquired the material means, and still retains the will, to establish and entrench the institutions of a humane and caring society which ensures a decent quality of life for all its citizens. We shall look forward to having Professor Smith chart its progress in that direction with another, equally sensitive and perceptive look at Kurusu in twenty years' time.

R. P. DORE

Preface

MY FIRST period of research in Kurusu in 1951–52 was supported by a grant from the Social Science Research Council. I went to Japan, then still under Allied occupation, as an associate of the Center for Japanese Studies of the University of Michigan. Many people were very kind to me, but I must acknowledge a special debt to the late Robert B. Hall, Sr., and to John W. Hall, now of Yale University. My return trip to Kurusu in 1975 was made possible through the generosity of Cornell University.

Many people have commented on earlier versions of the manuscript. For their patient and exemplary criticisms I wish particularly to thank Harumi Befu, L. Keith Brown, John B. Cornell, R. P. Dore, and Davydd J. Greenwood. Renée Pierce wrestled mightily with the draft and emerged triumphant with an impeccably typed manuscript. The Stanford University Press has once again provided the kind of help that every author needs. I am especially grateful to J. G. Bell and Peter Kahn, and to my editor Gene Tanke.

The foreigner conducting research in Japan is invariably the recipient of innumerable kindnesses. Among the many people who have been especially helpful to me over the years, I must single out my old friend Satoh Tetsuo, whose assistance in the first study was of inestimable value, and to all members of the Takao family, who have always made me welcome in their home on my visits to Kurusu.

My wife Kazuko was an equal partner in the 1975 restudy, but I have been unable to persuade her to accept coauthorship of this book. Her help and criticism during this project, as in all my undertakings, were indispensable.

A word is in order on some of the conventions adopted in this book. I have given all personal names in Japanese order, with the surname first, and have used the modified Hepburn system for romanizing Japanese words. Unless otherwise noted, all national and prefectural statistics are taken from the *Japan Statistical Yearbook*, published annually by the Bureau of Statistics, Office of the Prime Minister, Government of Japan. To avoid cluttering the text with figures, I have generally given wages, salaries, and costs of goods and services in *yen* alone. For comparative purposes, the reader may note that the exchange rate was fixed at 360 *yen* to one U.S. dollar from 1949 through August 1971, and that for the next six years it held at about 300 to one.

A special note on the matter of weights and measures. All recent Japanese publications have used the metric system, and by 1975 metric measures had almost completely displaced the old Japanese weights and measures that all Kurusu farmers had used in 1951. I have accordingly followed the new usage, except where conversion to acres and square yards serves to emphasize a relationship or draw a contrast for American and British readers. For convenience, the measures used most often in the text are given below:

Japanese	U.S.	Metric
1 *tsubo*	3.95 square yards	3.31 square meters
1 *tan*	.245 acre	9.92 ares
1 *chō* (10 *tan*)	2.45 acres	.992 hectare
1 *gō*	.384 pint	.18 liter
1 *shō*	1.92 quarts	1.8 liters

In 1975 everyone discussed farmland in terms of units of 10 ares rather than *tan*, but because of their similarity (1 *tan* = 9.92 ares) I have used the two measures interchangeably. American readers should bear in mind that both represent about a quarter of an acre. It will be helpful in understanding the scale of things if the reader keeps in mind that the average size of a Japanese farm family's holding is about nine-tenths of one acre (37 ares), whereas the average size of the American farm is about 200 acres. Building size is still expressed in terms of the number of *tsubo* of floor space. The average dwelling in Kurusu is about 20 *tsubo*, or about half the size of a typical American house with a floor area of about 1,500 square feet.

R.J.S.

KURUSU

Introduction

THIS BOOK is about a place called Kurusu and the people who live there. I first came to know them in 1951 and I last saw them in 1975. Because restudies in anthropology are still uncommon, if no longer rare, I should like to explain how I came to undertake this one, and why I decided to write about Kurusu in the way I have. In telling its story I have perhaps revealed more about their affairs than some of its residents would have wished, yet I know of no other way to communicate the quality of life in a place like this and the transformations it has undergone in the past quarter-century.

The author of a restudy usually begins with a previously published report, either his own or one by another person, to which he adds his newly collected materials. There are several ways to proceed, and the author's choice from among them is ultimately dictated by some combination of his personal preferences, the points he wishes to emphasize, and the nature of his material. (See the Bibliography for a short list of works that exemplify various approaches.) I have decided to write an entirely new book rather than to reissue previously published materials largely because I want to reconsider what I thought I knew about the place in 1951–52 in light of what I have learned about it during my most recent stay there in the summer of 1975.

It is tempting to cast a work such as this in the idiom of self-discovery. I have not found it difficult to resist this temptation, however, for I feel strongly that Kurusu and its people deserve something better than to serve as a mirror in which I may try to glimpse my own reflection. Readers who prefer their community studies straight may wish to skip the section on my personal involvement, although reading

it, I think, will do them no permanent harm. I offer the following remarks because I do not want to obscure the body of the account by
setting myself at the center of the narrative, which is not mine, after
all, but theirs. Unless he is hopelessly insensitive, anyone who returns
to a place he once knew well after nearly a quarter of a century will
inevitably discover some things about himself. The question is whether
the experience is of such intrinsic interest or value that it need be made
central to the analysis of the materials he has collected. I feel strongly
that the experience should *not* serve as the framework for a report of
this kind. In a day when narcissism has been elevated to the status of
an ideology, it is well to reflect on the considerable advantage of dis-
tancing one's self from the subject of inquiry.

I have therefore taken some pains to remove myself from most of the
action, believing that those who read this book in years to come will
not care very much about the interior states of its author. Nevertheless, I am bound to point out that my stance is in some ways a highly
partisan one. So that the reader will not have to keep his eye exclusively on me rather than on the people of Kurusu, I will state my bias
as clearly as I can. The farmers of Japan, and not the small-holders
alone, have been badly dealt with by their government. While they
have been treated very well indeed by the standards of Asian countries
generally, in comparison to other occupational groups in Japan they
have suffered economically, socially, and politically. It was only in
1960, after all, that the gap between the incomes of farmers and blue-
collar workers finally all but disappeared.

Moreover, the agricultural population, almost always at the low end
of the per-capita income scale, is regularly buffeted by an agricultural
policy that is well-meaning but often either incompetent or insensitive.
In all fairness, it must be pointed out that the entire blame for the
swings of policy cannot be laid to government indecision alone. In the
years immediately following the end of World War II, the government
encouraged production in a desperate effort to secure enough food for
the population of Japan. The farmers bent every effort to raise yields
and increase the amount of land under cultivation, and suddenly there
was too much rice. The series of bumper crops in the late 1960's led
to the adoption of a policy designed to take some land out of rice production altogether. The farmer would be paid not to grow rice—a concept I had discussed with a group of farmers in 1951, at which time

they found it completely incomprehensible. Then came the worldwide shortage of grains, and once again the Japanese farmer was asked to produce more rice. Despite all of these sharp swings from one extreme to another, the response of the farmer has been one of remarkable equanimity. Why should this be so?

The question raises a problem in writing about Japan that bears brief examination here. In the most general sense, it may be said that there are two strongly contrasting views of the character of that society. One holds that Japan is a restrictive and repressive society in which smoldering conflict is kept damped down only by the most odious forms of coercion. Proponents of this view sometimes maintain that dissent and outbreaks of violent opposition to established authority are common occurrences which are glossed over or concealed by the authorities, who are always at pains to foster the illusion that Japan is a harmonious and tranquil state. In this reading of the situation, the lives of working-class persons, including the farmers, are bitter, short, and brutish, and those of their exploiters, though equally brutish, are far more comfortable than they deserve.

The other perspective has it that to an extent rarely encountered in other industrial nations Japan really is a tranquil and harmonious society. These observers point out that not only are the indices of social disorder, such as rates of felonious crime, delinquency, divorce, and so on, remarkably low, but that many of them have remained stable or even declined in the past fifteen to twenty years. By world standards life expectancy for both men and women is very high, and the conveniences of everyday life are now almost universal, in a society where only a few years ago possession of even a radio was a luxury not yet attained by the majority of the population.

I raise this issue because I want to make my own position clear. However relatively deprived they may once have been, the people of Kurusu have never lived in abject misery. They neither fear the police nor commit serious crimes. Their health is generally excellent, and although they work very hard indeed, their lives are neither short nor brutish, and they are not dehumanized by their enthusiastic participation in Japan's consumer revolution. It is a tribute to their resilience and their essential graciousness that despite all the vicissitudes of their lives since the end of World War II they remain generally optimistic, cheerful, and civil. They are by no means paragons of virtue, of course.

There are among them the vain and greedy as well as the modest and generous, the hostile and frustrated as well as the acquiescent and passive. But it is not a cruel place; no one goes in fear of physical violence. The members of all its households can expect that in times of crisis others will rally round to help them out. As we shall see, even when the fabric of community life seems close to coming apart, these people still manage to activate the old hamlet-centered social usages which have for so long bound them together.

Because Kurusu is so small a place, I have kept some of its secrets. Almost all of them are known to virtually everyone in the hamlet, I suspect, but I can see no reason to give them wider currency. I once thought that I should respect confidences at least in part because only the speaker and I shared the knowledge that he was passing on to me. I am now convinced that this assumption was wholly in error. The anthropologist is far less likely to turn up information potentially damaging to his informants than some would have us believe. It is not entirely clear to me why it has been claimed with such urgency that anthropologists are privy to secrets, or that in the normal course of events they come into possession of uniquely threatening information. I strongly suspect that the claim serves largely to compensate for feelings of powerlessness on the part of the anthropologist, and to inflate his relatively unimportant role in the communities where he works.

To give an illustration from my own experience, when I was writing up the materials from my 1951–52 research, I deliberately suppressed all the information I had collected on black-market sales of rice. My reasoning was, I suppose, that in the unlikely event that what I had written were to be read by any person in a position of authority in Japan, he would learn nothing of this illegal activity by Kurusu residents from me. I now realize that the authorities were well aware of the black-market dealings in rice; in fact, they knew a great deal more about them than I could ever have hoped to learn, and for good reason. Grad (1952:33) points out that on paper the amount of land planted in grains, beans, peas, and potatoes actually *declined* by an incredible 595,200 hectares between 1939 and 1946. The reason was not that the farmers were concealing information from the authorities; it was that the local authorities were concealing the actual planted acreages from the central government. Crops from these unreported

fields could be excluded from the stringent national requisition program, thus providing more food for the prefecture's own population
and increasing the chances for profiteering by the local authorities
themselves. So much for my effort to protect my informants.

Yet there are limits beyond which I do not wish to go. Gossip is a
favorite pastime of some people in the community, and although its
purveyors and its subjects are about equally aware of this aspect of
their relationship, I have chosen not to report here what any resident
of Kurusu told me about another. The only exceptions are some of the
categorical denunciations made publicly in connection with the Clover
affair, which is discussed in detail in Chapter Eight. In order to blur
things a bit, therefore, I have taken a few liberties with the placement
of dwellings and the directions of roads and paths, as well as with
family composition and life histories. None of this information is
completely falsified, however, nor does it do such violence to the truth
of the matter as to distort the record in any substantive way.

It is not my intention to suggest that Kurusu stands for all of
postwar rural Japan (see Ishino 1962 and Norbeck 1961 for two early
commentaries on more general postwar changes), nor do I think it
profitable to pause long over the question of its representativeness.
Kurusu is representative to the extent that there is almost nothing in
the record of the past twenty-five years that would seem particularly
odd to anyone who knows rural Japan. At the very least, the materials
that follow would draw the comment, "Oh, so it's *that* kind of place."
Which is to say that its local festivals have been almost completely
abandoned (see Suenari 1972 for an account of the decline of ritual
between 1962 and 1971 in a community in northeastern Japan); that a
high proportion of its adult residents work outside the village; that
most of its children now graduate from higher-school; that very little
of its paddy-field land has been sold for other uses; that most families
have at least one automobile, a color television set, and many other
household electrical appliances; and that as its population has declined
the number of separate family residences has increased. Agriculture
has become less and less important as a source of family income, and
every year it accounts for a smaller fraction of the total. Nonetheless,
few families have given it up altogether, and it is one of the wonders of
the present that most of them have kept on farming. The agricultural

households cooperate on fewer and fewer occasions, and in recent years each of them has tried to assemble its own privately owned array of agricultural machinery. There has been no consolidation of lowland or upland paddy fields, and many of the upland fields have simply been abandoned.

It will doubtless seem to some readers that the picture of Kurusu we give dwells too exclusively on the decline of community and the disintegration of old bonds between its households. It could be argued that because the focus is on this smallest social unit of Japanese society, we have failed to see the emergence of integration within units of larger scale, such as the district or region. We would not deny the force of the charge, but that is not what we have set out to do. Kurusu is a very small place that once played a major role in the lives of all of its residents. How it has come to decline in importance, and how its residents have both precipitated that decline and dealt with its consequences, seem to us fully as interesting as the nature of their involvement with ever-larger social and economic entities.

The direction of change has never been in doubt, but it bears remarking that its pace has been far from uniform. When I went back to Kurusu in 1955 and 1958, nothing seemed to have altered much. In 1963, however, there were two passenger cars parked by the sawmill —the first ones I had ever seen in the hamlet. The shock was not lessened by the realization that one of them was an American car—a "Henry J"! Otherwise, visible change was minimal. There were many people about, and most of the houses looked pretty much as they had when I first saw them. The situation was much the same in 1968, but by 1972 it was clear that there had been dramatic and far-reaching changes. The turning-point had come in the very late 1960's and the early 1970's.

One hot afternoon in 1975, with the ubiquitous electric fan stirring the humid air but failing to cool the room, I was sitting in the Town Office with two or three men looking at the photographs of Kurusu I had taken when I had first been there. Almost every picture evoked some comment, and when we had finished one of the men looked at me and said, "You were here just as it was all coming to an end, weren't you?" He was referring primarily to the technology shown in the pictures. Many of the agricultural implements of 1951 are com-

pletely unknown to young people today; work cows, which I had pho-
tographed with an avidity that puzzles me now, are no longer to be
seen anywhere in the area. And, of course, he had been quick to notice
the absence of many things as well—there were no automobiles or
motorcycles on the hamlet road, and no electric fans, refrigerators, or
television sets in the households. Most of the houses had thatched
roofs, and there were no paved roads or paths.

In 1951 the people of Kurusu were a very long way from recovering
from the disaster of World War II, and the beginning of the economic
boom that was to lead to their present level of prosperity was years in
the future. Indeed, it was not until 1952 that the Japanese standard of
living of the mid-1930's was regained after the disastrous decline following the end of World War II. What had been ending in 1951 was
an agricultural way of life with a very long history indeed. I am not,
with that statement, joining the purveyors of the cliché that the Japanese farmer then tilled the soil as his ancestors had done since time
immemorial. Unlike his ancestors, after all, he had access to electric
power, kerosene, gasoline and oil, and chemical fertilizers, but he did
use some implements that appear in drawings and paintings centuries
old, and he shared with his ancestors an attitude toward the land that
made it much more than just the means by which he gained his livelihood.

That way of life and those attitudes have by no means been entirely
swept away. The pattern of the fields is not much altered, and the old
house-sites have changed little, although many of the buildings are
new and some of the old ones sport new roofs and television antennas.
And, as the Japanese proverb has it, even if the country is ruined, the
mountains remain (*kuni horobite sanka ari*), and every morning of
their lives the people of Kurusu look across the paddy fields, beyond
the river and the highway that separate them from the nearest settlement, to the mountains in the west. In the evening, the same shadows
fall across the hamlet, for here at least the ravages of the mountain-
levelers that have altered so many urban and some rural landscapes in
Japan are as yet virtually unknown.

The travel posters we saw in the summer of 1975 that touted Shikoku as "The Green Island of Japan" were part of an ambitious effort to

attract Japanese tourists seeking what is left of the natural beauty of their country. As it happens, most of Shikoku is beautiful still, especially the mountainous areas of the interior, where the population, always thin, has declined precipitously in the past decade. The full scale of the depredations wrought in the course of Japan's postwar economic development can also be seen on the island, however, especially along the northern coasts that border the Inland Sea, but great areas of it remain little explored or exploited by outsiders.

In 1951 the only way of reaching Shikoku was by the boat or ferry lines that linked it to the main island of Honshu and the southern island of Kyushu. The traveler can now fly in by commercial plane, but no bridges yet connect it with the rest of the country (see Map 1). Most of the water craft move through the Inland Sea, itself an extraordinarily beautiful body of water dotted with innumerable islands, providing views of far mountain ranges and great expanses of seascape.

Twenty-five years ago the hour-long Japanese National Railways ferry run from the port of Uno on Honshu to the city of Takamatsu in Kagawa Prefecture was a delight (see Map 2). While Uno itself was an unlovely town, the view from the ferry as it swung out into the main channel was of a succession of small islands of greatly varied shapes, some graced with gnarled plum and pine trees, others so dry that they were almost completely barren. Once past Onigashima, the island that claims to be the place where the legendary boy-hero Momotaro subdued the demons, the ferry slowed for its entrance into Takamatsu harbor. The small fishing boats were always much thicker here, but there were almost no freighters such as could be seen occasionally further out to sea. All along the shoreline up toward the great headland of Yashima were extensive salt fields. Ahead, just beyond the crowded ferry and railway station, could be seen the remains of Takamatsu castle, one of the rare seaside castles of the Tokugawa period (1615–1868), with its classic bent and twisted pines silhouetted against the sky.

Twenty-five years later, the crossing of the Inland Sea provides a vastly different prospect. Wherever the coastline has proved suitable, land reclamation projects have been carried out. On these great flat extensions of the land have been built industrial and marine installations of all kinds—petrochemical plants, oil refineries and storage

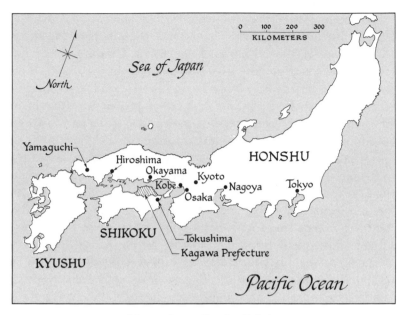

Map 1. Japan, Showing Shikoku

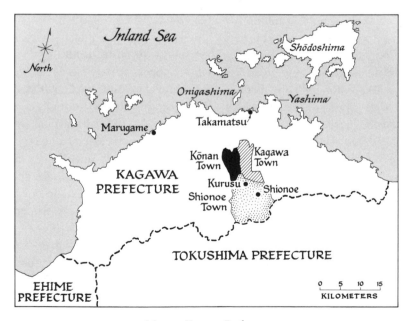

Map 2. Kagawa Prefecture

tanks, deepwater berths for tankers and freighters—all of which discharge their wastes into the air and into the waters of the sea. As a consequence, the Inland Sea has begun to die. On the very hot, humid and windless days of midsummer the view from the ferry is a nightmare. There are few fishing boats left, for most of the marine life that survives is inedible, but through the yellow-brown smog that blankets the entire passage on such a day one can see that there has been an enormous increase in the volume of commercial shipping. On a few islands the vegetation has died off completely, not from lack of water, but from the effects of pollutants discharged by the industrial plants that are everywhere up and down the coasts. Even the islands cannot be seen clearly any more, unless the ferry passes close by them. Over it all hangs a pale sun, sometimes a faint yellow, sometimes a pinkish orange, in whose diffused light objects cast no shadows. Onigashima remains, its identity proclaimed by a huge billboard, but the great evaporation beds of the salt fields have long since been converted to landfills for industrial and marine use. The trees of the castle grounds, still a public park, are almost completely obscured by the high-rise buildings near the harbor, and the Japan National Railways station, unlovely as ever, is infinitely more crowded than it used to be.

To make a crossing of the Inland Sea for the first time, perhaps on a day after an early autumn typhoon has cleared the air and stirred the filthy water to a semblance of white-capped purity, may still be the occasion for the enjoyment of great natural beauty. In the perspective of twenty-five years, however, the crossing is an infuriating reminder of the heedlessness of those who have poisoned the air and the water, seeing in every fair prospect only another place to erect a smokestack.

The Inland Sea was, then, a lovely place in 1951, and all the islands of Japan were green. Those who wonder why this was the case do not have far to look to find the answer to their question. The wartime destruction of Japanese industry, the sinking of virtually her entire merchant fleet, the shortage of fuels of every kind, and almost complete absence of passenger automobiles—these were the features of the country's situation that combined to make for an idyllic environment. It did not make for an idyllic life. The cost of pure air and water was very great, for people were hungry and enervated by extremely long working hours and poor nutrition. The standard of living had sunk far below the level of the prewar years. Life was very hard, and made worse because there seemed little prospect that it would improve.

Since those immediate post-surrender years, much has changed for the better. In terms of the individual's life expectancy, material comfort, and economic well-being, there can be no doubt as to which is the preferable time. No one who remembers 1951 clearly would willingly give up what 1975 has to offer. There are some who would wish that the present had taken a somewhat different form, but even they would not choose to return to the past as an alternative.

As we shall see, the Kurusu of 1975 also presents a picture drained of some of its earlier beauty. The consumer revolution has hit with a vengeance. Ubiquitous engines fill the air with noise and smell, and there are so many *things* now that not all of them can or need be recycled. Occasionally one can even see a junked household appliance standing outside a dwelling. The interiors are crowded with appliances and furnishings that are most remarkable for all being new. To a jaundiced American eye, it may appear that the people of Kurusu are the victims of runaway consumer-oriented production of goods and services. But their view of what has happened, I submit, is very different. It has been eloquently summarized for another population by the late Anthony Crosland, then Foreign Secretary of the British Labour Government (quoted in Rustin 1976:72):

My working-class constituents have their own version of the environment . . . which calls for economic growth. They want lower housing densities and better schools and hospitals. They want washing machines and refrigerators to relieve domestic drudgery. They want cars, and the freedom they give on weekends and holidays. And they want the package-tour holidays to Majorca, even if this means more noise of night flights and eating fish and chips on previously secluded beaches—why should they too not enjoy the sun? And they want these things not . . . because their minds have been brainwashed and their tastes contrived by advertising, but because the things are desirable in themselves.

Indeed, they *are* desirable, and the farmers of Kurusu want them or things very like them. They are likely to find as fatuous as I do the statement attributed to the President of Keidanren, the Federation of

Economic Organizations, in *Newsweek*, May 24, 1976: "As we look at the Western civilization we imported into Japan, we find that we placed too much emphasis on material progress, which is alien to Japanese culture. Now is the time to change this." A man who enjoys the kinds of comforts and perquisites that go with such a position may feel that now is the time to reduce consumption, but a farmer who has struggled all his life to maintain a decent standard of living—and sometimes fallen short of that—will continue to find "material progress" a worthwhile goal.

CHAPTER ONE

Shionoe Town

ON HIS RETURN from Nagasaki to Batavia in 1813, Dr. D. Ainslee wrote: "In Japan the Government pervades and animates every fibre of the frame of society, it identifies itself with its Subjects, and every Individual of its numerous population moves by its impulse" (Raffles 1971:155). These are the words of a shrewd observer, and we begin our account of Kurusu with a discussion of the town of which it is a part, for it is the government of Shionoe Town that most often administers the national and prefectural policies which extensively affect the lives of the people of Kurusu.

First, however, a brief explanation of the administrative context is in order. In 1951 the hamlet (*buraku*) of Kurusu was one of the 54 sub-units called *ko-aza* that made up Yasuhara Village (*mura*). There were 37 hamlets in the village, some of them so large that they contained two or three *ko-aza*. In the case of Kurusu the social and administrative units were coterminous. To handle its relationships with the village government and the office of the Agricultural Cooperative, the other chief administrative device by means of which national policies are carried out at the local level, Kurusu was required to select three officeholders. They were the hamlet head, a person responsible for collecting certain taxes, and an agricultural affairs liaison representative. Since the enactment of a 1953 law calling for consolidation of small administrative units, Yasuhara Village has disappeared. In 1956 most of it was incorporated into what is now Shionoe Town (*chō*). (See *Shionoe-chō shi . . .* 1970.) Kurusu lies in the area usually known as the lower Yasuhara district of the town. The old Yasuhara Village

Office was made the new Shionoe Town Office, and since it lies just across the river from Kurusu, no new problems of accessibility or new inconveniences have arisen as a consequence of the amalgamation program, both causes for complaints commonly heard in areas where the old village offices have been downgraded or closed altogether. Shionoe Town is located in Kagawa County, Kagawa Prefecture (see Map 3).

In 1975 the bulk of the town budget came from the national and prefectural governments, and its tax revenues accounted for only a fraction of its obligations. Because it had been designated a *kasochitai* (severely depopulated area), the town is eligible for participation in many special development programs and can borrow funds from the national treasury on terms so favorable as to represent almost an outright gift. Some of the many measures taken to try to stem the outflow of residents are discussed in the town's development plan, which will be paraphrased at length in a moment. A kind of chamber of commerce office has been established to organize the small shopkeepers whose stores are all concentrated along the highway. The larger businesses belong, too, but they are less involved in chamber activities, which are directed largely at helping small businesses make a go of it in the face of declining populations. The office has also been interested in promoting local industrial development, a complex task made even more difficult by the rise of public concern about the dangers of pollution. There has been increasing emphasis on attracting enterprises that are basically quiet and clean operations. There is good reason to be concerned, for the Kōtō River that borders Kurusu on the west is no longer safe for swimming, and the fireflies, which almost disappeared a few years ago, have only recently begun to come back in any numbers. The area used to be famous for a freshwater fish called *inago*, which during the food shortage of the immediate postwar years some people caught to feed to the children, for they are very rich in calcium. Today they have nearly died out and no one will eat those that do survive.

One of the most notable changes in the area is the paving of the roads. In Kurusu even mere trails have been asphalted. In his first successful campaign, the present mayor ran on a promise to pull the town out of the mud, and he has been returned to office partly as a result of carrying through on that commitment. Much of the cost of this pro-

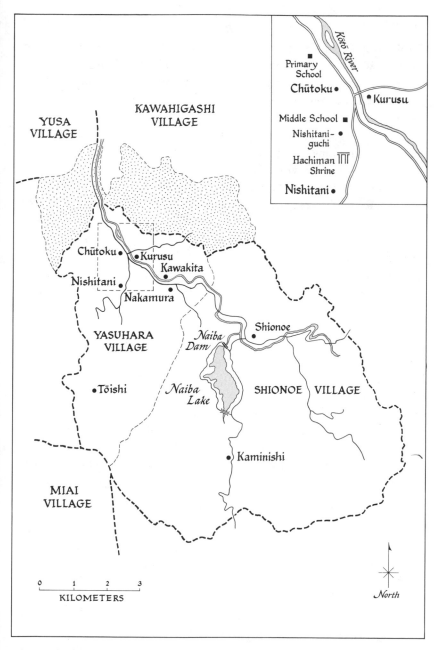

Map 3. Shionoe Town. The town incorporates the former Shionoe Village and lower Yasuhara Village. The dotted area represents the part of Yasuhara Village not included in Shionoe Town.

gram was borne by the national and prefectural governments, of course, with the aim of making it possible for people to commute to work in all weather, thus stabilizing the population to some degree.

Nevertheless, the entire area from Shionoe Town south toward the mountains is severely depopulated. The traveler will be deceived about the true state of affairs if he sticks to the main roads, for only the narrow strip along the highway has held its own and even developed a bit since 1951. Everywhere else the countryside is emptying out.

When the young people begin to pull out of the remote districts, the older ones tend to stay on for a while, but as they weaken physically and can no longer carry on alone, they follow one or another of their married children to the city. "They always say that they will stay here and die in their ancestral home," a young man told us, "but they don't. Most sell their house and fields to their neighbors and move away. You'll see them back at *o-bon*, when they return to visit the family graves. Usually they stay two or three days with relatives—everyone has relatives in the country—and then they go back to the city." Traditionally it has been held that the spirits of the dead return to their proper earthly homes at *o-bon*; today they are joined by the living, who themselves have left the family house and land for another kind of life altogether.

In 1974 the Shionoe Town Office issued a special report entitled "Plan for the Development of the Depopulated Region, Shionoe Town." An invaluable document, both for the data it contains and for its tone, it is abridged and paraphrased here in the interests of highlighting its major themes.

Only 7 percent of the land in our town is arable. A little over half is in wet-rice paddy fields and the remainder is dry fields where crops such as tea, flowers, nursery stock, and fruits are grown. The two kinds of agricultural land are unevenly distributed in the three sub-districts of Shionoe Town: the farm land in the Yasuhara area [where Kurusu is located] is mostly paddy; in the Shionoe area the land is about half paddy and half dry fields; in Kaminishi, it is mostly dry fields.

The average household has about 50 ares of land, but yields are low because the area is so hilly, the weather so cool, and the fields so fragmented. In our town, the average farm household's annual income is only ¥1,500,000, 75 percent of the average for Kagawa Prefecture as a whole. These figures represent income from all sources, including agriculture. The average per-capita income for a family with four working members is ¥370,000 in Shionoe Town. In Kagawa Prefecture the more usual case is the family with three working members and an annual per-capita income of ¥620,000. About three-quarters of our farm families depend on outside employment.

The situation in forestry is perhaps even more bleak. Ninety percent of the owners of forest land in Shionoe Town have fewer than five hectares. Charcoal making, once very important here, has almost disappeared. Those households that depend on forestry for their livelihood have either changed occupations or have moved away. There is no chance of a revival of the charcoal industry, and the reforestation projects have concentrated exclusively on varieties of trees suitable for lumber. In any event, the reforested areas are so recently planted that income from lumbering will remain very small for many years to come.

Because all local industries are of such small scale, it is virtually impossible for a household to derive an adequate income from one of them alone. As a result there is great diversification of any one family's subsistence activities.

It is imperative that we develop this area in order to attract tourists. The population density is low and we hope to keep the natural beauty unimpaired. For the past five years we have been improving the roads in the town, but much remains to be done to open up the more remote scenic and forest areas.

Goals. Both employment opportunities and the income level of the people in our town must be increased. To accomplish this aim, we have adopted a five-point program:

1. Improvement of the quality of working conditions in the local factories.

2. As alternatives to rice, to promote the cultivation of such crops as tea, flowers, nursery stock, and vegetables. Because it is cooler here than it is down on the plain, it should be possible to grow vegetables that can be marketed at good prices after the summer glut. A major problem in converting from rice to other crops, however, is that they require different kinds of irrigation techniques, which are very costly.

3. Capitalize on Shikoku's reputation as a place where tourists from the cities can discover something of the atmosphere of the *inaka* [this virtually untranslatable word is usually rendered "countryside" in English, but it means much more, including a way of life that is increasingly likely to be defined as "traditional" and therefore "Japanese"]. One possibility is to promote the growing of pick-it-yourself crops such as strawberries, mushrooms, chestnuts, and so on. We should emphasize the slogan *midori-taiyo-furusato* (greenery-sunshine-the old home place).

4. Develop the production of so-called "mountain vegetables" (*sansai*) like burdock, fern shoots, mushrooms, etc., with the slogan "Wild plants for your table."

5. Promote the development of recreational facilities that will exploit the beauties of our natural environment, such as hot-springs, hiking and nature trails, camping areas, and so on.

Accomplishments and Targets. The town roads are now 57 percent paved. In five years we plan to have paved 70 percent of them. So far, none of the agricultural roads (*nōdō*) or forestry roads (*rindō*) is paved. The five-year target is 20 percent for both.

In 1960 the town installed a universal broadcast relay system (*yūsen*) in every house. In 1972 the telephone system was put in. It became fully automatic in 1974 and 99 percent of the houses in the town are on it, the only exceptions being those located in extremely isolated spots. [The installation of the telephone system reflects the government's policy of providing amenities to residents of areas *because* they are losing population. There are, in fact, many settlements between Shionoe and Takamatsu where telephones are less common because there are no special funding programs that can be tapped by their local governments.]

In order to raise the standard of living, the town government must exert itself in several directions:

1. Education. The educational level here is low by national standards. Only 70 percent of our middle-school graduates go on to higher-schools. The facilities have been greatly improved, but we need more and better teaching materials at all levels. In recent years the auditoriums and swimming pools [all schools have pools now] have come to be used more and more by the general public, but we still need a community center and better sports facilities.

2. Health Care. The nearest hospital [operated by the prefecture and located in neighboring Kagawa Town] has no emergency facilities. All of our local physicians are aging and there is little hope of securing replacements for them. The people have been asking for a local clinic staffed by a doctor and a nurse, but it will be very difficult to satisfy this demand. Since we now must transport patients to the hospital the town needs a real ambulance or a clinic on wheels.

3. Human Waste Disposal. At present Shionoe has joined with the towns of Kagawa and Kōnan to deal with this problem, but the present holding facility cannot be used much longer. We must either develop a different one elsewhere or find an entirely new method of disposal.

4. Garbage Collection and Disposal. At present garbage is collected and buried in a landfill. But space for this purpose is severely limited and new disposal methods must be sought at once.

5. Drinking Water. In 1973 the town installed a vinyl-hose water system in 500 houses [including those in Kurusu]. The remaining households still use wells or streams. The service should be extended to all areas where the terrain is suitable.

6. Fire Protection. The town badly needs a new fire engine. At present we have only three small water pumps, fifteen hydrants, and twenty-six storage ponds. We need more of all of these. A major problem is that all of the volunteer firemen are getting old; young men cannot be counted on because they are away at work outside the town and cannot respond to alarms during the day.

7. Care for the Elderly. We must do everything in our power to improve the welfare of the old people of the town. Fortunately, we do have hot springs and the town government has been developing them [they are in fact a favorite kind of recreation spot for the elderly all over Japan]. We have also been promoting the cultivation of flowers and dwarfed trees, which old people can enjoy raising and from which they may derive some income.

There are several steps the town must take for the future:

1. Coordinate agricultural development. It is essential that farmers cooperate more in order to increase the efficiency of the farming operation. Both agriculture and forestry are on too small a scale here and new methods must be introduced in an effort to rationalize the exploitation of the land. The basic system of rice cultivation cannot be altered, but we must encourage crop diversification.

2. Promote the nursery business, with emphasis on cut flowers and ornamental plants. The carnation-*danchi* which was brought into town in 1974 is an example of tourist-oriented horticulture (*kankō nōgyō*). [It is hard to see how the author of this report came to this conclusion and harder to see why tourists would drive for miles to see acres of carnations blooming in scores of vast greenhouses.] Much more can be done along these lines and there are plans to promote the cultivation of rhododendron, which grow very well in this climate.

3. Improve the situation in forestry. The individual holdings of forest lands are so small that the owners will have to be organized and guided in the planting of different varieties of trees in accordance with the demands of a changing market. For example, broadleaf trees such as the two varieties of oak called *nara* and *kunugi* were once important for charcoal, but now are used only for growing *shītake* (a kind of cultivated mushroom). Demand for them is down sharply and all new reforestation projects will have to emphasize trees suitable for lumber.

4. Develop fish and fishing as a source of income. Despite pollution, sweetfish (*ayu*) is still plentiful in the natural state. They can be cultivated successfully, and fetch very high prices.

5. Continue to develop the roads. Three main purposes will be served by improving the town's roads. The first is to facilitate tourist access to our scenic areas. The second is to facilitate commuting to work so that residents of the town will not have to move out to be nearer their workplaces. The third is to make it easier to bring in heavy materials such as fertilizer, and to facilitate the marketing of products of the region.

6. Factories. In recent years, the town devoted intensive efforts to bringing in industries that would provide employment for local people. However, the recent interest in preservation of the natural environment has brought that program to a halt and we are concentrating on development of recreational facilities and tourism instead. Because there is much hostility toward indus-

tries that may pollute the environment, *no more factories will be invited to locate in Shionoe Town* [italics in original].

In 1973 the town proposed a four-year plan to develop tourism, especially up in the highlands along the Tokushima border. Many tourist attractions have been developed there and it would be very useful to have a bus that connects them all.

In 1973 we successfully drilled for new "hot-springs," which we want to develop for local people and for tourists. Care must be taken to observe all the new laws that now protect places of natural beauty.

In 1973, efforts to locate the Clover plant in the town failed after the local government had already acquired the building site. Part of the land will be used to build a facility devoted to the improvement of farmers' lives. It will be staffed by persons who can offer instruction and information on new agricultural techniques and materials, cooking and nutrition, the making and care of clothing, and so on. This will be the first such center of its kind in the town, and will be used by all our people until others are constructed, when it will serve only the Yasuhara area. The stimulus for this development is a law directed specifically at the improvement of the quality of life in agricultural households.

The town also has a long-range plan to build a processing plant where locally produced foods such as chestnuts, fern shoots, and so on, can be bottled, canned or preserved, permitting the growers to turn a greater profit because they would not have to sell the products fresh at low prices at the height of the season. Such a development would raise the incomes of farm households.

Although it is in many respects a public relations document, the report does speak of real accomplishments and pressing problems. Clearly the declining population and changes in the age distribution of the residents of the town are cause for serious concern. The following tables present some of the basic demographic information made available by the Town Office. Table 1 records a decline in population between 1956 and 1975 of just under 50 percent. Females have outnumbered males throughout the period, and the average family size has fallen from 4.9 to 3.7 persons.

Table 2 shows the changing age distribution of the population between 1960 and 1975, with the heaviest loss in the group fourteen years of age or younger. The only gain is in the number of persons over the age of sixty-five.

Table 3 gives the basic data on the proportions of the labor force engaged in various kinds of industry. The proportion of the total population in the labor force rose from 56.4 to 66.5 percent between 1960

TABLE I

Number of Households and Population by Sex in
Shionoe Town, 1956–75

Year	Population			Households	Average size of household
	Males	Females	Totals		
1956	4,509	4,709	9,218	1,875	4.9
1960	3,250	3,489	6,739	1,469	4.6
1965	2,747	3,113	5,860	1,404	4.2
1970	2,477	2,824	5,301	1,377	3.9
1975	2,278	2,560	4,838	1,324	3.7

and 1975, largely because of the decline in the number of children under the age of fourteen. The postwar baby boom was over and in the intervening years legalized abortion, combined with the gradual spread of the use of other birth-control measures, had sharply reduced the birthrate.

During the same period the proportion of the labor force engaged in agriculture and forestry fell 60 percent, while that of those engaged in secondary and tertiary industries rose 134 percent and 36 percent respectively. These increases are attributable almost exclusively to the availability of employment opportunities within relatively easy commuting distance of the town.

As the town's plan for development shows, there are a great many other pressing problems that must be dealt with. In the sections that follow, we shall take up some of them, dealing first with a national problem that has affected Kurusu directly: the necessity for finding new ways to handle the disposal of human waste. Next we consider the impact of the town's plan to build a housing development in a hamlet up-river from Kurusu. And finally we discuss at somewhat greater length the three major issues of education, welfare services, and recreational facilities—which are concerns shared by all the depopulated areas of the Japanese countryside.

The Human Waste Storage Facility

A new problem for the Japanese, traditionally recyclers par excellence, is how to dispose of human waste. The problem has arisen not only because the population of the country has grown enormously

TABLE 2

Age Distribution of Population in Shionoe Town, 1960–75

Age group	1960		1965		1970		1975		Overall change, 1960–75
	No.	Pct.	No.	Pct.	No.	Pct.	No.	Pct.	
Under 15	2,377	35.3%	1,648	28.1%	1,254	23.7%	940	19.4%	−60.1%
15–64[a]	3,803	56.4	3,584	61.2	3,391	63.9	3,219	66.5	−15.4%
Over 64	559	8.3	628	10.7	656	12.4	679	14.1	+21.5%
TOTAL	6,739	100.0%	5,860	100.0%	5,301	100.0%	4,838	100.0%	−28.2%

NOTE: When the town was created in 1956 the total population was 9,218. The 1975 figure thus represents a decline of 47.5 percent.
[a]Labor force, not all gainfully employed.

TABLE 3

Size of Labor Force by Economic Sector, Shionoe Town, 1960–75

Economic sector	1960		1965		1970		1975		Overall change, 1960–75
	No.	Pct.	No.	Pct.	No.	Pct.	No.	Pct.	
Primary (agriculture and forestry)	2,353	69.0%	1,877	61.4%	1,543	50.5%	935	34.6%	−60.1%
Secondary (manufacturing and construction)	338	9.9	430	14.0	685	22.5	792	29.3	+134.3%
Tertiary (clerical and service)	720	21.1	752	24.6	826	27.0	979	36.1	+35.9%
TOTAL	3,411	100.0%	3,059	100.0%	3,054	100.0%	2,706	100.0%	−20.1%

since the end of World War II, and has concentrated chiefly in the cities, but also because the farmers of Japan have gone over completely to chemical fertilizers. Kurusu has been directly affected by this development, primarily because of the bridge at the entrance to the hamlet, which can carry heavy vehicular traffic from the Takamatsu highway across the Kōtō River. Properly called the Tsukimi Bridge, it is known locally as Kangetsu Bridge or simply the cement bridge. What seemed a boon when it was first constructed several years before World War II has in recent years proved to be the means by which a great volume of unwanted traffic gains access to areas beyond the community toward the hills.

The waste storage facility, built jointly in 1972 by Shionoe and two other towns, is located on the small road up in the hills behind the hamlet. Built underground, only the ventilating pipes and the ground-level covers are visible to travelers on the road. There is absolutely no odor, but many people in Kurusu complain about the small tank trucks that bring in the waste and pump it into the holding tanks, and about the larger trucks that come in periodically to remove the waste and transport it to the boats on which it is loaded and dumped far out in the Pacific off the southern coast of Shikoku.

The facility is located on land sold to the town by a Kurusu family. Other residents of the hamlet think they got a good price for what had been upland paddy fields, but the family members themselves say that they simply could not resist the intense pressure brought to bear on them by town officials. Many people in Kurusu were upset by the proposed development, pointing out that it would provide no new jobs to compensate them for the likelihood of offensive odors and the certainty of increased truck traffic that would be both noisy and dangerous. The Kurusu hamlet association met on the issue several times before it was finally settled, and it is likely that it was the seller's unhappy experience in this affair that led him to keep out of the Clover affair later (see Chapter Eight).

The hamlet eventually agreed to a five-year trial period on condition that the town give them one of the two small houses built in 1953 for repatriates, and located on land that had reverted to Yasuhara Village when the rail line was closed down. The building, now the meeting-house of the hamlet association, lies within the boundaries of Kurusu, across the road from the sawmill. Because there was so much opposition to the building of the waste storage facility, the five-year period was agreed to in hopes that an alternative disposal system will have been developed by the expiration of the period. The town government is painfully aware that time is running out, for one hears frequent references to the problem of relocating the facility or devising some new disposal method. Relocation will not be easy, for when the original planning was in progress, the town had to rule out two prime sites—one in Shionoe, where the hot-springs are located, and the other in Nishitani, where the town had already constructed a crematorium. The general opinion locally is that Kurusu will not grant an extension of the present agreement.

The Kawakita Housing Development

The Shionoe Town government is planning to build a small housing development about two kilometers south of Kurusu on the same side of the river. Originally they had hoped to construct another vehicular bridge at Kawakita, to replace the footbridge that crosses the river there. But since local governments are now strapped for funds, the town has opted for a less expensive road-improvement project at a projected cost of six million yen.

The town bought the wasteland in Kawakita cheaply, but it has proved very costly to prepare it for the houses, all of which will have electricity and water and will be sold at cost to individuals. This is an excellent example of the lengths to which local governments will go in their efforts to slow the rural exodus from remote districts directly to the cities. In many isolated places in the town, so many inhabitants have moved out that there are now abandoned houses and fields overgrown with brush. The town hopes that resettlement schemes like the one at Kawakita will prove attractive enough to keep some of these families in Shionoe, in easy commuting distance of the industries of Takamatsu and its satellite towns.

Again, it is Kangetsu Bridge that exposes Kurusu to this incursion from the outside of interests not at all connected to the community or the lives of its people. The main road through Kurusu can accommodate the additional traffic that will be generated by the housing development, but only to the place where it branches and crosses the smaller bridge that lies inside Kurusu. The southerly branch will be widened from two to four meters. The expanded right-of-way will have to be taken from some of the best paddy fields in Kurusu. People say that they have no choice but to sell, even though they all doubt that they will get a fair price for the land.

The fields of ten families will be affected by the plan to widen the road, which was scheduled to start in the fall of 1975. Since only two of the families are residents of Kurusu, the Town Office consulted with the group of ten rather than with the Kurusu hamlet association. Two major issues were the level of compensation and the possibility of harmful effects on the irrigation system. While it is true that individuals could refuse to sell—for unlike the higher levels of government, the town does not possess the right of eminent domain—the powers of persuasion of the authorities are considerable. The irrigation system is by far the more important concern, however, for the housing development lies between Kurusu and the spot upstream where a diversion channel leads off from the river, which is the hamlet's principal source of irrigation water. The widening of the road will also necessitate some redesigning of the gravity-flow system that feeds water to the paddy fields downstream, and everyone will have to put up with the problems posed by still more vehicular traffic passing through the hamlet. They do not relish the prospect, but their distaste for it is somewhat offset by the agreement of the town to put in some new irrigation channels and repair several of the old ones, a windfall for members of the Kurusu Irrigation Union (see Chapter Seven), which will not have to pay for the materials or labor.

Education

Among the many problems of the depopulated areas, that of maintaining an adequate educational system is especially acute. Without the special subsidies provided by the national government, even more local schools would have shut down than have already done so. One teacher commented on the irony of the current situation: "The classrooms in Takamatsu are seriously overcrowded, while ours are half-empty or worse. Many of the local schools would have closed years ago if it were not for the national policy of keeping them open in hopes that more families will decide to stay or perhaps even move back from the city."

In 1951 there were three schools in Yasuhara Village: a primary school, its branch located in a remote area of the hills, and the newly built middle-school located not far from the village office. Table 4 shows the total enrollments in 1951, when there were 27 Kurusu children in school; in 1975 there were only 10. It was estimated at that time that about one-third of the middle-school graduates in Yasuhara went on to higher-school (grades ten through twelve), but no Kurusu resident had ever had more than the compulsory years of education. By 1975 it was estimated that the proportion of local middle-school graduates going on to higher-school had risen to roughly the national average of 90 percent, while the remainder sought employment directly after graduation. From higher-school about 25 percent of the graduates seek to continue their education, at two-year or four-year colleges and universities. This compares favorably with the national rate of 30 percent.

In 1975 there were four primary schools and a consolidated middle-school in Shionoe Town, but no higher-school. Those who wish to continue their education beyond middle-school may choose from among several higher-schools that can be reached fairly easily by bus. The old Yasuhara Primary School is at the same location; its main building was extensively remodeled in 1956 and the gymnasium was put up seven years later. Part of the old wooden building was moved to Kurusu where it is used as a tea-processing factory (see Chapter Four). The former Yasuhara Middle School now houses the Hani Pajama Factory (see Chapter Four); the new consolidated middle-school is in Nakamura, a short bus trip or bicycle ride for the Kurusu children who attend it.

There are two national government policies aimed at maintaining the rural educational systems in places like Shionoe Town. On the one hand, schools are consolidated wherever possible; on the other, there are subsidies for schools in severely depopulated areas so remote that the children cannot commute. In Shionoe Town the four primary schools are: Yasuhara, with an enrollment of 144, including the 8 Kurusu children of primary school age; Tōishi, with only 18 pupils, which is actually a branch of the Yasuhara school, subsidized by the

TABLE 4

School Enrollments in Yasuhara Village, 1951

Grades	Yasuhara			Kurusu only		
	Male	Female	Total	Male	Female	Total
Primary (1–6)	226	209	435	13	9	22
Middle (7–9)	136	124	260	3	2	5
TOTAL	362	333	695	16	11	27

NOTE: See Table 5 and the discussion in Chapter Two concerning the heavy preponderance of males of school age.

government because it serves the most isolated area of the entire town; Kaminishi, consolidated with the two other primary schools, which now has 103 pupils; and Shionoe, newly constructed in 1975, and the largest, with an enrollment of 166 students.

The Kaminishi situation is grave, for a projection of present enrollments shows so sharp a drop in 1977 that two grades will have to be combined in one room. The people who formerly lived in the three areas whose primary schools are now consolidated at Kaminishi were primarily engaged in forestry and went out as seasonal labor, especially to Okayama Prefecture for the harvest of the rushes used to weave the coverings for tatami. It was a hard, marginal existence, and in recent years these people have moved out of the area lock, stock, and barrel.

The law forbids combining more than two grades into one class, so that even a tiny school like Tōishi requires three teachers to handle its six grades. Obviously such schools could not stay open were it not for heavy governmental subsidy, for in terms of number of students alone, the school has dropped well below the size for which three teachers would normally be supplied.

In 1953 the Yasuhara Village government constructed a nursery school at the edge of Kurusu close to the Kangetsu Bridge. It was built on village land that once had been a part of the right-of-way of the defunct rail line. The school was run by the village for a time and was then taken over and operated by a nearby Buddhist temple, whose young priest had recently returned from the university. The priest in turn abandoned his efforts there, and the school reverted to the village. As a result of the creation of Shionoe Town, when part of what had

been Yasuhara Village was incorporated into Kagawa Town, the enrollment at the kindergarten at the Yasuhara Primary School dropped
so sharply that for a time its remaining pupils were sent to the nursery school. They were subsequently separated once more.

In 1975 there were three nursery schools in Shionoe Town, the
largest of which was the old Yasuhara school in Kurusu. Until 1972
each had its own principal, but sagging enrollments and declining
budgets forced the appointment of a single principal for all three. The
government supplies about 80 percent of the budget for the operation
of the three schools, which run two buses to pick up the children and
take them home. The principal takes justifiable pride that there has
never been an accident in the twenty years that the bus service has
operated over the large area it must cover.

When the nursery school in Yasuhara opened in 1953 it had an
enrollment of more than 70 children and employed from four to five
teachers. In 1975 the enrollment had dropped to 44 and there were
only 55 children in the other two schools in Shionoe and Kaminishi. It
is anticipated that the downward trend will continue, and that the
schools will soon have to be consolidated, probably in Shionoe. When
that happens, the town government has tentative plans to convert the
Yasuhara facility into a center for old people's activities.

Rural parents expect much of education, which they hope will fit
their children for productive lives, and as a consequence they expect a
great deal of schoolteachers. In 1975 there was a new problem, the
preponderance of female teachers. Local educational officials are especially worried about the declining number of men in what they regard
as the crucial age-group between thirty-five and forty-five, which is felt
to include the bulk of the responsible and vigorous members of the
teaching profession. The number of women teachers has been increasing steadily for a decade. The parents, especially those who have boys
in school, do not like it and are vociferous in the expression of their
opinion that women teachers are less effective than men.

Actually, although the teaching staff of a small primary school may
be made up of equal numbers of men and women, it is inevitably the
case that all the women will be actively teaching, whereas some of the
men will be devoting much of their time to administrative tasks. Invariably, both the principal and the head of teachers will be male. Thus
the direct influence of women teachers on the children is dispropor-

tionately great. The situation in 1975 contrasts sharply with that in 1951, when the teaching staff of the primary and middle-schools attended by Kurusu children was predominantly male. Why do men avoid the profession today? Level of income is not the sole issue, for in 1974 a new law raised teachers' salaries to the levels of those of other civil servants. The move was part of a general effort to make many unpopular occupations more attractive, but it has had little discernible effect. Only about 10 percent of those entering normal schools in Kagawa Prefecture are men.

If salary upgrading fails to entice men into the teaching profession, it is clear that there must be other negative aspects of the job that keep them away. One of these is said to be the peculiar character of the relationship between the teacher and the community. There surely have been few societies in which the teacher traditionally has been accorded such immense prestige and respect. The prewar ethic emphasized the unrepayable, limitless debt owed one's ancestors, parents, and teachers. One of the costs to the occupant of this exalted position was that he was expected to lead an exemplary life. While the prestige of teachers has sunk to new lows in Japanese society, and while public censure of a teacher's misconduct may not be as severe as was formerly the case, the public nonetheless stands ready to condemn with special severity the teacher whose public behavior is considered less than exemplary or whose private life is deemed unacceptable in any way. It is widely agreed that because the same behavior would hardly be noticed were the individual a company employee, men are understandably likely to choose company employment over teaching.

A second unappealing feature of the teacher's role is that he is often caught between the children and their parents. Should he violate the regulations forbidding corporal punishment, he may well find himself denounced as a brute. If children seem undisciplined, the PTA may take a hostile stand against the teachers, especially in rural areas like Shionoe Town, accusing them of failing to do their jobs. It is no wonder that the profession fails to attract more men, who are unlikely to be prepared to put up with any of this. The vacuum they have left is willingly filled by women, for whom the position of teacher represents a considerable improvement over many other kinds of jobs for which they can qualify.

The decline in the number of male teachers is by no means the only problem faced by the school district, for it is doubly difficult to attract teachers of either sex to the schools in Shionoe Town. An education official commented: "It's because they think that anything south of Kagawa Town is really rural, even though it's only ten minutes further down the highway by bus. Most of our teachers come from Kagawa Prefecture, but there's a high turnover rate nonetheless. It's very unusual for anyone to spend more than three years here, and only a few stay as long as ten."

Welfare

A major concern of the Town Office is what is seen as the growing problem of families and individuals who require welfare assistance of some kind. In 1975 seventy families, 5 percent of those in the town, were judged to be sufficiently impoverished to qualify for full welfare support. Very low-income families received supplemental benefits, which included a telephone, now defined as an absolute necessity. Children of these families also received all expenses for the nine years of compulsory education, including a clothing allowance, books, and supplies. Needy but not indigent families with four or more children received ¥4,000 per month for each child, a sum intended partly to help meet the cost of education.

In 1972, when my wife and I were back in Kurusu on a very brief visit, an older woman had told us that there were many places in the area where there were only old people left. She expressed reservations about the adequacy of the town's program of having regular visitors look in on these elderly people periodically. By 1975, the town had twelve public welfare workers and two home-helpers. The welfare workers, all non-professionals, are good, responsible people, many of them retired, who receive nominal compensation for their services. Each is assigned a district, whose size is determined by a combination of topography and population density, and travels about checking on client families and applicants for assistance. They make their recommendations to the Welfare Section of the Town Office as to eligibility, level of support required, and the general situation of those already enrolled. Basically, the cut-off point, below which a family is considered eligible for welfare support, is a very low monthly per capita income of ¥15,000. In addition, there are many special programs, such as relief for fatherless families, care for the bedridden elderly, services for the retarded and disabled, and the like.

In a 1975 survey of Shionoe Town it was found that there were 24 bedridden old persons, none of whom lived alone, and 60 persons over seventy years of age living alone but still able to care for themselves. All of the homes for the elderly available to Shionoe Town residents are financed by one or another level of government. One of them, located in Kagawa Town, was built and is maintained jointly by two counties and the city of Takamatsu. It is located near the prefectural hospital only about twenty minutes by bus from Kurusu and offers specialized care, but its capacity is limited. Another institution, somewhat more distant, accepts the elderly from Shionoe Town, but none are there now. Most such special-care facilities charge a nominal fee only if the individual can afford to pay; most of their residents are admitted free of charge.

Many families on welfare have one physically handicapped or mentally retarded member, but by far the most common variety is the household consisting of two elderly persons. The two types are not infrequently combined in a family consisting of an elderly husband and wife and a handicapped offspring. There are public facilities for the care of both the elderly and the handicapped, but the welfare workers have found it very difficult to persuade people to take advantage of them. In the case of the handicapped, it is likely that either the individual or the other family members, or both, will refuse to take the step. As for the old people, they are likely to object that going to a home is like going to prison, or to argue, not unreasonably, that they are places where people are sent to die.

The services of the home-helpers, who provide minimal care for such families, are available free of charge to all who require them. The positions are supported by national government funds, and the welfare officials in Shionoe Town complain only that they need more. The home-helpers are neither nurses nor cooks. They visit the houses of the elderly and the handicapped, but not usually the houses of those temporarily laid up as the result of accidents, and do the laundry, bathe helpless people, and spend some time talking with those who are lonely. There is one physician from Kagawa Town who makes regular weekly calls on bedridden old people. His rounds, made in his automobile, have been made much easier since the paving of all the major roads. And there are, of course, staff physicians at the prefectural hospital about twenty minutes by car or bus down the highway toward Takamatsu.

What gets an ordinary family into such trouble that it must seek welfare assistance? One official was of the opinion that alcoholism is a major contributor in the bulk of cases. He attends many conferences on welfare problems, and he said that although he had heard many discussions of amphetamine abuse in the cities, the problem did not exist in Shionoe Town. There are welfare cheats, ordinarily people who have been receiving assistance and have found jobs that they have not reported to the authorities. They thus receive both their wages and welfare payments, and it is the task of the welfare workers to keep checking on the employment status of their clients. "In America do people ever *ask* to be removed from the welfare rolls?" one social worker inquired.

It would be fair to say, however, that at the level of most direct contact between the welfare system and the poor, the concern is far less with cheating than with the inadequacies of the program. Virtually everyone we talked to felt that much more needs to be done, especially for the retarded and handicapped. Their problems are not solely attributable to inadequate government programs; much remains to be done to educate the public, including members of their own families, to adopt a different attitude toward them. Most people are ashamed to expose the retarded to public view. The physically handicapped do go out now more often than they used to, but it is said that the only time one can get a good count of the mentally retarded in an area like this is on election day. "They bring them out then all right, when every vote counts." It is still difficult to arrange a marriage locally for a child of a family in which there are any mad or retarded members. We encountered a young man from such a family whose solution to the problem was to go to Osaka to take a job, where he eventually met and married a young woman. Only then did he bring her back to his home.

Many of the more thoughtful welfare workers are also concerned that the law, or at least the administration of the programs it provides, be made more flexible. In this connection one of them cited the following case as an example of the problem:

There is an elderly couple in my district who used to be fairly well off. They had two sons, and the future looked secure. But the first son died while he was away at college. The second son married and he and his wife had two children before he suddenly died of cancer at a young age. The old couple are left without support and obviously need help, but they are disqualified because they own some forest land. They don't want to sell it for a very good reason. It was pretty badly cut over and is not worth much in its present state. It has been reforested, however, and they want to hold on to it and leave it to their grandchildren, for whom it may have some proper value. They are too old to farm, so they are really hard up. They ought to be able to get the help they need. It is only a quirk in the law that puts them in this desperate situation.

A related issue is the feeling of many workers that welfare assistance should be provided to some persons who have incomes slightly above the maximum allowed. One gave the following account of a case that she feels requires discretionary action:

In one complicated case in my district there is a family that now consists of a grandmother and her grandchild, whose father—the old woman's son—has a job in Matsuyama. She steadfastly refuses to move to the city, as he wishes her to do; he refuses to come back to the country as she wishes he would. She does a little piecework for one of the factories, but cannot do much and is paid very little. These two are living on about ¥13–14,000 per month, which is clearly substandard. They need more money obviously, but even so there are some tough welfare officers who would reduce her payments in a flash if they found out about the small extra income she gets. It's not right. They ought to be more flexible.

In such cases it is always the practice to contact the children and siblings of a person before putting him on the welfare rolls, but they are not bound by law to help out. One man told us that he knows of two or three cases in Shionoe Town where an elderly couple have been abandoned by all of their children. "I cannot understand how young people can do such things. That children should accept responsibility for the care of their parents is an admirable Japanese custom, but it seems to be dying fast."

Recreational Facilities

The provision of recreational facilities for the local populace was anything but a major concern of local government in 1951. Several developments have combined to make it one today. With rising levels of income (by mid-year 1975 Japanese workers were receiving an hourly compensation only slightly lower than that received by British workers, and half that being paid U.S. workers), the attraction of relatively higher wages and salaries in the city, and the recognition that there is no future in farming, the rural population has been draining out of places like Shionoe Town at an alarming rate. One of the many attractions of city life is the increased availability of amusement and entertainment as contrasted to their almost complete absence in the rural areas. Both the town government and private entrepreneurs have moved to try to fill the gap.

The classic vacation trip in Japan has involved going to a hot-springs inn, or more recently a hotel. Three "hot-springs" developments have been undertaken. Actually, there are few hot-springs on Shikoku; most of the island's resorts are located near springs, to be sure, but the water is heated. The settlement of Shionoe has long been a resort town patronized by people from Takamatsu. This was one of the reasons for putting the gasoline-powered railway in; its southern terminus, which stood abandoned in 1951 and has since been pulled down, was in Shionoe. The only full-fledged inn (*ryokan*) there, the Hanaya, burned to the ground in 1974 and there were no plans to rebuild it. It is in the Shionoe district that all three recreational developments centering on hot-springs have taken place.

The first is about ten minutes from Kurusu by car, and provides a heated bath and a limited range of amusements for its patrons. The handsome new building was put up largely with government funds. Admission is ¥500 and there are special lower rates for the elderly and for children. It is a very popular spot, as evidenced by the sizable parking lot that has been put in, and Kurusu people often come here on Sundays.

The second is located far up in the mountains almost on the Tokushima border. Built in 1975 with a combination of town and national government funds, this facility is defined as part of the town's effort to provide the amenities for its remaining population. Its rates for the general public are very low and even less for the elderly. Few Kurusu people had yet visited the place, but everyone had heard about it and many were planning to go at the first opportunity.

The third is a privately owned establishment called Shionoe Hot Springs Hotel. It is financed by Osaka capital, as are many Shikoku enterprises, and has been open for only a very few years. It has had no real competition since the Hanaya burned. The clientele of this astonishing establishment is quite varied and includes Kurusu people. The hotel has two major components. The upper level, which has twenty-two tastefully decorated rooms, half in the Japanese style and half in the Western style with beds, couches, and chairs, is for overnight guests. Most of these are travelers from the cities who arrive in their own automobiles, either for the weekend or on an overnight stop on their way to more distant destinations such as Tokushima or Kōchi. The rates are high, from ¥6,000 to ¥6,800 per day with two meals. Unless special arrangements are made, all meals are served on a rigid schedule in a public dining room. Virtually all dishes, including those on special order, are Japanese. This upper level has nothing to do with the people of the surrounding rural communities, who never have occasion even to enter it or its large swimming pool unless by some rare chance they come as members of a larger party (*dantai*).

The dantai are groups of people who arrive by chartered bus, hired car, or taxi. They come for the public bath (enticingly named the jungle-bath), usually have one meal in the large banquet room, and return before nightfall. These groups are of considerable variety—they may be employees of a government section or agency, farm machinery salesmen, entire kindergarten and primary-school classes with their teachers, or a women's club. The group is charged a fixed per capita rate, which includes all services. Sometimes schoolchildren on excursion stay overnight; the hotel staff lays out bedding for them all in the banquet room, which has a tatami floor and can sleep one child to a mat. Smaller groups of people often use the place for day-long conferences or meetings.

To serve the male guests who wish to take their meals in their rooms, the hotel employs professional women (called *o-nakai-san*) from Takamatsu. They come up by taxi, change into kimono, and perform the services traditionally expected of them. That is, they pour *sake* for the guests, converse with them, and if arrangements have been made in advance they play the *shamisen* and sing, but they do not stay at the hotel overnight. It is said that they are generally middle-aged or older because younger women dislike this kind of work and will not learn to play the shamisen "because it is too difficult."

The women who clean the rooms and the male members of the hotel staff are drawn from nearby communities; most of the women work on a part-time basis. No women from Kurusu work here, although it is in easy commuting distance and many of the hotel employees travel much further by bus or motorbike. Most of them do not particularly like the work, but say that it is not too demanding physically and has the great advantage of being part-time, so that they can be home when the children return from school and keep up with their own house and farm work as well.

The lower level of the hotel is designed for the general public and especially for the local people. There is a parking lot where one may leave one's car free of charge. For ¥500 per adult (half-price in the evening) and ¥200 per child one is admitted to the hotel grounds. There is a spacious paved playground (actually the original parking lot, which proved to be too small) with swings and other equipment for the small children. On weekends booths are set up at one end of the playground, and a variety of food and drink is available.

Inside the building at this level are the jungle-bath, a room filled with coin-operated game machines, and an enormous dining room, partly Western style with tables and chairs, partly Japanese style with tatami mats, cushions, and low tables. At the souvenir and snack counter, one may purchase tickets for a variety of dishes and drinks, which are brought to the table by waitresses, local girls and women who also work part-time. A color television set is kept on at all times. It was invariably turned to one of the commercial channels, never to the Japan Broadcasting Corporation (NHK) channels whose programming the rural people generally dismiss as too dull. Along one wall of this room are coin-operated machines that dispense cold soft drinks, beer in cans, ice candy on a stick, Japanese rice-cracker snacks, and peanuts. There is even a machine that dispenses tea.

At the far end of the dining room is a modest stage where on weekends vaudevillians and musicians perform twice nightly. One Kurusu man who had recently been at the hotel and seen a Sunday night performance said that the pair of comedians had been pretty amusing, but added, "They don't charge much, you know, which is probably why they can only get the students of students of students of the professionals." This array of amusements draws families, groups of friends—almost invariably all male or all female—and co-workers, and an occasional couple on a date. The busiest times are the weekends. The lower level closes at 10:00 P.M.; none of these customers ever stays overnight.

I have dwelt on the Shionoe Hot Springs Hotel because it is a kind of place that had absolutely no analogue in 1951. The hot-springs inns that did exist then were considered prohibitively expensive (even though my bill from the Hanaya in 1958 shows that a room with two meals then cost ¥800), and almost no one enjoyed such a quantity of leisure time. To one accustomed to the quieter pleasures of an earlier day, it is an extraordinary experience to see the weathered faces of the old people and the small family groups of Kurusu who have driven up by car in such gaudy surroundings as these.

All around the hotel are scores of summer homes, all only two or three years old, belonging to city people. They range from modest prefabs to quite imposing establishments. Most have gardens, some in the Western style, with clumps of white birch designed to evoke the atmosphere of the northern mountain countryside. Local people have no connection whatsoever with this particular aspect of the new affluence.

CHAPTER TWO

Kurusu's Population and Its Families

VIEWED FROM across the river, the houses of Kurusu lie in a long arc between the skirt of the hills that rise to the west behind the settlement and the area of fields containing some of the best wet-rice land in the entire district. The most direct access is by the road that leads into the hamlet across the Kangetsu Bridge. The visitor walking through Kurusu will find that virtually all of the fields lie on his right and all but five houses on his left, most of them up a fairly steep grade, set against the hillsides. Three of the five houses on the field side were probably built during the last century, and each of them represents an early decision to take some paddy land out of cultivation. One of the two older houses bears the house-name *dendai*, an apparent reference to the unusual circumstance of its location in the paddies (see Map 4).

In this chapter we shall discuss the people who live in the hamlet's 23 dwellings, with emphasis on changes in age and sex distribution and family composition. We shall conclude by describing what has happened to four Kurusu families since 1951, and by introducing one that has moved into the community recently.

Demography

Between 1951 and 1975 the population of Kurusu declined about 20 percent and the number of households fluctuated between 20 and 23. The scattered evidence from the intervening years suggests that the exodus was a gradual one, with no sharp break, and that families which left were replaced by newcomers. In the course of decline in the absolute numbers of people in Kurusu, there has also occurred a

TABLE 5
Population of Kurusu by Age and Sex, 1951 and 1975

Age	Male	Female	Total	Pct. each age	Pct. male in each age group
1951					
Under 10	20	9	29	47.7%	71%
10–19	16	6	22		
20–29	6	8	14	26.2	43%
30–39	6	8	14		
40–49	6	5	11	16.8	56%
50–59	4	3	7		
60–69	1	3	4		
70–79	3	3	6	9.3	40%
Over 79	0	0	0		
TOTAL	62	45	107	100.0%	
Percent	57.9%	42.1%	100%		
1975					
Under 10	10	9	19	34.1%	46%
10–19	3	6	9		
20–29	4	4	8	26.8	45%
30–39	7	9	16		
40–49	4	4	8	23.2	47%
50–59	5	6	11		
60–69	4	5	9		
70–79	2	0	2	15.9	46%
Over 79	0	2	2		
TOTAL	39	45	84	100.0%	
Percent	46.4%	53.6%	100%		

change in the composition of the population, as shown in Table 5. First, the population is older. In 1951 almost half of the residents of Kurusu were under twenty—the age of legal majority in Japan. Twenty-five years later, this group made up only one-third of the population. Second, the proportion of males to females had almost reversed. In 1951 males outnumbered females by a substantial 58 percent; in 1975 females made up 54 percent of the population.

The differential between males and females was most marked in 1951 in the age group of those under twenty, of which 70 percent were males. Indeed, two-thirds of all the males then resident in Kurusu were under thirty years of age. I am at a loss to explain this situation, but we have seen (Table 4 in Chapter One) that school enrollments for the

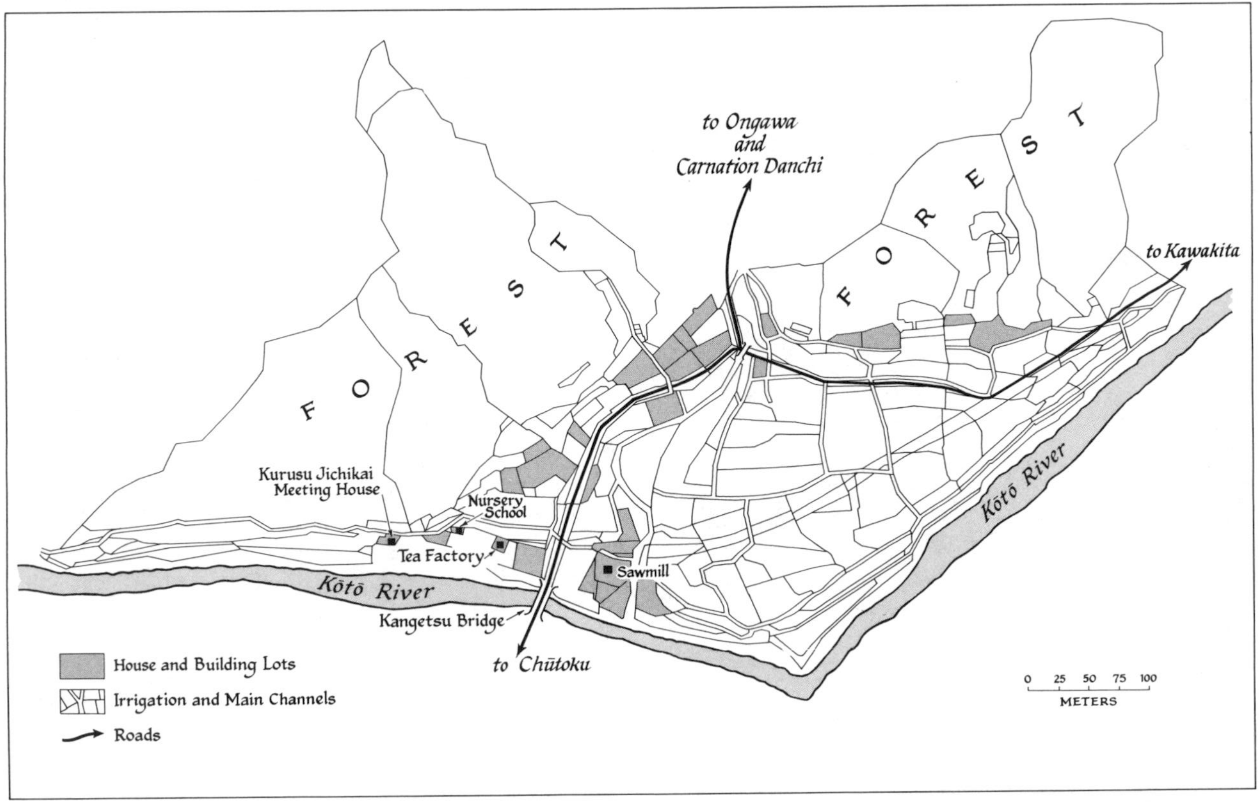

Map 4. Kurusu

House and Building Lots

Irrigation and Main Channels

Roads

to Kawakita

to Ongawa
and
Carnation Danchi

Kōtō River

FOREST

FOREST

FOREST

Sawmill

Nursery
School

Tea Factory

Kurusu Jichikai
Meeting House

Kangetsu Bridge

to Chūtoku

Kōtō River

0 25 50 75 100
METERS

village as a whole reflect the same imbalance. In 1975, males accounted for only 46 percent of those under twenty. Furthermore, the distribution of males in the total population by age group is quite different at the two times. In 1951 males made up only 43 percent of the age group twenty to thirty-nine, a clear reflection of the war's toll. In 1975 the proportion of males in every twenty-year grouping is about 46 percent, their percentage of the total population in that year.

The household register for Kurusu records 116 deaths between 1872 and 1952 (see Table 6). Of these almost half were children under ten years of age and almost three-fourths of all deaths claimed people under thirty. Since 1953, nineteen men and women have died in Kurusu, 79 percent of them over the age of fifty. Half of the total number of deaths were of people over seventy. As has been observed repeatedly, the sharp decline in infant and childhood mortality in the postwar period has been a major factor in the decision taken by married couples to limit the number of children through legal abortion or the use of contraceptives. The old pattern of having many children was primarily a device for insuring the survival to maturity of at least two or three of them, a precaution that has not been necessary for a generation.

TABLE 6
Age at Death of Kurusu Residents,
1872–1952 and 1953–75

	Deaths			
	1872–1952		1953–75	
Age group	No.	Pct.	No.	Pct.
Under 10	56	48.3%	2	10.5%
10–19	10	8.6	–	—
20–29	17	14.6 [a]	2	10.5
30–39	8	6.9	–	—
40–49	3	2.6	–	—
50–59	5	4.3	3	15.8
60–69	9	7.8	2	10.5
70–79	5	4.3	6	31.6
Over 79	3	2.6	4	21.1
TOTAL	116	100.0%	19	100.0%

[a] Eight men from Kurusu died in World War II. One of them was in the age group 10–19; six were between 20 and 29; one was in his forties.

In 1951 there were fifteen women in Kurusu who had married into hamlet families from outside. Because marriages were almost universally arranged in those days, the places of origin of Kurusu brides were generally within a fairly narrow geographical range. Four came from other hamlets in Yasuhara Village; eight were from places in Kagawa County; three were from other parts of Shikoku. None came from more distant places in Japan.

There were also five adopted husbands (see Chapter Six): two from Yasuhara Village, one from Kagawa County, one from Tokushima Prefecture on Shikoku, and one a Korean who had come to the area originally as a member of the construction crew that built the gasoline-car rail line in the 1920's.

Between 1952 and 1975 eighteen women married men who at the time of the wedding were registered as residents of Kurusu. Not all of them now reside in the community, but their places of origin are nonetheless of considerable interest. Six are from Shionoe Town, eight from other places in Kagawa Prefecture, one from elsewhere on Shikoku, and three from other parts of Japan. The expanding area from which brides are taken is not a reflection of the broadening horizons of the go-betweens, but rather a result of the participation of Kurusu men in the urban labor market. "Work-place marriages" (*shokuba-kek-kon*) seem to be increasingly common, and since firms and factories hire without regard to place of origin, people from widely separated parts of the country increasingly meet and marry.

There were five adopted husbands in Kurusu in 1975, as there had been in 1952. The man from Tokushima Prefecture and the Korean were still there; the three who had come in since 1952 were all from Kagawa Prefecture.

Households

Table 7 shows the number and size of Kurusu households in 1951 and 1975. The number rose from 22 to 23, while the population declined from 107 to 84, bringing the average family size down from 4.86 to 3.65. This contrasts with the national figures for rural households of 6.1 and 4.68, respectively.

At the beginning of 1945, just as the destruction of the cities of Japan began to flood the rural areas with evacuees, there were sixteen

TABLE 7
Number and Size of Kurusu Households,
1951 and 1975

Persons per household	1951		1975	
	Households	Persons	Households	Persons
1	2	2	2	2
2	3	6	7	14
3	3	9	3	9
4	2	8	4	16
5	3	15	2	10
6	3	18	2	12
7	3	21	3	21
8	1	8	0	0
9	1	9	0	0
10	0	0	0	0
11	1	11	0	0
TOTAL	22	107	23	84

NOTE: The average number of persons per household was 4.86 in 1951 and 3.65 in mid-1975. By the end of 1975 there were 25 households; the population was 89 and the average household size was 3.56.

households in Kurusu. According to the old men and women, only six of them had been in the hamlet for as many as four or five generations. This does not mean that the settlement itself is of recent date, for there are many gravestones in Kurusu cemeteries that bear family names no longer found anywhere in the district. All of the rest of the heads of families that were here in 1951 are at most the third-generation head of their respective households to live in Kurusu. The old-timers still refer to them as "the new households." Of the six with the longest residence, it is said, only three were ever financially well-off by local standards: one is the owner of the sawmill, and the other two were agricultural households with enough land to give them a comfortable living.

Such at least is the claim, and there are two incontrovertible pieces of evidence that bear it out. Alone of the pre-World War II houses, these are built on a plan that includes a garden through which guests must pass to reach the main sitting room. One of these has been pretty much abandoned for lack of hands and funds; the others are still well maintained. All the other prewar houses have dooryards except for the few built right against the hillside, where the slope is too steep to allow much open space in front or in back of the dwellings, but none has a garden. The other piece of evidence is to be found in the possessions of the family, especially in the furnishings of the house. In only these three are there any old pieces of good furniture or anything that might be called ornamental objects such as old charcoal braziers, tables, vases, plaques, and so on. In all the other houses everything is new, purchased during the very recent years of the new prosperity.

In 1951 all of the households that had been resident in Kurusu at the end of World War II were still there, although sadly depleted of young men. There were also six additional families, two of them branches (*shinya*) of the original sixteen; three were evacuee families who, un-like the dozen or more others who had been living with one or another of seven of Kurusu's households, still had not managed to move back to the cities they had fled; one was a family that had been repatriated from Taiwan where they had gone to settle before the outbreak of the war.

The remaining evacuee families deserve special notice. One came from Takamatsu and was composed of only the husband and wife. She was usually alone in Kurusu; her husband was a blind singer who traveled with a small theatrical troupe. They were considered so pitiful a case that although they lived in a tiny dwelling outside Kurusu's borders they were counted in as members of the hamlet association. The second, also a married couple, had fled Osaka after the great incendiary raids, and shared a house with another family. The two women were usually alone, since both men were away from the hamlet for long stretches during the agricultural off-seasons. The third couple represent a different kind of case altogether, for he was a native of Kurusu who had become head of his household and married a woman from Yasuhara in 1923. A few years later they had moved to Kobe and transferred their official domicile there. At the end of the war they had left the city, which was extensively burned over in the incendiary raids, and in 1951 had only just transferred their domicile back to Kurusu.

By 1975 seven of the twenty-two families had disappeared and eight new ones had been created or had moved in. The seven no longer residing in Kurusu include the three evacuee families, two others that have died out (both were widows living alone), and two that had moved away. The eight new families include three that have moved in, two branch-families (brothers of the head of an old Kurusu household), and three newly created successor families that occupy housing separate from the main dwelling. Two of these are sons of their respective families and one is an adopted husband. In tabular form, the changes are as follows:

Out between 1945 and 1951:	In by 1951:
None	3 evacuees
	2 branches (*shinya*)
	1 repatriate

Out by 1975:	In by 1975:
3 evacuees	3 in-migrants
2 died out	2 branches (*shinya*)
2 moved out	3 newly created successor families

By way of introduction to the remainder of this chapter let us review briefly the character of the Japanese domestic group. The family in its ideal form is what is usually called the "stem family." The residential unit consists of a senior married couple and a married child with his or her own spouse and children. Such a family unit may include as many generations as are alive, but there can be only one married couple in each generation. While succession is ideally primogenitoral, a great variety of options can be exercised to secure the succession to the headship of the family. All other children in every generation marry out; the sons establish their own nuclear families, and the daughters marry into the houses of successors or become the wives of sons who establish neolocal residence. Thus, in any given community one may expect to find many conjugal families as well as those of the stem type. It is important to bear in mind, however, that every conjugal family was what may be called, following Yamane and Nonoyama (1967: 785), a temporary conjugal family or a potential stem family.

Under the prewar Civil Code the household (*ie*) had a legal definition. Its head exercised legal authority over all its members, and it was conceived to represent an unbroken continuum from the founding ancestor through the present membership on into the indefinite future. Among the sacred duties of the head, who controlled the destiny of its living members, was that of preserving the descent line unbroken. He was responsible for passing on, enlarged if possible, the goods and property that he had inherited, and it was his task to see to the proper veneration of the ancestors. It was not the marriage bond that was sacred, but rather the descent line (Kawashima & Steiner 1960:216).

This was roughly the situation until quite recently. Now, however, there is some reason to believe that the household ideal has been abandoned in favor of the ideal of the conjugal family (Goode 1963:7–10), which is no longer a stage along the way to the establishment of a stem family. Certainly the number of nuclear families has increased greatly. A government report on the number of households in Japan that classified them as either "nuclear families," "nuclear families with elderly member," "elderly couple only," or "elderly person living alone" revealed significant shifts in the relatively short period 1967–71. The total number of families, defined as residential entities, rose 9.7 percent. The number of nuclear families was up 11.9 percent; nuclear families with an elderly member, up 14.8 percent. The number of elderly couples living alone rose an astonishing 42.7 percent and single-person households consisting of one elderly person rose 31.6 percent (see Table 8).

There are at least three major reasons for the rise in the number of elderly persons and couples occupying separate residences. One is the desire of young married couples to set up independent households in order to be free of the responsibility of caring for elderly persons. The second can be traced to the policies of the Japan Public Housing Corporation and the practices of the private entrepreneurs who build the vast apartment complexes that are the hallmarks of the postwar cities of Japan. Apartments, generally designed to house nuclear families, are too small even for that purpose in the view of many. It was not until the early 1970's that the Japan Public Housing Corporation at last initiated a plan whereby the senior and junior couples of a stem family could rent paired apartments, and plans were proceeding to offer double apartments with shared kitchens and baths. The third of the major reasons for the changes in residential patterns is the lengthening of the life-span of the individual. In 1975 the average for Japanese women was 77 years, for men it was 72 years.

As is the case in all industrial societies, Japan's aged women greatly outnumber men—they account for 60 percent of the age-group of sev-

TABLE 8

Number of Japanese Households of Different Type, 1967 and 1971

(thousands)

Year	Total households	Nuclear families[a]	Nuclear families with elderly member(s)	Elderly couple only	Single elderly person	Other
1967						
No.	28,140	15,600	7,970	1,030	570	2,970
Pct.	100.0%	55.4%	28.3%	3.7%	2.0%	10.6%
1971						
No.	30,860	17,460	9,150	1,470	750	2,030
Pct.	100.0%	56.6%	29.7%	4.8%	2.4%	6.5%
Rate of change	+9.7%	+11.9%	+14.8%	+42.7%	+31.6%	−31.7%

SOURCE: Economic Planning Agency (1973: 45).

[a] Families with intact married couples are not distinguished from those with only one surviving parent.

enty and over. The extraordinary change in the life cycle of the typical woman between 1940 and 1972 sheds some light on the circumstances that have made for very different patterning of the domestic unit in the two periods (see Table 9). While she marries about three and one-half years later, the Japanese woman now lives almost twenty-six years longer. Two major changes stand out. The first is the drop in the number of children from five to two. The second is that all of the events from the entry of the last child into college through the last child's marriage formerly occurred well *after* the deaths of both parents. But in 1972 both husband and wife survive the marriage of their last child by many years. And although the average length of married life has doubled from 22 to 44 years, the length of widowhood is about the same. The major difference is that widows today are old women, chronologically and physically, and very much more likely to be dependent on others than they were when the average widow did not live to be fifty years of age.

While cross-sectional analysis shows a marked decline in the average size of the Japanese family, the duration of cohabitation of the individual in a full two-generation stem family has increased greatly. In 1930 the two married couples lived together on the average only 5.5 years before one member of the senior couple died. The period of coresidence had almost tripled, to 15.7 years, by 1960 (Morioka 1967: 597–98). As we saw in Table 8, between 1967 and 1971 there

TABLE 9
The Life Cycle of the Typical Japanese Woman,
1940 and 1972

Event	Age based on data for:	
	1940	1972
Completion of education	14.5	18.5
Marriage	20.8	23.1
(age of husband)	(24.8)	(26.2)
Birth of first child	23.2	25.3
Birth of last child	35.5	27.9
(number of children)	(5)	(2)
Last child enters primary school	42.0	34.4
Last child enters college	56.0	46.4
Last child graduates from college	59.0	50.4
(age of husband)	(63.0)	(53.5)
Husband's retirement	52.0	51.9
Marriage of last child	58.3	52.5
Death of husband	42.9	67.1
(age of husband)	(46.9)	(70.2)
Death	49.6	75.5

SOURCE: *Jinkō mondai shingikai, Nihon jinkō no dōkō* (Tokyo: Okurasho, 1974), p. 116. Cited in Yamamura and Hanley (1975: 116).

was an actual increase of 14.8 percent in the number of families consisting of elderly people and their adult children. The government reported that in 1973, 80 percent of all rural residents over the age of fifty lived with either a married child (55 percent) or an unmarried one (24 percent), and that more than three-fourths of all persons over seventy lived with a married child (69 percent) or an unmarried one (8 percent). There were more than four times as many households of this type in which the parents live with a son's family than with a daughter's.

In a major contribution to our understanding of the Japanese family, Koyama (1962) identified what he called six family types (see Table 10), which are more profitably viewed as stages in the domestic cycle. In a study of a set of village household registers for the years 1802–61, he found that the classic household cycle was from 7 to 6 to 3 to 4 and back to 7. By contrast, the contemporary conjugal family of the western industrial countries moves from 2 to 3 to 2 to 1, when it terminates.

Koyama's types are set forth in Table 10 with the corresponding figures for Kurusu families in 1951 and 1975. This cross-sectional view reveals an increase in the proportion of conjugal families, from eleven to sixteen (50 percent of the total in 1951 and 70 percent in 1975), and a striking drop in the proportion of three-generation stem families from 32 percent in 1951 to 13 percent in 1975.

Such are the changes in family types analyzed cross-sectionally. More interesting by far are the cycles through which they have moved during the past generation. In Kurusu there are fifteen families who were present in 1951 and 1975. In Table 11 we give a brief account of these families and the course of development through which each has gone.

Koyama's classic pattern (7–6–3–4–7) did not occur at all in Kurusu between 1951 and 1975. There were no families of Type 7 in 1951, and only one in 1975. Furthermore, the two families that did pass through this stage then went to Type 2 and Type 1, respectively,

TABLE 10

Distribution of Kurusu Households
by Koyama's Family Types, 1951 and 1975

Family type (Koyama's numbering)	Households	
	1951	1975
1. Single member	2	2
2. Husband and wife	4	7
3. Husband and wife + unmarried child	7	9
4. Husband and wife + married child	2	1
5. Husband and wife + lineal ascendants	–	–
6. Husband and wife + lineal ascendants and descendants	7	3
7. Household including collaterals	–	1
TOTAL	22	23

TABLE II

Longitudinal Changes in Fifteen Kurusu Families, 1951 to 1975

Changes in type	1951	Intervening changes in type		1975
4–3–7	A▲⊤ B○⊤ C D	B●⊤ C D	B●⊤ C E D	B●⊤ C○⊤▲E ○D F G H
6–3	A△⊤ B●⊤△C D E	B●=△C D E F G		B○⊤▲C E F G
6–3	A△⊤○B C▲⊤○D E	C▲⊤○D E	⊤●D E	⊤○D ▲=○ E F	E▲⊤○F G H
6–2	⊤○A B●⊤▲C D E F G	B●⊤▲C D E F G		B●=△C
6–2	A△⊤ B▲⊤○C D E	B▲⊤○C D E	B▲⊤○C △=○ D F E	B▲=○C
6–3–2	A△⊤ B▲⊤○C D E F G H I	B▲⊤○C D E F G H I		B▲=○C
6–6	⊤○A B▲⊤○C D E F G	⊤○A B▲⊤○C △=○ D H		⊤○A B▲⊤○C D△⊤○H ○○ I J

TABLE II (*continued*)

Changes in type	1951	Intervening changes in type	1975
3-5-3	A▲ ⊤ ○B △ C	A▲ ⊤ ○B △=○ C D ⊤ ○B ▲=○ C D C▲ ⊤ ○D △ △ E F	C▲ ⊤ ○D △ F
3-3	A▲ ⊤ ○B ○ C		A▲ ⊤ ○B △ D
3-3	A▲ ⊤ ○B ○ ○ ○ △ △ △ C D E F G H	A▲ ⊤ ○B △=○ F I ⊤ ○B F▲ ⊤ ○I △ J	F▲ ⊤ ○I △ ○ J K
3-6	⊤ ●A ○ △ △ B C D	⊤ ●A △=○ C E	⊤ ○A C▲ ⊤ ○E △ ○ △ F G H
2-6	A△ = ●B	⊤ ●B C△ = ○D	⊤ ○B C▲ ⊤ ○D ○ △ E F
4-1	⊤ ●A ⊤ ○ ○ ⊤ △D B C △ △ ○ E F G		= ●A
3-4-6	A▲ ⊤ ○B △ △ ○ C D E	A▲ ⊤ ○B △=○ C F	⊤ ○B C▲ ⊤ ○F ○ ○ △ △ G H I J
6-2-7-1	⊤ ○A B▲ ⊤ ○C △ △ △ ○ D E F G	⊤ ●C △ △ △ ○ D E F G ⊤ ●C △=○ ○ D H G	= ●C

NOTE: Family head is shown in black. In only one case, the last family listed, does the elderly person live entirely alone, with no nearby kinsmen. All of the elderly couples and the other widow have established a married child in a new-style successor's house in Kurusu. (See Chapter Six.)

rather than to Type 6. On the other hand, there are no instances of a simple conjugal family pattern either (2–3–2–1). By far the most common shifts are from the three-generation stem family toward conjugal forms, and from these back to three-generation stem families again. All eight new families in 1975 were one or another of the conjugal types.

In Japan during the past twenty-five years there has been an increasing tendency for newly married couples, including the successor and his wife, to take up neolocal residence. There has been an increase in the number of conjugal families in Kurusu as well. As we have already noted, in 1951 half of the households were composed of a married couple with or without children, the classic conjugal family, whereas in 1975, 70 percent of families were of this type. But there is a fundamental difference between the two situations, for in 1951 the members of a conjugal family assumed that it represented only a stage on the way to the development of a stem family, consisting of either (1) a husband and wife (or one of them) with one married child with or without children, or (2) a husband and wife (or one of them) with parents of one of them and their own children. These two stages differ in regard to the age of the head of the family; in the first stage, he is a member of the oldest generation, whereas in the second stage he belongs to the middle generation. In 1951 the four families of Kurusu consisting only of husband and wife were either newlyweds or childless couples. In 1975, however, there were seven such families, of which only two were newlyweds and five were couples whose children had left the community altogether or lived in separate dwellings in the hamlet. Furthermore, the nine conjugal families made up of husband and wife (or one of them) with unmarried child(ren) were by no means clearly on their way to becoming stem families. Indeed, most people in Kurusu assumed that when the successor married, the outcome, at least to begin with, would be the creation of *two* kinds of married-couple families—an elderly couple living alone and the newlyweds living in a separate dwelling not far away.

Perhaps the most striking shift of all has occurred with respect to families consisting of husband and wife (or one of them) living with both lineal descendants and ascendants. Seven of the twenty-two households in 1951, but only three of twenty-three in 1975, were of

TABLE 12
Number of Generations per
Household in Kurusu,
1951 and 1975

Generations per household	Households	
	1951	1975
1	5	9
2	8	9
3	9	4
4	0	1
TOTAL	22	23

this type. This is, of course, the classic stem family, composed of two married couples in different generations and the unmarried children of the junior couple. This particular stage of the family cycle is an especially difficult one for the Japanese farm family, for only the middle generation is fully productive.

There remains only to look into the question of the generational depth of Kurusu families, shown in Table 12. In 1951 there were five one-generation families, eight two-generation families, and nine with three generations. By 1975 there had been a sharp shift toward shallower depth, with nine one-generation, nine two-generation, four three-generation, and one four-generation families.

On the other hand, the number of families with no intact married couples in any generation had declined from six in 1951 to two in 1975, while the number of families with at least one intact married couple had risen slightly, from fifteen to nineteen (see Table 13). Nonetheless, the stem family was found in only two of the twenty-three households in Kurusu in 1975, and not at all in 1951.

Does all this mean that the household ideal has disappeared completely? Under the requirements of the old system we should have expected that elderly parents would live out their lives in continuous residence with one or another of their married children. But the household lost all of its legal supports with the adoption of the postwar constitution and Civil Code. Although the position of the household head was abolished at the end of 1947, the household register still designates one individual as the "ranking family member," who is the nom-

TABLE 13
*Number of Intact Married Couples
per Household in Kurusu,
1951 and 1975*

Couples per household	Households	
	1951	1975
0	6	2
1	16	19
2	0	2
TOTAL	22	23

inal head of the family. Clearly some consideration must be given to the ways in which the questions of succession and inheritance have been handled in recent years. In 1951 there had not been enough time for the provisions of either code or constitution to have any measurable effect on the agricultural households of Kurusu. Their principal concern was with the long-range effects of the abolition of impartible inheritance and primogenitoral succession. Many people rather casually predicted that the reforms would lead to the fractionating of the already tiny farms of Japan, and that there would be a great deal of trouble among siblings about the inheritance. This grim forecast reckoned without the force of the restrictions on the disposition of agricultural land, however.

It is often said that the equal-inheritance provision of the Civil Code did not lead to the breakup of holdings because of the inertia of tradition or the lack of interest of the children in obtaining small pieces of an already small operation. Both may have been important considerations, but the import of legal restrictions must not be overlooked. Under the law, non-farmers could no longer own agricultural land and no one was permitted to own agricultural land located outside the administrative unit in which he resided. As a consequence of these restrictions, sons who were in wage-earning or salaried positions were ruled out as successors, as were married sons who had established residence outside the village, and daughters who had married out. As a rule, the successor remained in his natal home and inherited the land; other children received some money or property at the time of their marriages and moved away. In any event, the law also required that no agricultural holding be reduced to a unit of less than two *tan* (19.84 ares) in size. Since the agricultural holdings of Kurusu families rarely exceed four *tan*, there was little room for the relevant provisions of the Civil Code to have any effect on Kurusu's already fractionated lands.

Nevertheless, twenty-five years and one generation later, some notable changes in inheritance and succession patterns have occurred, not all of them in predictable directions. Ten family headships have changed between 1951 and 1975. The outcomes are as follows. (1) With the death of the household head, an elderly widow, her surviving son closed down the house in Kurusu and went to the city. (2) The widow of the deceased head has been unsuccessful in securing the succession as yet. She had persuaded her son and his wife to move back into the house with her, and has made extensive improvements on it, but they quarrelled and the young couple moved out. (3) The present head is the daughter of the former head. She had married out, but returned as a widow to live in her natal house. Her elder daughter has taken an adopted husband into the family. (4) The headship passed to the adopted husband of the deceased head's adopted granddaughter, through whom the succession passed. (5) The head's grandson, first son of the head's fourth son, succeeded him many years after the head's own sons had established separate households of their own. (6) The widow of the deceased head has passed the headship on to their first son; and in four cases the son of the head has succeeded directly to the headship of the family and inherited the property.

Thus in only two cases have the families of Kurusu failed to find someone to carry on. Although only four of the eight successions have been directly from father to son, none of the variations represented by the other cases is a violation of the range of traditional options. There is, however, a more recent development of special interest. Several families are facing up to the necessity of finding a successor in the not-too-distant future. Some of them have opted for, or say that they are planning to opt for, a new style of uxorilocal marriage; others have devised a new way of housing the senior and junior generations of the family.

Before we turn to a consideration of these devices, let us review the situation as it was in 1951. Almost all of the heads of families then had been heads of households under the old Civil Code. Although their

legal position had changed, authority relations within the family were
not much altered, despite quite a lot of complaining by older people
about the evil effects on the young of the new postwar educational
system and the democratic reforms promoted by the American Occupation. Older males still enjoyed positions of prestige and influence in
household and community alike; women and younger males were generally deferential, and however outspoken they were on some issues,
they were careful not to press their expressions of independence too
far. Ten of the twenty-two family heads were sons who had succeeded
their fathers; three were adopted-husband successors; and four were
widowed women whose children had either died or were not yet old
enough to assume responsibility for family affairs. Of the remaining
five, one was the granddaughter of the head who had adopted her after
his son was killed in World War II, another the grandson of the former
head, one the son of the former female head of the house, one a
nephew who succeeded his uncle, and the fifth an adopted daughter of
the former head, whose own adopted husband had not yet been designated family head. In short, not quite half were sons of previous heads.
The situation has not changed dramatically, then; finding a successor
has never been a routinely simple matter.

As an example of the continuing character of the problem, let us
look at the adopted husbands (*muko yōshi*). When a family reaches an
impasse in its efforts to secure the succession by regular means, one
alternative is to take a husband for one's daughter. The groom enters
his wife's house, takes her name, and eventually becomes the successor. Clearly there are severe strains on the occupant of such a position,
resulting largely from the role-reversal of husband and wife. The
difficulties of the adopted husband are reflected in the local version of
the old saying, *konuka san gō motta nara muko ni iku na* (As long as
you have three measures of rice bran, don't go as an adopted husband). They are in a disadvantaged position in their wives' families,
and they are often criticized by members of their communities. As one
man told me in 1951, "That *yōshi* over there is a wretch. He has
caused a lot of trouble here because he doesn't know how we do
things. But my neighbor's *yōshi* is a fine young man who has fit in very
well."

In 1951 there were five such men in Kurusu. Three of them were
family heads; the other two, while de facto heads, were not registered

as such. As we have seen, there were five adopted husbands in 1975 as well. Two of them were family heads; two still occupied junior positions in the family, but were quite influential in its affairs because the head in both cases was a widow; one was married to a woman who has never relinquished the headship of the family and is not likely to do so. Although five may seem a large number of adopted husbands for so small a community, Kurusu is not unusual in this respect. Befu (1962:37) summarizes data from several communities which shows that about one-quarter of all successions were secured through adopted husbands. Nonetheless, given the peculiar relationship of these men to the communities in which they live—they are potential or actual family heads who are not native to the place—there is reason to believe that the proportion is too high for Kurusu's own good, a conclusion arrived at recently by several of its residents (see Chapter Eight).

Five Kurusu Families

In the remainder of this chapter we will try to give some sense of what has happened to four of the older Kurusu families in the past twenty-five years and what one of the newest is like. Because family secrets are among those we have tried to keep, none of the five will be found in the longitudinal analysis of households given in Table 11. None of the events discussed in these vignettes is pure invention, however; they have simply been rearranged.

The Tsurutanis

When I first went to Kurusu in 1951, one of my early encounters was with a man named Tsurutani Teruo, who was then fifty-five years old. He and his wife Hideko, who was six years his junior, had had six children, three of whom had died in infancy. The surviving children, all sons, were Haruo, twenty-four; Akira, nineteen; and Tsutomu, seventeen years old. The eldest, who was not yet married, lived with his parents and his youngest brother. The nineteen-year-old visited home frequently from his job with a construction company not far from Takamatsu.

The Tsurutani house was a substantial one but was in need of some maintenance they felt they could not afford. The family had lost the land it owned in another village as a result of the land reform, leaving them the 44 ares they owned in Yasuhara Village. While they were comfortably off by Kurusu standards of the time, with an annual gross income of about ¥160,000, they had suffered a considerable decline in their standard of living.

The household was run on what Kurusu people of today are inclined to think of as traditional lines. The father was unmistakably head of the house, yet because his wife did so much essential agricultural work, she was likely to speak her mind when she thought it important to do so. All the outward rules of decorum were observed, however. When guests were in the house, Hideko served them and her husband, and would have never considered eating with them. She fetched tea, beer, and food at the orders of her husband, and fell silent in the company of men. The two boys were moderately deferential to their father, and had a healthy respect for their mother's opinions about agricultural matters, which Haruo often sought.

Haruo, the eldest son, was married in 1954 to a woman from a village about six kilometers from Kurusu. The marriage was arranged, and they saw each other only twice before the wedding. Haruo, whose chief characteristic is his hair-trigger temper, had the good fortune to marry a woman of remarkably calm and pleasant demeanor. Her name is Shizue, and she is a year older than her husband. Within their first six years of marriage they had three children, a boy and two girls. Teruo, the head of the family, died suddenly in 1968. Haruo, who is now forty-eight, became the family head and presides over a household consisting of his seventy-three year-old mother, his wife, and their three children—Ichirō is now twenty, Sadako is nineteen, and Junko is fifteen. Haruo and his wife can do all of the agricultural labor, except at the peak seasons, because they own all of the major new agricultural machines. He works occasionally as a plasterer, a trade he was taught during his military service, but the jobs are irregular and the family cannot count on the income from them. The grandmother does some gardening, but a leg injury resulting from a fall a few years ago makes it impossible for her to do heavy work of any kind.

Their son Ichirō has been employed as a bus mechanic for the past three years, and commutes daily by car—a four-cylinder Subaru—to the company barns. They had very much wanted to send him to college or a technical school after he graduated from higher-school, but they could not afford it. Nineteen-year-old Sadako commutes by bus to her job in the offices of a trucking company in a nearby town. She also finished higher-school, where she was enrolled in the commercial course, and got the job through a man who works for the bus company that employs her brother. Hideko thinks that this man may very well serve as go-between for both children, although it is a little early to be thinking about their getting married just yet. Ichirō makes the payments on his car and Sadako is known as a dedicated saver. She confesses that she would like to save enough money to take a charter-flight vacation to Hawaii, but in more sober moments she says that she is saving for her marriage. Her ambition is to be able to take with her a handsome array of household appliances which will make the housework easier. Since she plans to continue working until she has children, and does not expect any help with domestic chores from her husband, this not unreasonable goal is shared by a great many young Japanese women in her position.

The younger daughter Junko is still in school. As the youngest child she is much indulged by the whole family—in Japan the last-born child (*suekko*) is characterized in much the same way that only children are in the United States. She is charming and lively, and is very popular with her classmates, so popular indeed that her grandmother complains that she is seldom home.

The Tsurutanis are worried about the future. The parents wonder if Ichirō will continue to live in Kurusu after his marriage, and they are anything but sanguine about the prospects for agricultural operations as small as theirs. Neither parent expects that either daughter will take even a new-style adopted husband, apparently, in order to bring in a man to carry on the family. As long as Haruo and Shizue remain vigorous they will continue to farm, for they have no other skills that are readily marketable. One day as we sat talking about Kurusu and its problems, Haruo said, "If I knew of any sure way of making it work, I'd sell out as soon as the children are all married. But it's just too risky. If Ichirō stays on, we may be all right, but we have not really talked it over, and I'm not sure what he wants to do."

The Sawamuras

Among the farmers of Kurusu who benefited significantly from the land reform, the Sawamuras are a rather typical case. They owned about one-fifth of the land they cultivated prior to 1946, and were tenants on the remainder. Fortunately, much of the land they rented belonged to a man who lived in another village and Sawamura Yoshio was able to purchase all of it for cash. When I first met him in 1951 he was forty-nine. His wife Kyōko was forty-seven, and they lived in a modest house with his seventy-nine-year-old mother and their two sons, Kiyoshi and Yoshiharu, then twenty-nine and twenty-two. Their second son, who would have been twenty-seven, was killed in the South Pacific during the closing weeks of World War II.

The head of the family, Yoshio, was working part-time as a carpenter and used to bicycle to his local jobs or wait for a truck to pick him up when he was working at more distant locations. His wife was one of the hardest-working women in a place where everyone worked hard. She was a morose woman, and it was rumored that she had a great deal of trouble with her first son's wife. Indeed, their relationship seemed almost a paradigm for the mother-in-law vs. daughter-in-law problem that figures so prominently in Japanese fiction and drama.

The first son Kiyoshi and his wife lived with his parents, as all successors and their wives then did. Their four-year-old daughter Chiyoko was a special favorite of her grandfather's. Yoshiharu, the unmarried son, also lived at home. Both young men occasionally worked with their father on carpentry jobs. Kiyoshi had in fact gone to Osaka, where he worked for about three years for a distant relative, but he had come back to Kurusu and married Tamako, who was from a farm family in Shionoe. The same age as her husband, she was known as a physically strong, somewhat stubborn woman, and most people said that she was not to blame for most of the trouble she had with her mother-in-law.

In most respects the family was better off in 1951 than it had ever been, with about one-half hectare of land and three men with some side-jobs that brought in cash. Yoshio was confident about the future and often congratulated himself on having a fair amount of land for this district and two hard-working sons. But for a time things did not go well at all. In 1960 Kiyoshi moved away to Takamatsu with his long-suffering wife and their two children. A son had been born in 1953, and it seemed for a while that Kyōko's attitude toward her daughter-in-law was softening. Trouble soon developed again, however, and the chance of a regular job in a construction company was all the excuse that Kiyoshi needed, and they moved out.

By this time Yoshiharu was married, and he and his wife lived in a small apartment in Hiroshima, where he worked in a shipyard. They had two sons, born in 1961 and 1963. The parents, left alone, continued cultivating their land, buying the usual complement of machines and hiring labor when they needed it. Increasingly embittered, Kyōko grew more and more difficult and at length suffered a nervous breakdown, following which she became quiet and withdrawn.

In 1969, the situation changed dramatically. Yoshiharu's wife, who had taken a part-time job as soon as her second child entered school, found her accumulating responsibilities too heavy. The couple had been unable to find a place to live with more room for the children, and Yoshiharu seems to have had some trouble at work. After a visit to Kurusu at New Year's, when the two brothers had discussed the situation with their father, it was decided that Yoshiharu would be designated successor. His father offered to build a house for him and his family at the side of the compound. The senior couple would continue living in the main house; the new one, much roomier than most urban apartments, would be for the exclusive use of the young family. The plan was effected in 1971.

Yoshio, now seventy-three, still works in the fields and hires some labor at peak seasons. His wife stays in the house most of the time, but looks after a small vegetable and flower garden. Yoshiharu and his wife are both employed by a small company in a town not far from Takamatsu, to which they commute by car. Their son and daughter are both in school, and spend a great deal of time with their grandmother. Yoshio thinks that they will stay in Kurusu. When we asked him if he thought that the farm operation would continue, he looked at me for a long time and said, "If you had asked me that before, I'd have thought it a peculiar question. Now I have no idea how to answer it."

The Okazakis

There have been significant changes in the fortunes of the Okazaki family, most of a nature that would have been very difficult to foresee in 1951. The head of the family had died unexpectedly in 1940, leaving his thirty-year-old widow Ayako with two small sons. Fortunately, the family then owned about 25 ares of excellent paddy land and exercised rights of tenancy on another 60. Being widowed, Ayako was able to call on the other families of Kurusu for help with her agricultural operation. She was managing fairly well until the land reform in 1946, which deprived her of most of the rented fields, which she was unable to purchase because they were located outside Yasuhara Village. By 1951 her financial situation was quite precarious, but on more than one occasion the hamlet had rallied to her support by making up the quota of rice that she was legally required to deliver to the government, so that she would be able to keep enough to feed her family and even sell some on the still-lucrative black market. Her sons, Fumio and Takashi, thirteen and fourteen, respectively, were both in middle-school, and while she complained about the high cost of education, she hoped that one or both of them would be able to go on to higher-school. Neither did, however; both sought employment instead. Takashi commuted to work in a nearby town by bus. Fumio was sent to an uncle who had a small shop that made lathe-turned chair and table legs; he returned to Kurusu after about five years.

In 1965, at the age of twenty-seven, Takashi married a woman from Takamatsu who had been a fellow-employee for a time, and she moved into the house in Kurusu. Ayako was pleased with the arrangement; for twenty-five years a widow, she at last had her first son and his wife with her in the family home. There would be someone to carry on. Her younger son stayed on for a few months before moving to a small city in the west of Shikoku, where his uncle had found him a job.

For a little less than a year Takashi and his wife commuted to work in Takamatsu by automobile. She stopped working shortly before the birth of their first child, and it was not long before tensions developed between mother-in-law and daughter-in-law. Ayako comments with some bitterness on the selfishness of "that city girl" and accepts little of the blame that led eventually to the departure of Takashi and his family. Hurt and disappointed, Ayako nevertheless called in some outstanding debts and helped the young couple relocate nearer their place of employment. In the summer of 1975, their only child was staying with her in Kurusu, where his parents were frequent visitors.

Shortly after the rift, Ayako, now approaching sixty, began what her neighbors describe as an artful campaign to persuade Fumio to come home. He did return finally in 1973 with a pregnant wife, one child, and a car of his own. Ayako has had the house extensively remodeled, making the greater part of it over into nearly private quarters for the young family. Fumio and his wife have nothing to do with agriculture, and both work full-time in a town near Takamatsu. Ayako cares for both children during the week, and tries to schedule her household chores and occasional visits to see nearby relatives during school hours. She no longer farms, having let out her land to a man who cultivates many scattered plots with a full complement of agricultural machinery.

In 1975 she was deeply concerned about the succession, and was hoping that her sons and their wives could be persuaded to decide among themselves who would ultimately live in the Okazaki house in Kurusu. Early in our stay it was widely believed that whatever the decision, neither son was likely to remain for long after her death, for the house is in need of extensive repair and there is very little agricultural land at stake. But in the late summer of 1975, faced with a sharply reduced income and endlessly rising consumer prices, it appeared that Takashi and his family might come back to Kurusu—perhaps only to wait out the recession, perhaps to stay. Ayako seemed to have once again within her grasp her dream of a regular succession. Failing that, it was clear that she would settle for what many of her generation have been unable to secure—a married child living close by who would look after her in her old age.

The Kawabes

The house looks much as it did in 1951, although the thatched roof has given way to a blue tiled one. But the Kawabe family is gone, and a younger couple from near Shionoe lives there. In 1951 Kawabe Seiichi, his wife Hamako, their five children, and Seiichi's parents were among the poorest of Kurusu's families. Even though they had gained a little land as a consequence of the land reform, it was not nearly enough to support so large a family adequately. The children, all of school age, were of little help, and Seiichi's parents were too old for heavy agricultural labor. The Kawabes were just at that point in the domestic cycle which is the most disadvantageous for a farm family: neither its most senior nor its most junior generation is fully productive, and the entire burden falls on the adult couple of the middle generation. Seiichi worked as a casual laborer at the Naiba Dam construction site when he was not in the fields, and Hamako had just started weaving *kamasu* mats for sale to the Agricultural Cooperative in hopes of bringing in badly needed cash income.

As the children finished middle-school, all but the eldest son Takao found work outside Kurusu. He joined his father in construction work, and like other unmarried teenagers who stayed at home, was a full participant in the agricultural operation as well. Two other sons eventually went to Osaka, and the two daughters, who continued to live at home, were employed at the offices of the Agricultural Cooperative. In the late 1950's both of the grandparents died and Seiichi began to look for a bride for his eldest son. In 1960, a foreman at the construction company he was then working for told Seiichi of a likely marriage prospect for Takao. The negotiations went smoothly and the wedding was held that same year. Emiko was the daughter of a farm family in Yamaguchi Prefecture who had been sent to Matsuyama in Shikoku to work as a clerk in a cousin's food processing business. Although accustomed to rural life, she did not much care for Kurusu, which she is reported to have found too hostile or aloof toward a young woman marrying in. Nevertheless, she stuck it out, and one by one all of the other Kawabe children moved out. Takao had found a fairly good job in a cement plant, and Hamako had utilized her Matsuyama connections to secure a clerical position in a hotel office in Takamatsu. The family's economic position had improved greatly, and everyone commented on how well the Kawabes seemed to get along; older women in particular were openly envious of the good relations between Hamako and her daughter-in-law.

Then, in 1969, with almost no advance warning, Takao and Emiko moved away to Yamaguchi, where a relative of hers had offered to set them up in business. Kurusu was awash with rumors about the reasons for this unexpected turn of events, but all that is known for certain is that Takao went as the successor to a couple who were either childless or who had been unable to persuade a child to carry on their business. Seiichi and his wife, by now quite elderly, stayed on in Kurusu for about a year; in 1974 they sold their house to outsiders and their small landholdings to a Kurusu family and moved to Osaka to live with their third son and his family. It was a swift end to a household that by all accounts had been in Kurusu for at least four generations.

Opinion about the affair in the community is divided. Many older people, seeing in all this a future that they are unwilling to contemplate, are sharply critical of Takao and his wife. Most of the younger people, even those who found the details of the affair somewhat bizarre—"after all," they said, "he *is* the eldest son!"—professed to approve of what they seem to interpret as a set of perfectly reasonable decisions on the part of all concerned that in the long run will prove to have been to everyone's advantage. In 1975 at *o-bon*, Seiichi and his wife returned to visit the family graves and called on some of their former neighbors. They stayed with relatives in Nakamura and spoke no ill of any of their children.

The Handas

The Handas, one of Kurusu's newest families, are a young couple with an infant daughter. Tomoo is twenty-five; his wife Kimiko is twenty-three. Their brand-new house was built on a paddy field owned by Tomoo's father, who lives up the highway a few miles. He deeded Tomoo the land and the young man took out a low-interest government mortgage on the house. It has four small rooms, all wood-floored but one, including what in Japan is called a DK (for "dining kitchen") with table and chairs, which both find more comfortable than sitting on the tatami mats, for like almost all Japanese their age, they have spent most of their school and working lives on chairs. Beside the house is a combined garage and storage building of concrete-block construction.

Tomoo drives a small car to his job with a tool-and-die firm about twenty-five kilometers away. He says that the gas consumption is low and the trip takes only about thirty minutes, not a great distance at all compared to that traveled by some of his coworkers who commute from Tokushima Prefecture. His wife quit her job in Takamatsu when the child was born, and she hopes to stay home only until she can get her into the local nursery school or until the little girl is old enough to be left with her husband's mother during the day.

They both say that they prefer the clear air and cool summers of Kurusu to the smoggy heat of Takamatsu, where they would otherwise have to live, and both are quick to point out that with land prices so high they could never have hoped to have a house in the city. Kurusu is not the place where either of them was born, it is not the place where they earn their living, and the worries of its agricultural households are not their worries. They represent, in all these respects, the newest kind of Kurusu resident, a kind who one day may well outnumber the farmers.

CHAPTER THREE

The Decline of Agriculture

MUCH OF what has happened in Kurusu over the past twenty-five years can be understood only against the background of the development of Japanese agriculture during that period. The people of Kurusu are farmers of a sort, after all, and their forebears settled there because of the unusually good paddy-field land. In this chapter we give an overview of conditions in 1950 and 1975 in Japan and Kagawa Prefecture, and in Yasuhara Village in 1951 and Shionoe Town in 1975. Wherever possible, we have used figures and statistics for these three calendar or fiscal years, but in a few cases the vagaries of data collection or publication have made it necessary to use materials for other years.

Japan

Between 1950 and 1975 the ratio of rural to urban dwellers has almost reversed, from 62:38 to 30:70. In that same period, extraordinary changes have occurred in the agricultural population with respect to the proportions of farm families engaged in full-time and part-time farming. Table 14 tells the story. The proportion of full-time agricultural households has declined steadily; those classified as part-time farmers dependent primarily on agriculture have decreased less dramatically; and there has been an astonishing rise in the proportion of those families in agriculture who depend primarily on non-agricultural occupations.

Between 1970 and 1975 the number of people engaged in agriculture dropped 23.6 percent, from 10.4 to 7.9 million, more than double

TABLE 14
Percentage of Japanese Farm Families Engaged in Full- and Part-Time Agriculture, 1950–75

Employment	1950	1955	1960	1965	1970	1975
Full-time agriculture	50.0%	34.8%	34.3%	21.5%	15.6%	12.4%
Part-time, dependent mainly on agriculture	28.4	37.7	33.7	36.7	33.7	25.4
Part-time, dependent mainly on non-agr. income	21.6	27.5	32.0	41.8	50.7	62.1

NOTE: In the 1970 census, a farm household is defined as one cultivating 5 ares (0.13 acres) or more (in Western Japan), or one with smaller holdings which earned more than ¥50,000 from agricultural pursuits. A full-time farm household is one which has no member employed off the farm for more than 30 days or who grossed more than ¥30,000 from non-agricultural employment. The distinction between the two types of part-time farm households turns on whether agricultural income accounted for more or less than half of total household income. (All calculations were based on the situation reported for the year preceding the census.)

the rate of decline in the preceding five-year period. In 1975 more than 70 percent of those engaged in farming were men over sixty years of age and women. In the five years between 1970 and 1975 the number of farm families dropped 8.3 percent to 4,953,000, the first time that the figure has fallen below five million in Japan's modern history. The rate of decline, 6.5 percent, was greater than the 5.7 percent drop between 1965 and 1970, but not so dramatic as that in the number of people engaged in agriculture (*Nōgyō hakusho* 1976:129).

While the degree of dependence of the farm household on non-agricultural sources of income has grown steadily in recent years, both side-employment and the taking of wage-work to supplement agricultural income have very long histories. For example, data recorded in the early 1840's for an area in the extreme south of the island of Honshu show that more than half the income (about 55 percent) of a population defined as 82 percent agricultural was derived from sources other than farming. Similar roughly contemporaneous materials from scattered places in southern Japan speak of work away from the village as providing substantial income to agricultural households. In some cases, up to 20 percent of the total population, and thus an even higher proportion of the labor force, were reported by the census taker to be living and working away from home on the day of the enumeration (T. Smith 1969). It is further worth noting that "the dominant type of off-farm occupation ... since the 1930's has been that of a wage- or salary-earner who resides on the farm and commutes by various means of transportation to his off-farm job" (Misawa 1969: 252–53).

The smaller the size of the operation, the more likely the family is to leave agriculture altogether. The number of households tilling less than 2.5 hectares dropped significantly in the period under consideration, while the number of those tilling more than that amount increased. Nonetheless, the average area tilled was only 1.1 hectares in 1974, and 68 percent of all farm families cultivated less than one hectare.

Kagawa Prefecture

Shikoku is the smallest of the four main islands of Japan and Kagawa is the smallest of its four prefectures. Indeed, after the urban prefecture of Osaka, Kagawa is the smallest administrative unit in the country. The population of the prefecture in 1950 was 946,000, yielding a density of about 506 persons per square kilometer. With one or two exceptional years, the population fell steadily to a low of about 895,000 in 1966, when it began to rise annually to the 1975 figure of 960,000, with a density of 513 persons per square kilometer. Thus, during the period when the population of the country as a whole grew 35 percent, that of Kagawa went up only 1.5 percent. In its recent reversal of population outflow Kagawa joins the other prefectures in Japan which until 1974 reported annually a net loss of people; in 1975 none recorded an absolute decline. The unbridled growth of the metropolitan areas had finally slowed.

The proportion of Kagawa's population living in cities has increased, but the rate of urbanization is not dramatic. The only three urban places with more than sixty thousand inhabitants accounted for 38 percent of the population in 1960, 40 percent in 1965, 43 percent in 1970, and 45 percent in 1975.

In 1970 there were 242,568 households in Kagawa Prefecture as compared to 191,288 in 1950. The average size of households had dropped from 4.9 to 3.9 persons. The proportion of agricultural households in 1970 had declined to 78,961 (33 percent) from 93,048 (49 percent) in 1950. Between 1950 and 1974 the average number of persons per agricultural household fell from 5.8 to 4.5.

The shift to part-time farming, long a marked feature of Kagawa agriculture in any event, has been dramatic. In 1950, 49 percent of all agricultural households were classified as full-time farmers, 30 percent were part-time depending primarily on agriculture, and 21 percent were part-time farmers depending primarily on other sources of income (*Kagawa ken chō* 1951:52). In 1974 only 10 percent were full-time farmers and the other percentages had shifted to 19 and 71 respectively.

Kagawa Prefecture has long been known for the extremely small size of its family-farm operations. In 1948 the average area cultivated was only 53 ares, the smallest in Japan (Yabe 1949:8). At that time three-fourths of the cultivated land was in paddy. In 1973 the amount of cultivated land in the prefecture had dropped by about 4 percent and the average area cultivated was 47 ares. About three-fourths was still paddy. Nearly a third of the agricultural households farmed less than 30 ares in 1950, about 20 percent cultivated between 30 and 50 ares, and just under 40 percent between 50 ares and one hectare (*Kagawa ken chō* 1951:45–46). The distribution in 1975 was substantially unchanged.

As a result of the land reform, whose local effects are discussed below, the percentage of landowning farm households in Kagawa rose from about 25 to about 70, while the proportion of pure tenants declined from 31 percent to 3 (*Kagawa ken chō* 1951:46).

Yasuhara Village, 1951

In 1951 the total area of Yasuhara Village was 33.75 square kilometers. Its population in 1950 was 4,215 with a density of 125 persons per square kilometer. The average household size of 4.97 persons was about the same as the figure for the whole of the prefecture. Of the village's 848 households, 78 percent were agricultural. They cultivated an average of 50 ares, a figure not very different from that for the prefecture as a whole (*Kagawa ken chō* 1952:271–74).

The 663 agricultural households were classified as follows: only 12 percent were full-time farmers, 69 percent were part-time farmers depending primarily on income from agriculture, and 19 percent were part-time farmers depending primarily on non-agricultural sources of income. As for the area under cultivation, some 23 percent farmed less than 30 ares, 27 percent from 30 to 50 ares, and 45 percent between

50 ares and one hectare. They had fared far less well than the average Kagawa farmer in the land reform, for in 1950 only 52 percent were classified as landowners and 6 percent remained pure tenants (*Kagawa ken chō* 1951:45–49).

After rice, the second most important crop was the grains called by the generic term *mugi*, which include wheat, millet, barley, and naked barley, followed by sweet potatoes, Irish potatoes, tobacco, and a great variety of garden vegetables raised almost exclusively for home consumption. Most of Yasuhara's land was in forest, much of it severely cut over during the 1930's and 1940's, which yielded lumber, fuel, and three important food crops—bamboo shoots, a kind of mushroom called *matsutake*, and chestnuts.

Small-scale industry was almost nonexistent except for a number of sawmills scattered widely over the area. The one located in Kurusu, which like most of the others produced lumber for building construction, box staves, wooden parts for agricultural machinery, and serving trays, was opened in 1938 by a Kurusu family.

Shionoe Town, 1975

Table 15 gives the figures for the agricultural households of Shionoe Town in terms of the degree of their involvement in agricultural pursuits. The proportion of full-time farmers fell from 22 percent to 12 percent between 1960 and 1970 and rose slightly by 1975. In 1960, 51 percent were part-time farmers whose income was primarily agricultural and 29 percent were part-timers engaged primarily in non-agricultural activities. These percentages had shifted dramatically by 1975, when only 30 percent were in the former and 57 percent in the latter categories. Throughout the 1960's the average number of persons per farm family remained at just over 4.3, but dropped to 4.1 in 1975.

At the Agricultural Cooperative they estimated that the only member households which make a decent living from agriculture alone are those near enough to Takamatsu to make it possible to raise a variety of vegetables for the urban market as well as the rice crop. The remainder still engage in some agriculture, but it accounts for a smaller and smaller proportion of their total income. The membership is classified as follows:

TABLE 15
Agricultural Population of Shionoe Town, 1960–75

					Overall change, 1960–75	
Statistical category	1960	1965	1970	1975	No.	Pct.
Agricultural population	4,852	4,428	4,200	3,524	−1,328	−27.4%
Total farm households	1,123	1,025	956	868	−255	−22.7%
Agriculture only					−126	−52.3%
Number	241	242	119	115		
Pct. of total	21.5%	23.6%	12.4%	13.2%		
Part-time, primarily agriculture					−308	−54.3%
Number	567	437	363	259		
Pct. of total	50.5%	42.6%	38.0%	29.8%		
Part-time, primarily non-agriculture					+179	+56.8%
Number	315	346	474	494		
Pct. of total	28.0%	33.8%	49.6%	57.0%		
Persons per household	4.3	4.3	4.4	4.1		

1. Full-time farm families: 7 percent of the membership. Assuming a family of five or six persons with about one hectare in rice, vegetables, and tobacco, the annual income ought to be three to four million yen.

2. Part-time farm families: 93 percent of the membership. These break down into two subcategories:

(a) Type 1: 15 to 20 percent of this category. These families are primarily dependent on agriculture, but have a major source of additional income. By and large this supplementary income, while important, is less than that derived from agriculture.

(b) Type 2: 80–85 percent of this category. These families, said to farm primarily to keep their land or because they treasure it as more than a mere capital asset, obtain most of their income from non-agricultural employment. They often spend as much as ¥100,000 to ¥150,000 annually on agricultural equipment. It is in such cases that one frequently hears that agriculture has become the by-employment, for two-thirds or more of their total income is non-agricultural earnings.

While there has been a steady decline in the number of full-time farm households in Shionoe Town, and a growing dependence of part-time farmers on supplementary income, Ogura (1967:61) has pointed out that "The propertied farmers [created by] the land reform persist, because the cultivated land provides a form of social security, because land ownership acts as a hedge against possible inflation, and because other opportunities for obtaining stable employment adequate for the family may be limited in the near future." Indeed, the oil crisis of 1973 precipitated just such a situation as that envisaged by Ogura, and we shall consider its effects below.

Land

Local Effects of the Land Reform

In 1946 the Japanese government enacted a land reform law. In Kagawa Prefecture the maximum holding was set at 2.6 *chō* (2.589 hectares) of which only 6 *tan* (59.52 ares) could be rented out. According to the records of the Yasuhara Village Land Reform Commission, as of November 1945 there were 338.2 hectares of agricultural land in the village, of which only about 6 percent was in the hands of absentee landlords. Of the remainder, 46 percent was cultivated by its owners, and 54 percent by tenants. Following the reform, as of August 1950, there were 343.3 hectares of agricultural land in Yasuhara, the increase resulting from a combination of factors including re-surveying, the "discovery" of unregistered plots, and small-scale reclamation projects. Only 11 percent of this land was tenanted; 89 percent of the village's agricultural land was being cultivated by its owners.

A total of 105.8 hectares—about 31 percent of village farm land—had been sold. As was generally the case throughout Japan, the sales had the chief result of transferring title of a given piece of land from its owner to the erstwhile tenant who had been cultivating it prior to the reform. Prices were set so low that 87 percent of all sales in Yasuhara were for cash. Land ownership, as it had been for a very long time, continued to be on a molecular scale.

We have noted that the land reform law specifically prohibited ownership of agricultural land by persons not resident in the administrative unit in which it was located. In this provision lay great misfortune for Yasuhara's landowners, for while only about 20 hectares of the farmland in the village belonged to absentee owners, residents of Yasuhara owned approximately 150 hectares in other villages. The net loss of land was considerable here, as it was in other similar mountainous areas.

In 1952 the land register listed 170 plots of agricultural land in Kurusu. These included paddy fields and dry fields (many of which had names of their own just as the oldest houses did), cemeteries, grassland, and waste land. The total area of the paddy fields was 5.16 hectares (12.6 acres). The largest was 20.9 ares, the smallest just under four square yards. There were 33 dry fields with a total area of 69.5 ares, averaging about 250 square yards in size.

Before the land reform 8 of Kurusu's 17 households were pure tenants who owned minuscule amounts of land or none at all, and five were small holders who rented out some land to others. About 72 percent of the land in Kurusu was tenanted; by 1952 the figure had fallen to 15 percent. The seventeen households cultivated a total of 6.3 hectares prior to the reform, an average of 37.06 ares each. Although the same families were cultivating a slightly smaller average holding—36.82 ares—in 1952, Kurusu had become a hamlet of owner-cultivators, albeit on an extremely small scale. In the process of transition, only three of its families had been forced to sell small amounts of land. In 1952 about a third of the fields lying within the borders of the community were cultivated by fifteen families who lived elsewhere, eleven of them just across the river in Chūtoku. Most of these people had formerly been tenants on the plots to which they had obtained title under terms of the reform.

Because subsequent developments in agriculture have centered so heavily on mechanization, it is worth emphasizing how very small the holdings and field size are in Kurusu. In 1953 a national survey which excluded the northern island of Hokkaido where the fields are very large by Japanese standards, revealed that the average farmer cultivated 5.86 separate plots of land whose average size was 14.7 ares (Ogura 1967:59). Kurusu's farmers cultivated an average of 8.5 paddy fields and 3.1 dry fields with an average size of 3.3 ares in 1960, rendering consolidation all but impossible because of the complexities of the irrigation and drainage systems and the wide variability in quality of land making up each family's holdings. The extreme case in Kurusu is that of a family that cultivated 18 separate paddy fields of which the largest was 14.9 ares.

It is hardly surprising, therefore, that no progress had been made toward consolidation and rationalization of fields in this district. Not only are there places where ten ares of paddy land are divided up into as many as fifty fields, but the landholdings of a given family are widely scattered; all but two of Kurusu's farmers have fields located in other hamlets. Indeed, a little less than half of the land they cultivate lies at some distance from the community, requiring time-consuming and tiring travel on foot. The most distant are two miles away, making the transport of any equipment other than hand tools extremely difficult. (Today, seventeen families own one or more automobiles, but they are not suitable for carrying the new agricultural machines.)

Forest Lands and Forest Products

It has been widely held that the failure of the framers of the post-war land reform program to force the redistribution of both forest and agricultural lands would perpetuate fundamental economic in-equalities in the rural population. Two issues were the basis for this charge: first, control of access for collecting fuel, grass, and other forest products, and second, income to be derived directly from fores-try. As things turned out, with the shift to non-agricultural occupa-tions and the introduction of many household appliances, the matter of differential access to woodlands has become irrelevant. Indeed, some people attribute the decline in the wild mushroom of the type called *matsutake*, a very valuable crop, to the fact that the floor of the pinewoods is now so little disturbed by collectors of needles, twigs and branches that it no longer affords optimum conditions for growth. An-other view, less commonly subscribed to, is that something else has happened to greatly reduce the growth of the mushrooms:

I think it's all the automobiles and those agricultural chemicals that have pol-luted the area so heavily. Some people say that it is because no one clears the forest floor any more, but I know a man who used to cultivate the mushrooms and he says that he hasn't had a decent crop in years. It is a great change from the old days, when I used to go mushroom gathering. Why, I had to take along a carrying-pole and two big baskets to bring back what I picked. It was no trick to fill them every time I went out.

Whatever the cause of the decline, it is true that people no longer need the kinds of fuels they once collected, nor do forest lands have the potential they once held for enriching their owners. The problem is that the market for forest products has changed drastically since the end of the war. The demand for deciduous hardwoods has dwindled to almost nothing, for these trees were best suited to the production of charcoal and firewood. In 1951 virtually all of Kagawa Prefecture's production of these two commodities came from the villages of Yasuhara and Shionoe (*Shikoku chihō* . . . 1950:91), but with the widespread adoption, in rural areas as well as in the cities, of electricity, oil, and propane gas, the market for these forest products collapsed. Almost no one buys these trees any longer, although the Forestry Association did say that about forty families in Shionoe Town raise *shītake*, a mushroom that commands a very high price and that can be grown only on certain hardwoods. There are no charcoal makers left.

The emphasis now is on growing evergreens for lumber, but raising timber is a long-range affair. While the town government does hire laborers to reforest some fifty hectares every year, one official of the Forestry Association said, "The problem is that although the war ended thirty years ago, reforestation has lagged, and the forests have a long way to go before they are ready to harvest. *Sugi* (cryptomeria), for example, takes fifty years before it is ready for cutting." The government does offer small subsidies to those who will reforest their own lands, but Kunimoto (1973 : 96) correctly expresses impatience with national policies that have had the effect of letting Japan's forested areas, amounting to at least three-fourths of the country's land area, go to waste while the imports of lumber continue to rise. There are now very strict laws governing the cutting over of forest lands for building sites, and a major interest of the local government is in developing natural recreation sites. Since these latter sites often involve privately owned land, the association has been helping with the laying out of projected hiking trails and campsites.

In places to the north like Kagawa Town, on the other hand, some forested areas have become extremely valuable, not for the timber, but for the land itself, which in these foothills can be converted rather easily into building lots. For about one-third of the purchase price all the necessary expenses of surveying, installation of utilities, and roadbuilding can be met. But in Yasuhara, where the hills are much steeper, the cost of preparing land for development is generally prohibitive. It is not good for housing, and there is almost no other use that forest land can be put to. In fact, the far more common practice has been to sell upland paddy fields rather than forest land, for the terraced fields can easily be converted to building sites. Nonetheless, the critics of the land reform program were right in charging that failure to include woodlands would perpetuate old inequities, but they did not foresee that it would be the land itself rather than its products that would come to have enormous asset-value. Many landowners in other parts of the prefecture who were stripped of their excess agricultural lands have profited hugely from the sale of their unredistributed forests.

Changes in Land Ownership

Since the completion of the land reform program there have been some sales of land in Kurusu. Table 16 shows the amounts of land owned by the residents of the community in 1952, 1960, and 1975. There have been modest declines in the figures for paddy-field and dry-field land, but the amount of forest land owned has apparently dropped by over 16 percent. Although we could confirm the sales of some forest land, primarily to the Town Office for various other uses, we were unable to account for the bulk of the decline, and cannot say if it is a real or a paper phenomenon.

According to the Land Register there were thirty land transactions in Kurusu between 1951 and 1975. The amount of land involved is quite small, as Table 17 shows. The nine house lots total 520 square meters, the fourteen paddy fields 82.3 ares, and the seven dry fields 13.3 ares. All told, sixteen of the purchases were made by residents of Kurusu, fourteen by outsiders. It is difficult to discern a consistent pat-

TABLE 16
*Amount and Type of Land Owned by Residents
of Kurusu, 1952, 1960, and 1975*
(hectares)

Type of land	1952	1960	1975
Paddy field	5.68	5.06	5.39
Dry field	1.29	1.10	.99
Forest and other	15.66	12.65	11.56
TOTAL	22.63	18.81	17.94

TABLE 17
Land Transactions in Kurusu, 1952–75

Purchaser	House lots		Paddy fields		Dry fields	
	Total area purchased (*sq. meters*)	No. of lots purchased	Total area purchased (*ares*)	No. of fields purchased	Total area purchased (*ares*)	No. of fields purchased
Kurusu resident	400	7	57.5	8	1.5	1
Non-resident	120	2	24.8	6	11.8	6
TOTAL	520	9	82.3	14	13.5	7

TABLE 18
Land Transactions in Kurusu by Year and Type of Land,
1951–75

Period	Type of land			
	House lot	Paddy field	Dry field	Total
1951–59	3	7	0	10
1960–69	0	4	1	5
1970–75	6	3	6	15
TOTAL	9	14	7	30

tern, partly because both the number of transactions and the numbers of households involved in them are very small. There has been very little conversion of agricultural land to other uses. In the four cases of which we can be certain, the change has been from field (paddy or dry) to house lot; it has usually represented a move by a family to incorporate a small field into its compound so as to make possible construction of a new house for the successor. One other case of conversion of dry field to house lot is that of the fields bought by a non-resident entrepreneur who has built houses on speculation.

The timing of the land transactions is more clearly patterned and in many ways of more interest than their scale. As Table 18 shows, in the 1950's ten parcels of land changed hands. In the next decade only five sales were recorded, and between 1970 and 1975, fifteen more, half of all land sales. The table also reveals that in the 1950's and 1960's the majority of transfers were of paddy-field land, while in the 1970's there has been a marked readjustment of house lots and dry fields.

In the next chapter we discuss the issue of land prices and the comparative advantages of selling at today's very high prices or retaining title to what has become the most valuable asset of the farmers of Kurusu.

Mechanization of Agriculture

In the last century three great events have transformed the Japanese countryside. Each in its own way was revolutionary in its impact. The first was the reorganization of the local governments in the 1880's; the second was the land reform of the immediate postwar years; the third was the overwhelming mechanization of the agricultural process over the past decade.

It is not that there were no mechanical devices in use prior to the middle 1960's, but rather that the kinds of machines and the level of capital investment in equipment altered so dramatically. It would be a serious mistake, therefore, to begin a discussion of the adoption of the internal combustion engine and electric motor without calling attention to the history of other kinds of mechanization that have long characterized Japanese agriculture. Some of these early technological changes had just as profound effects and ramified just as completely throughout the production process as have the more recent ones. Since it is not within the scope of this study to take up the changes of even the last one hundred years, let us consider only one or two examples.

The hand-operated rotary weeder provides an instructive instance of ramification. Invented in the 1880's, this very simple machine cut the time required for hand-weeding in half. It could be used only on fields where the rice had been planted uniformly in straight rows, however, which required use of a frame with the intervals marked or strings to guide the transplanters. Thirty years later both the weeder and the planting method it mandated were in use throughout the country (Takane 1961:122). In the past fifteen to twenty years the weeder has been completely displaced by the universal use of herbicides, and the straight rows of plants at regular intervals are produced by the very newest mechanical device, the rice-transplanting machine. Harvesting is done by yet another new machine, the binder.

From the seventeenth until early in the twentieth century, a comb-

toothed thresher was in general use. By the late 1920's it had been
displaced by a pedal-powered machine that was shortly improved to
combine the winnowing and threshing operations. In the 1950's the
thresher, huller, and polisher were all on the way to being powered by
the internal combustion engine or electric motor, which were mass-
produced from the early 1920's on (Takane 1961 : 123–25). As late as
1961, however, Takane could still comment on the remarkable fact
that over the preceding century there had been no progress whatsoever
in the mechanization of harvesting rice, for farmers were still reaping
by hand with a sickle. The astounding transformation of the entire rice
production process was yet to come.

   In 1950, 393 (59 percent) of the households in Yasuhara Village
owned work cows, 10 households (1.5 percent) reported owning an
electric motor, and 523 (79 percent) owned an internal combustion
engine (*Kagawa ken chō* 1951 : 59–61). In Kurusu there were eight
work cows, and five households each owned an internal combustion
one-horsepower engine, which cost from ¥20,000 to ¥35,000. None
had an electric motor because utility rates were very high and because
the available power was both weak and unreliable. In addition to the
engines, each of the five households had a threshing machine (*dak-
kokki*) and one of them owned a huller (*momisuriki*); this was all of
the mechanized agricultural equipment in Kurusu. All of these machines, many of them second-hand, were purchased in 1950 and 1951.
In spite of the very modest scale of mechanization, people did comment in 1951 that all of the new machines and the new techniques that
were being introduced had greatly reduced the amount of physical
labor the farmer had to perform. The hand-operated drill for seeding
mugi, for example, eliminated stooping altogether. At the time the full
complement of other labor-saving devices consisted of a plow and
straight-toothed and rotating harrows—all drawn by a work cow—a
hand-powered weeder, and a number of sickles. However, the Agricultural Cooperative had installed electric-powered grain processing
machines toward the end of the war and just after the surrender, and
people took their grain there for polishing, cracking, pressing, and
conversion to flour, noodles, and other products.

   Before the heavy mechanization of the rice production process, it was estimated that the labor requirement from plowing to baling was between 130 and 230 man-hours per ten ares; in 1953 the national average was 187. By 1971 it had fallen to 110 (Shimpo 1976:41). Less labor was required, of course, in the lowland areas where the fields were larger and holdings more compact than they are in places like Kurusu, whose farmers in 1952 estimated an input of about 250 man-hours per ten ares of land. In 1975 they estimated about 120–140 man-hours, a figure far higher than the national average of 82. Part of the explanation for the decline lies in the introduction of labor-saving devices into the process of preparing and cultivating the fields, which cut the amount of time required by more than half. Subsequent important savings have been made with the mechanization of the harvesting process.

When the agricultural census of 1960 was taken, however, these profound changes still lay in the future. Kurusu's seventeen agricultural households listed eight engines and eight threshing machines, one of which was owned jointly by three households. There was still only one huller. That Kurusu was in no way unusual in this respect is confirmed by the following observation from a village near Osaka in the late 1950's: "There are few areas in which mechanization can supplant hand labor either because of the expense of machinery or because the fields are too small to make it practical" (Yoneyama 1967:224). Yet only fifteen years later, Fukutake (1974:47–48) wrote: "At the present time Japan leads the world in mechanized power used per unit area. Mechanized agriculture also means excessive capital investment for the farm family," and a growing gap between the *agricultural* income of the large and small farmers. As a consequence there has been a tendency for the large farmers to seek land that they can rent in order to secure a larger return on their investment in equipment. There has even been a slight increase in the number of successors of such families returning to agriculture from other employment for this reason.

Table 19 shows the phenomenal increase in ownership of machinery by the farmers of Japan over the past fifty years. The residents of Kurusu have been full participants in this surge of mechanization, despite their miniscule holdings of land. In 1975 ten families were still

TABLE 19
Farm Machinery in Japan, 1927–75
(thousands)

Year	Electric motor	Kerosene or gasoline engine	Tillers and tractors	Threshers	Hullers	Power machines				
						Combines and reapers	Sprayers	Dusters	Dryers	Trans-planters
1927	–	–	–	30	39	–	–	–	–	–
1935	47	96	0.2	92	104	–	0.6	–	–	–
1945	152	262	7	352	177	–	–	–	–	–
1950	601	383	18	828	379	–	16	–	–	–
1955	956	1,134	90	2,038	696	–	76	11	12	–
1960	1,070	1,663	519	2,458	800	–	232	73	37	–
1965	1,366	1,903	2,175	3,085	827	18	494	206	724	–
1970	–	–	3,452	–	–	308	961	1,215	1,229	32
1975	–	–	3,926	–	–	1,671	1,315	1,291	1,496	740
Percent of households owning in 1951	10%	5%	0.3%	16%	6%	–	0.3%	–	–	–

SOURCE: These figures are taken from Bureau of Statistics (1975: 113), Fukutake (1967: 20), Takane (1957: 69; 1961: 125), Tsuchiya (1969: 156), and various reports of the Ministry of Agriculture and Forestry.

sufficiently involved in agriculture to warrant the purchase of farm machinery, and they have done so on a scale that is startling (see Table 20).

It is significant that almost all of the machinery now found in Kurusu has been purchased since 1965, about the time that substantial numbers of men began to seek full-time employment outside the community, a trend followed shortly thereafter by women as well. The older pattern had been that of *dekasegi*, seasonal work that took a man out to work elsewhere in the agricultural slack seasons, but permitted him to come back home for at least the transplanting and harvest. Full-time employment initially meant a six-day week, and while a few people are now employed by the kinds of enterprises that give their employees six days a month off, for most the only time available for work in the fields is on weekday evenings and Sunday. Thus every family must try to get its own work done in the small amount of time available to all. Cooperative endeavor becomes impossible because there literally is not enough time to permit the sharing of labor. It also becomes extremely difficult to work out a schedule for the use of the machines.

Nevertheless, everyone is perfectly well aware that there are communities whose residents have bought machines and farm the entire area of their holdings on a cooperative basis. We have already discussed the nature of local holdings, which is the reason most commonly given for their inability to contemplate any such step. There is some truth to the argument, for the fifteen or sixteen riding tractors in use in the district served by the Yasuhara Agricultural Cooperative are all found to the north on the plain, where rectangular fields of twenty ares have been created out of the old mosaic of plots.

Even if they could consolidate, many people protest that jointly owned machines are not cared for properly by all who share in the right to use them, especially nowadays when one is always pressed for time. Lest we mistakenly assume that such sentiments are entirely new, representing the emergence of a complete shift in morality, let us quote from the account of Kurusu twenty-five years ago (R. Smith 1953:270):

There is . . . only one cooperatively owned machine. Three residents of Kurusu joined with two non-residents who cultivate land [there] to buy a threshing machine. One of the Kurusu men has already dropped out, having bought a machine of his own. Being of recent formation, this group has not yet resolved all the problems of maintenance and use-order, and other people feel that it is better to own a machine individually than to rent one.

Or, we should add, than to purchase one jointly with neighbors. A case in point is that of the three families—the Hiranos, the Fukudas and the Izumis—who reported in the agricultural survey of 1960 that they owned some farm equipment jointly. They are identified as households number 3, 4, and 5 in Table 19. At that time the heads of the first two families, since deceased, were older men bound to one another by long-standing ties of obligation and responsibility. The third family, the Izumis, had been incorporated into the group when they returned from Taiwan after World War II. This small group, whose rather brief history belies the intensity of their relationship, was almost destroyed by the quarrel over the proposal to locate the Clover food-processing plant in Kurusu. Crucial as the event may have been, it was by no means the sole cause of their troubles, for they

TABLE 20
Farm Machinery in Kurusu, 1975

Machine	Number owned	Household									
		1	2	3	4	5	6	7	8	9	10
Straw cutter	10	x	x	x	x	x	x	x	x	x	x
Brush cutter (*kusakari-ki*)	9	x	x	x	x	x	x		x	x	x
Dryer (*kansō-ki*)	9	x	x	x	x	x	x	x	x		x
Thresher (*dakkokki*)	8	x	x	o	o	o	x	x	x	x	x
Cultivator (*kōunki*)	6	x	x	o	o	o	x	x	#		
Sprayer (*misutā*)	5	x	x	o	o	o	x	x			
Binder (*baindā; inekari-ki*)	3	x	x	o	o	o					
Transplanter (*taue-ki*)	3	x	x	x							
Huller (*momisuri-ki*)	2	x							x		
TOTAL[a]	55	9	8	8	7	7	6	5	5	4	4

NOTE: The symbol o designates single machines owned jointly by households, 3, 4, and 5; the symbol # designates a machine owned jointly by household 8 and a relative not resident in Kurusu.
[a] Because of the joint ownership of some machines, the numbers to the right add up to 63 rather than 55.

had already experienced considerable difficulty in organizing the joint use of the machines after their purchase. A major bone of contention appears to have been the inherent inequality of the labor exchange, for although both Fukuda and Hirano have four children, in one family the three eldest are girls, in the other family they are boys. Furthermore, all four men in the Fukuda family have full-time jobs and thus are free to work only on Sundays. The Izumis have only two children, one a boy who is seldom available to help out because he is frequently called away from Kurusu in connection with his work.

But all such cooperative endeavors may suffer from just such imbalances of family composition and age distribution of members who are able to carry full work-loads. There is, in fact, another more fundamental reason for the difficulties in which these three men find themselves. Hirano said on one occasion, "It is very hard to see why the old relationship with Fukuda should continue now that the two old men are dead." It was one of the few occasions on which anyone made any comment that touched directly on the issue of former landlord-tenant relationships. In the past tenants or families obligated in some other way to their erstwhile landlords frequently were called upon to assist them in a variety of ways. The subordinate party was referred to as *de-iri-mono*, meaning roughly "those who serve." The only clear-cut case of such a relationship in Kurusu involved old Hirano, who in the past had been aided materially by the father of the present head of the Fukuda family. The extent of the help was so great that its recipient had placed himself at the service of his benefactor, who once said to me, "It is unusual for these things to go on so long. When the old man dies his children probably won't feel obligated to keep it up" (R. Smith 1953 : 149). He was right, for the present head of the Hirano family is an adopted husband and that of the Fukuda family succeeded to the headship in 1969 when his father died. It is easy enough to understand Hirano's desire to sever the bonds that formerly united the two families and hardly surprising that he has moved to do so on more than one occasion.

The pattern of equipment purchases by individuals in Kurusu, where the fields are much as they were twenty-five years ago, shows how risky predictions about the future of Japanese agriculture can be. An official of the Kagawa Prefectural Agricultural Cooperative Office told me in 1951, "They will never be able to use the hand tractor up there in places like Yasuhara because the fields are so narrow and broken up." It did not even occur to him that one answer might be to enlarge the farm unit by collective management, nor could he have guessed at the motivations that were to lead to the rapid mechanization of agriculture fifteen years later, despite the lack of alteration in field size and shape.

The head of one family gave us the following accounting of the pattern of acquisition of farm machinery. He had purchased a tiller and a thresher in 1965, a huller and a dryer in 1970, and a two-row binder and a transplanter in 1971. The last two were the first such machines owned by anyone in Kurusu, he told us. He was particularly impressed with the speed with which the transplanter operates, but said that he could see no difference in the yields produced with the use of machines. Formerly it had taken him about five days to hand-transplant his 42 ares of paddy land, but with the machine it is only a day's work. Nevertheless, he felt that the mechanization of agriculture had brought a host of problems in its wake.

The machines are so expensive! They break down at the most inconvenient times—when you're using them, and can't afford the time to have them repaired—and they only last for about ten years. These days most of the income from agriculture around here goes to buy and maintain the machines. It's hardly worth it, but this is the machine age and no one here has begun to sell off his land yet. So we have to have machines in order to keep going, and if the field dividers here were not so high, you can be sure that people would have bought even more and larger ones. The only thing that stopped them is that you can't get the big machines up and down from field to field.

Another family head, who has long maintained a written record of his household's income and expenses, provided us with the following information about his purchases of farm machinery:

Machine	Year of purchase	Cost	1975 Replacement cost (estimated)
Cultivator	1967	¥246,000	¥450,000
Thresher	1967	52,000	130,000
Straw cutter	1967	19,500	54,000
Sprayer	1969	33,000	57,000
Brush cutter	1969	35,000	44,000
Binder	1973	167,000	230,000
Dryer	1973	52,500	120,000

Thus the total cost of the seven machines was about ¥600,000, and he calculated that he could not replace the lot in 1975 for less than a million yen. Actually, since most of the equipment was quite new, he was more interested in purchasing additional machinery than in replacing any of the items that he owned, but admitted that his fields were too small to justify buying, for instance, one of the new combines.

What I would really like to do is buy a transplanting machine next year. It doesn't really pay unless you have at least 120 ares of land, but I might get one anyway. The government has a low-cost loan program for the purchase of farm machinery through the Agricultural Cooperative. It's all connected with their plans to modernize agriculture. Transplanting by machine is a lot faster than doing it by hand, and the work is not so hard. I could hire a machine but the fee is too high. We still transplant by hand with some help from hired labor. It's the cheapest method at about ¥2,000 per day for women and about ¥5,000 for men.

This man was not alone in his desire to purchase new machinery, for the government reported that in 1975 investment in agricultural machines continued to rise, especially among the small-holders of Western Japan who were buying the small-scale equipment of the kind so heavily invested in by Kurusu farmers already (*Nōgyō hakusho* 1976: 139). In this connection, it must be pointed out that although the nominal prices of tillers and rotary cultivators, for example, have risen 2.1 and 2.5 times, in real terms they decreased by 32 and 15 percent, respectively, between 1960 and 1975. During the same period the price of rice rose 4 times in nominal terms and 1.3 times in real terms.

Only two families in Kurusu have bought hullers. Most people thought it a poor idea, arguing that the machine is used at most five or six hours a year. For that reason most preferred to hire a man from the neighboring hamlet to bring his machine around by pick-up truck and hull the grain on the spot for a fee fixed by weight processed.

The fan dryers, which are either electrical or oil-powered, have become extremely popular in a very short period. The new models can handle large amounts of grain, making it possible to complete the process in a matter of two or three days. Most households had put off buying a dryer as long as they could. Its major disadvantage is said to be that it is very expensive given the amount of use that can be made of it, but that is also true of most of the machinery now employed in the production of rice. A second difficulty is that machine-dried rice is thought to be markedly inferior in taste to sun-dried rice. According to a technician at the Agricultural Cooperative the flavor is inferior because most people over-dry, reducing the water content below the recommended 17 percent.

There is also general agreement that cooking machine-dried rice in an electric rice-cooker (as every household in the hamlet now does) completes the ruin of what used to be the best rice grown anywhere. Why do they do it, then? The answer invariably is that it is faster and more efficient. Rice cooked over a wood fire is a luxury that few can now afford, for there is no one to gather firewood, build and tend the fire, and watch the pot. With the electric rice-cooker, one simply flicks the switch and the thing shuts off automatically when the rice is done. A more important consideration leading to the abandonment of sun-drying the grain, by spreading it out on mats in the dooryard, is that someone has to be at home all day to rake and turn the rice and bring it in out of the rain if the weather changes. In 1975 there were very few houses left with anyone who could take the time or who had the strength to carry out this once-universal task. Among the last to give it up is one elderly grandmother who said that when her strength had finally failed her two or three years before, they had folded up the mats and stored them away in an outbuilding with other relics of her generation's agricultural endeavors.

The second farmer, whose purchase record appears above, first bought a small cultivator in 1964, but he found it so hard to handle that he traded it in on his present machine three years later. With this machine he can cultivate his land in about half the time it used to take with his work cow and plow. People routinely plow a paddy field two or three times to break up the soil and get out the weeds, which are very bad these days since the fields are allowed to lie fallow over the winter. After many passes with the cultivator, water is let into the field, which is then plowed once more. Few families cultivate their upland paddies, most of which have been abandoned to weeds and brush, because they cannot get to them with the machines. "All of that backbreaking work that went into making them in the first place—for nothing," one man said.

Probably no mechanical invention of the postwar period is as startling on first viewing as the rice transplanter. Transplanting proved to be the step in rice production most resistant to mechanization, and the machines were not mass-produced until 1968. By the end of 1974 one in seven of all rice-farming households in Japan owned one, and about half of all rice land was being planted by machines. They are expensive (the 1975 price was about ¥250,000) and are needed for only a very few days a year; and unlike the tractor cultivator, which can be used to prepare land for any kind of crop and has other uses as well, the rice transplanter is adaptable to no other task. The Ministry of Agriculture and Forestry reports that the distribution of these machines among farm households like those of Kurusu, whose holdings are under fifty ares, is only one in fifty-three.

The clumsy prototype of this most specialized of all the new machines required elaborate preparation of very young seedlings taken from a standard seedbed. The models now on the market are designed in such a way that seedbeds no longer need to be made at all. The owner of the transplanter purchases flat pans already filled with dirt and fertilizer, to which he adds his seed. The pans are put in a dark place in an outbuilding or under vinyl and later set out in the light; the process is very like that of growing bean sprouts. When the time comes, the pan, now filled with seedlings, is mounted directly on the machine and the transplanting is done mechanically, in single or double rows depending on the model.

Where it has been widely adopted, the transplanter has eradicated at a stroke the part of the process of rice production most heavily involved with ritual and cooperative behavior. Gone are the cooperative seedbeds and the striking sexual division of labor in which the men carried the bundled seedlings out to the fields where the women's work-group thrust the seedlings into the rich muck. In 1951 no one sang the old work songs, to be sure, but there was an air of gaiety and excitement at transplanting time that contrasted sharply with the rushed seriousness of the harvest. In 1951 the seedbeds of Kurusu were still adorned with offerings to Jichin-san, the hamlet's tutelary deity, designed to insure a good harvest. As of this writing, however, the transplanters have not completely displaced older patterns of production. Many Kurusu farmers still perform labor exchange at transplanting time, but only one of them erects the rice-field deity's offering on the edge of the seedbeds. As the transplanters increase in numbers, or as more and more people hire them to plant their fields, the quintessential activities of rice transplanting will all disappear here, as they have long since disappeared in many other parts of Japan.

Adoption of the transplanter has other consequences as well. Kurusu farmers say that if it is used to set out the seedlings in the flooded paddy, the rice cannot be harvested by hand, for the distance between the plants is not right. To do the job properly, they claim, one must have a binder which also comes in single- or double-row models. In 1975 the combined cost of the two machines was about ¥450,000. Automatically tied with nylon cord, the rice bundles are still hung up by hand to dry on the bamboo racks set up in the fields.

What has led these small scale, part-time farmers to invest in such a dazzling array of agricultural machinery? One school of thought emphasizes the non-rational character of the decision. Tsuchiya (1969:157–59) cites several studies and summarizes their conclusions with respect to the runaway adoption of the power tiller. First, they charge that this is a case of "overinvestment," by which they mean that without taking into account the finances of the family agricultural enterprise, the farmers bought power tillers as though they were consumer goods rather than aids to production. Second, since the power tillers were underutilized, it is clear that the demonstration effect must have played an important role in the decision to make the purchases. Third, the young people insist on having these machines; the older people buy them as a means of keeping the young people on the farm, and especially in order to attract the intended successor. Fourth, the labor that is saved is used for leisure and recreation, rather than farming more intensively or increasing the amount of income earned from part-time employment. And last, these analysts note what seems to them to be a lamentable decline in physical stamina resulting from the long period of schooling. Before the war, they say, twelve-year-olds who completed the compulsory six years of education were already inured to hard labor, but now they are not, and so it has become necessary to purchase mechanical devices to do the really hard work.

Perhaps the most extreme view of the role of the hamlet in encouraging the purchase of farm machinery is that expressed by Ishida (1971:57):

The villagers as consumers, whether they are farmers or not, are still under the constraint of the village and hamlet. In the late 1950's I was told by a farmer in a famous rice-growing area that it was less efficient for him to own his own cultivator than for him and his neighbors to share a better one, but that it was necessary to have one because all the others had them. The same can now be said about vacuum cleaners and washing machines and other appliances.

Thus the hamlet, which formerly exercised such strong constraints on production, now is charged with exercising similarly strong constraints on consumption.

We do not doubt that the demonstration effect is pronounced and that as soon as one family acquires a new machine or a more recent model of an old one, its neighbors will not rest until they have one too, but there are other far more compelling reasons for a farmer to go into debt to buy equipment that he can never hope to return a profit on.

The city person's easy assumption that the farmers are a simple lot, bedazzled by the full-color advertisements (often showing a pretty girl got up in chic work clothes, or, more appealingly, a young couple— clearly the successor and his wife) or motivated by a gnawing envy of their neighbors, is an insult to the intelligence of the farmers. Tsuchiya (1969:159) reports on a study that seems to us to be much nearer the mark in suggesting that there are at least four major reasons for mechanizing. The first is that there has been a sharp decline in the marginal valuation of cash because so many farm families have increased incomes from by-employment; second, the price of power tillers declined over a period of several years until the oil crisis of 1973, bringing them within the reach of more and more farmers; third, the tillers greatly increased the amount of work a man could do, obviously recommending their use; and fourth, it became increasingly difficult to hire agricultural laborers capable of heavy work. Indeed, the shrinkage of the farm labor force, both farm family members and hired hands, was cited as the main reason for purchasing a power tiller by 84 percent of about two thousand families surveyed in 1963–64, even though the cost in 1964 was very high relative to average farm household income (Tsuchiya 1969:160). It may also be noted that before the tillers became almost universal, a man could always hire out himself and his machine to cultivate land for others.

One final comment on the adoption of the tiller is in order. Because it actually tills less deeply than the old Japanese plow, its use might have brought about a reduction in yields. That they have risen instead is largely owing to the lavish application of fertilizer and pesticides and the introduction of new strains of rice (Sawada 1969:152). Kurusu farmers have thus been able to maintain high production levels despite the shrinkage of the active farming population and its increasing average age. The cost has been great here, as it has been throughout the country, but they see no alternative to a system which now requires heavy investment in both machines and chemical products if they hope to continue in agriculture at all.

As all of the foregoing strongly suggests, changes in the process of rice production have been so far-reaching that what I wrote about it in 1951 retains primarily historical interest today (R. Smith 1953:83–89). I had some intimation of this when I was back in Kurusu briefly in 1972. It was a warm summer day and I met an older woman I knew on the road. She said that she was on her way to visit a neighbor. I thought this odd because fifteen years earlier she almost certainly would have been out weeding the paddies. When I expressed my surprise at seeing her dressed up and out of the fields on such a day, she registered equal surprise. "We don't have to weed any more. We just put herbicide in the water at transplanting time and that's that. It's a lot easier now than it used to be." There can be no doubt that things are much easier; nowadays after the rice seedlings are transplanted, pellets containing fertilizer and herbicide are simply scattered in the flooded fields.

Although the spraying of insecticides is also much easier than it was in 1935 when the first chemicals were applied to a Kurusu field by a man using a hand-operated sprayer, we were to discover that use of the new mechanical sprayers posed some new problems. Ten ares can be covered in a matter of a few minutes, and as a consequence some families spray on a cooperative basis. The machine requires at least two operators and those families that prefer to spray only their own fields ordinarily do so in the early evening after work or on Sundays when there are enough hands to do the job. Down on the plain the farmers with large holdings use a motorized sprayer; in Kurusu almost every family has a small backpack sprayer.

The schedule for spraying insecticides, usually three times after mid-July, is set after consultation between the Town Office, the Agricultural Cooperative, and the Prefectural Agricultural Experiment Station. The station operates a network of insect traps, one of which is located in Kurusu. A higher-school student, from one of the farm families, earns ¥10,000 for the summer by checking it periodically. He counts the number of male and female insects and reports every ten days by postal card. If the report is not received on schedule the experiment station telephones for the information. After the data are analyzed, the station notifies the town office of the recommended spraying dates. After making certain that there are no special local conditions that require alteration of the schedule, it is read over the broadcast relay system. While it is in theory up to the individual farmer whether or not he adheres to the schedule, in practice everyone does so in order to avoid difficulties that might arise between those who had sprayed and those who had not. While somewhat less mandatory than cooperation in the use of irrigation water, the parallels are obvious.

It is very difficult to think of any way of dramatizing the full impact of all these changes in agricultural technology on anyone who first knew rural Japan in the years just after World War II. Perhaps one way is through the unlikely medium of the tables of the *Japan Statistical Yearbook*, in which there are many clues to the qualitative as well as quantitative changes that have been wrought. One such place in the 1950 edition is the enumeration of farm implements. In its entirety the list is as follows: electric motors, gasoline engines, pumps, threshing machines, barley-hulling machines, rice-hulling machines, plows, spades, and sickles. The 1976 edition lists none of these, not even the electric motors and gasoline engines, which have been displaced long since by the new self-powered equipment found universally in rural Japan today.

CHAPTER FOUR

Making a Living

IT WAS THE hope of the planners of the land reform that a major consequence of the redistribution of agricultural land would be the eradication of social and economic inequalities in the countryside. The inequalities had been very real. As one Kurusu man told me in 1951, "When we met our landlord on the path we stopped, put down whatever we were carrying, greeted him and bowed low. He usually nodded and passed on. Not any more! If you want two stories about the land reform and its effects, ask a man who got land and one who lost it." In 1951 most of the former landlords were still lamenting what they regarded as the confiscatory prices they had received for their land, and most of Kurusu's former tenants were happily in possession of fields on which they had enjoyed only the rights of tenancy before the reform.

In 1975 questions about this whole matter were usually dismissed rather lightly. One middle-aged man put it succinctly: "The land reform was a whole generation ago. No one makes anything of the old landlord-tenant distinction any more. It has nothing at all to do with life here today." That this is a general feature of life in Japan's countryside is borne out by the remark of Fukutake: "Now hierarchical status relationships between families based on the landlord-tenant tie are increasingly thought of as a tale of the distant past" (1974:34). The Shionoe man quoted above is himself from an old landlord family, however, and it may be that he is likely to make light of an old but still painful memory of vanished eminence. As we shall see, some former tenants still remember the distant past, and seldom miss an opportunity to demonstrate how far they have risen in the world. In 1951 I was told: "The future? The farmers will gradually lose everything they have gained under the land reform. The landlords will soon have it all back again." But this has not happened. They have not got the land back—and partly because they do not want it, having put their capital into far more lucrative enterprises.

It may be said with some justice that in many ways the hardest hit of all were the medium-sized and small resident landowners and owner-cultivators. It is they who were left with holdings just large enough to tie them to the land, but inadequate to provide them a living from full-time agriculture. The former tenants, who did not acquire enough land even to tempt them to try full-time farming, sold out and moved to the city. Some years ago it was noted that the per-capita income, both agricultural and disposable, of farm households with between 50 ares and 1.5 hectares of land was barely equal to, or even less than, that of families cultivating less than 50 ares. "This is probably because farmers in the latter class depend more on side-work in the form of permanent employment, with the resultant higher hourly income. . . . Such differences must have arisen from circumstances which prevented the farmers in the 0.5–1.5 *chō* category from allotting their labor to subsidiary jobs" (Kawano 1969:394).

The farmers of Kurusu faced a host of serious problems in the immediate postwar years, some of which were directly attributable to their new status as landowners. Their concerns were almost precisely those outlined by Raper and others (1950:182–91) in their classic report on Japanese agricultural communities in 1947 and 1948. The farmers were worried about the increased tax burden and inflation, and they feared the onset of a serious agricultural depression. Taxes were not nearly as burdensome as the old rents had been, of course, but they had to be paid in cash, which was very hard to come by, and they seemed always to be rising. The black market was fading, substantially reducing their illegal incomes, and they were worried at the prospect that the government would impose even heavier grain requisition quotas that would require an ever-greater proportion of their rice to be delivered at the low official price. In addition to the eternal problems of having too little land broken up into too many separate scattered plots supporting too many people, the farmers of twenty-five years ago complained about the scarcity of work clothes and some critical fertilizers. Many wanted more technical assistance from the government and improvement in the agricultural extension services.

In 1975 the people of Kurusu expressed many of these same concerns. Taxes, inflation, government price supports, too little land too broken up into minuscule plots—all of these and other disturbing matters figured in our conversations. The *Asahi Shimbun* of August 13, 1975, commenting on the state of Japanese society as the thirtieth anniversary of the end of the war approached, noted editorially that the people were anxious about the immediate future. Real wages were declining while savings had reached their highest level since 1965, and nationally there was a trend toward purchasing low-priced goods in almost all categories of food, clothing, and appliances.

Agriculture as a Livelihood

Rice

Rice cultivation and agriculture have long been virtually synonymous terms in Japan, and the production of other grains has always been a secondary enterprise. Between 1950 and 1974 the number of Kurusu families selling rice for cash declined, but the amounts sold by them increased dramatically, as did their cash value. Two factors contributed to the rise in sales of "surplus" rice. One is the great increase in yields, the other the sharp reduction in the domestic consumption of rice.

For the country as a whole, rice yields rose almost 50 percent between 1950 and 1975 (*Nōgyō hakusho* 1976:29). At the same time the per-capita consumption of rice in 1974 was down about 30 percent from prewar levels. In the early 1960's it rose somewhat above the levels of the preceding decade, but never recovered its prewar highs before starting to decline. As we shall see, this discrepancy between production and consumption has had far-reaching implications for the course of the government's agricultural policy.

In 1950 the average yield of rice in Yasuhara Village was about 273 kilograms per ten ares, as compared with the prefecture-wide yield of 333, which was about the same as the national average. Similarly, Yasuhara yields of wheat and naked barley were about a third lower than those for the prefecture as a whole (*Shikoku chihō* . . . 1951:6–19). At this period Kagawa alone of the four prefectures of Shikoku exported rice to other parts of the country. What were called "the three whites of Sanuki" (the old province name) were rice, salt, and sugar; in an earlier time, when other cash crops had been important, they had been cotton, salt, and sugar (Yabe 1949:37). It was said that one *shō* of Kagawa rice cooked up to 30 bowls full, while ordinary rice made only 25 bowls. The people of Kurusu were especially proud of their rice, as are most people of most communities in Japan.

The average yield of rice in Kurusu in 1951 was the highest in the village, 336 kilograms per ten ares. Very good paddy land yielded 390 and very poor only 180. The official price for first-quality rice in 1950 was ¥1,800 per 60 kilograms. One man told me that he had grossed ¥9,000 on his crop, but that his production costs had been ¥3,500. The net profit on his nearly 50 ares of paddy land was so small that in order to support his family of six one of his sons worked at a nearby sawmill for ¥190 per day, earning about ¥3,500 per month.

In 1975 the average yield nationally was 523 kilograms per ten ares, a historic high, and Kurusu farmers were estimating a gross of about ¥115,000 per ten ares. A farmer with from 30 to 50 ares would therefore receive from ¥345,000 to ¥575,000 from rice alone. This does not compare favorably with income from wages or salaries, yet eight Kurusu families still grew enough rice to be able to market a surplus in 1975.

The amount of rice sold by Kurusu households for the years 1950, 1962, and 1974 was as follows:

	1950	1962	1974
Amount sold	4,184 kg	5,400 kg	6,900 kg
Total sales	¥202,286	¥432,010	¥1,381,942
Income per household	¥20,228	¥43,200	¥172,742

In 1950 the system of imposed delivery quotas on rice was still in effect. The quotas for that year, representing the amount that had to be sold directly to the government, was 42.3 percent of production, the highest in the postwar period. By 1955 production had risen so dramatically that the government abandoned the compulsory quota system and offered to pay its controlled price for as much rice as the farmers chose to sell. In that same year, because of the bumper crop (almost one-third again as large as that of the preceding year), the black-market price of rice fell from immediate post-surrender highs of thirteen to fourteen times the official price to a mere 5 to 10 percent more (Dore 1959:231).

The 1975 price for rice was set at ¥15,570 per 60 kilograms. Several farmers remarked that a price of ¥20,000 "would not be too high." One man who has over five *tan* of land was especially upset by what he considered to be the government's niggardly attitude, but the smaller holders in Kurusu, who produce little or no rice for sale, did not support the efforts of the agricultural unions and associations to force the setting of an even higher price in 1975. They correctly argued that since all other prices follow the rice price upward, "it would simply mean that everything would cost more and we would be no further ahead than we are now." The annual struggle over the official price of rice to be paid to the producer is matched in intensity by the struggle over the official price for the consumer. Every year the press devotes extensive coverage to the negotiations between the Ministry of Agriculture and Forestry and representatives of the farmer's organizations, which are often conducted in the new style of open and angry verbal confrontation. When the producers' price is settled attention turns to the equally strident public meetings between government figures and the representatives of the major consumers' groups. Donnelly (1977) offers an excellent account of the intricacies of the negotiations and analyzes the political aspects of the trade-offs made by the participants. Having set the price to the producer at ¥15,570 per 60 kilograms in 1975, the price for the consumer was set at ¥13,799, up 19 percent over the preceding year, thus creating a huge deficit in the government's Special Food Account. It is estimated that one-half of the entire budget of the Ministry of Agriculture and Forestry now goes for the rice subsidy (Trezise & Suzuki 1976:773).

Determination of both prices represents an uneasy compromise between the clash of consumer interests, which would prefer of course that the retail price be held down, and the political interests of the Liberal Democratic Party, whose remaining in power depends in large part on securing the rural vote. More than 300 of the 511 seats in the lower house of the national Diet are rural and town districts, although most of the population now resides in cities. As long as the electoral districts established in 1946 remain unrevised, the LDP will continue to raise the subsidy and force up the retail price, for it is precisely that policy that brings in the vote on which it so heavily depends. In general, Kurusu farmers take a predictably cynical view of the whole matter, and it is clear that the government party is slowly losing its hold on them.

The peculiarities of agricultural policy were highlighted by the embarrassment of a bumper crop in 1975, 7 percent higher than the 1974 figure. The ensuing spectacle only served to heighten the farmers' sense of the essential bankruptcy of the policy, for the situation completely unhinged the government's plans. After the price is fixed in the summer, the government places advance orders for the grain. In 1975 the surplus far exceeded the willingness of the government to raise the already swollen deficit of the Special Food Account. The agricultural organizations were furious at the decision to handle the problem by treating the surplus as free-market rice, which commands a lower price than that purchased by government contract. The Ministry of Agriculture and Forestry moved belatedly to press for further reduction in the acreage of rice, raised the producer price for all other grains in an effort to encourage their production, and urged the use of more rice in school-lunch programs after years of pushing consumption of wheat products. For a scathing indictment of agricultural policy, see Iinuma's (1976) commentary on rice monoculture and its consequences for both producer and consumer.

Barley and Wheat: The Winter Grains

The story of the winter grain crops in Kurusu is quite different. In 1952 the favored crop was naked barley, but some wheat was grown on the 55 percent of the paddy fields that could be double-cropped. For the past several years, however, fewer and fewer farmers have bothered to put in a winter crop at all. According to the people at the local Agricultural Cooperative, while yields of mugi have risen nationally from 175 kilograms per ten ares in 1950 to 270 in 1973, they have gone up less dramatically than rice because almost all of the new technology has been developed for rice. This may be true for local growing conditions, but in fact there has been a greater improvement in yields of mugi than in yields of rice nationally. The former was up 54 percent from 1950 to 1973, the latter only 43 percent. Nonetheless, in 1975 most people were even claiming that local mugi yields had been declining because the farmer devoted less time and effort to the care of those crops. This echoes some comments to the same effect made to me in 1951 by farmers who even then were saying that their return on mugi was discouragingly low. Whatever the perceptions of the yield, the current situation of the winter crops in Kurusu reflects the national trend. In 1950 there were 1.8 million hectares planted in mugi; by 1965 the area had plunged to 137,000 hectares (Sawada 1969:152).

In 1951 the average yield for naked barley in Yasuhara was 151 kilograms per ten ares, lower than the national figure of 175. In Kurusu official reports show an average yield of 184. The official price for mugi of the top grades averaged out to about ¥1,900 per 60 kilograms in 1951. Thus a man with 40 ares of rice land, of which perhaps 15 ares could be double-cropped, would gross about ¥12,000 a year from his winter crop. In 1975 the average price per 60 kilograms of naked barley was about ¥6,000. Assuming a high yield of 375 kilograms per ten ares, the same farmer would gross about ¥56,000. A local rule of thumb is that mugi nets less than half as much per ten ares as a good monthly wage.

In light of these figures, it is no wonder that so few farmers put in a winter crop, although during the same period the diet of Kurusu people, like that of all Japanese, came to include ever larger components of wheat products, displacing rice. The complexities of agricultural policy and the exigencies of international trade led not to a boom in production of wheat but to importation of the grain on a massive scale, while the farmers turned to non-agricultural sources of income with which to purchase it.

Cash-Crop Alternatives

Some people have turned to the cultivation of cash crops other than rice. It has been many years since the farmers of Japan have been required either by laws like the Staple Foods Control Act or by circumstance to plant rice in all suitable fields. They have long experimented with crops that could be grown as alternatives to winter wheat and barley, rather than rice. In 1952, for example, one Kurusu family tried to grow the variety of rush used to make the covering for tatami, in hopes of developing a profitable cash crop. Nothing came of the experiment, which seems to have been abandoned after only a year's trial. For a time tobacco seemed to have promise and several families in Kurusu grew it. Indeed, this effort involved construction of two drying-sheds, but by 1975 the enterprise had been abandoned. The tobacco harvest falls at the end of July, leaving enough time to put in a crop of an early- or medium-maturing variety of rice that is highly sensitive to day-length; the yield is about 60 percent of a normal crop, but a major disadvantage is that transplanting of such fields must be done by hand. The profits to be had from the sale of tobacco did not offset this and other disadvantages, at least in the experience of the Kurusu people who had tried to make a go of it.

There were two abandoned orchards in Kurusu in 1951, one of persimmon and one of chestnut, both begun as commercial ventures some time before World War II. But the city of Takamatsu, the intended market, was too far away and the production too small, and both entrepreneurs had simply let the orchards go wild. One man was raising tree seedlings for reforestation under a program sponsored by the Yasuhara Forestry Association, but profits were not large enough to attract others to this specialized enterprise.

Many crops are no longer grown at all, either because there is so little demand for them or because they are economically unfeasible. These include soybeans, formerly planted along the raised paths between the fields, rape seed for oil, and sorghum. The process of experimentation with various crops has a long history. Around the turn of the century, for example, some cotton was grown locally and many families spun their own thread. Many of the efforts to supplement agricultural income were extremely short-lived, largely because the farmers have so narrow a margin on which to operate. A prefectural agricultural official put it very well: "These people are not afraid to experiment, but they'll drop any new thing the minute they see that it is not proving out."

At every level from town to nation, government programs have been developed to encourage the rotation of crops and the production of crops other than rice in recent years. Appalled by the bumper crops of 1967, 1968, and 1969, which exceeded fourteen million tons annually even in years of poor growing conditions, the government took emergency measures to reduce production of rice. Beginning in fiscal 1970, a program was instituted that would pay farmers to take some land out of rice production. The target for the first year was a 10 percent reduction in the harvest. The program was voluntary and offered compensatory payments in the neighborhood of ¥40,000 per ten ares of land left fallow or planted in another crop (Kunimoto 1970:444). The program was successful in some respects, and in combination with other disincentives to rice production, resulted in the 1971 harvest, which was the smallest since 1954 (Anonymous 1972:11). In fiscal 1974 the program was terminated and the acreage of land planted in rice rose four percent. In fiscal 1975 it rose 1.5 percent, as a consequence of the reduction of the target level for conversion to other crops (Anonymous 1976c:12).

Only a few Kurusu farmers took advantage of the subsidy programs, and those who did so generally opted for the cultivation of alternative crops rather than fallowing. Almost universally throughout the Yasuhara area, the emphasis was on cucumbers because people had experience in growing this vegetable and conditions were generally favorable for good harvests. Cucumbers are grown primarily for the Takamatsu and Osaka-Kobe markets. It is the government's hope that widespread diversification of production might stabilize the price of fresh vegetables, which is subject to sharp fluctuations from year to year and from the beginning to the end of a single growing season. Diversification is stressed as the best means for preventing overproduction of one or two vegetable crops and the resultant sharp break in prices paid to the producer.

In 1975, however, the program was meeting with limited success. The subsidy paid to the farmer who converted from rice to cucumbers was set at ¥35,000 per ten ares, a figure that proved so attractive an inducement, especially in the context of the general economic downturn, that many farmers entered the program. The unintended but entirely predictable result was to drop the bottom out of cucumber prices, which fell almost 40 percent between 1974 and 1975.

For the farmer who has a good year cucumber production is a risk well worth taking, for the gross profit is about two and a half times that realized on rice. In the case of vegetables, however, about one-half of the gross may go to production and marketing costs, and everyone complained in particular of the high cost of packing and transportation. Nor has the government yet been able to correct for at least one major element of risk. With vegetables there is a substantial effect on prices of a modest rise or fall in overall production. The Agricultural Cooperative estimated, for example, that if production of cucumbers rises ten percent, the market price declines by half; if production falls ten percent, the market price doubles.

One Kurusu family has been especially active in its efforts to capitalize on the opportunity to convert part of its land from rice to cucumbers. Their experience is instructive. They had about five *tan* (49.6 ares) of paddy land and because of their family composition (four of the seven members are not in the labor market) are more heavily dependent on agricultural income than most. In 1971 they converted two sizable paddy fields to cucumber cultivation at an initial investment of ¥50,000 for the aluminum pipe frame and nylon cord netting, sold at a special price by the Agricultural Cooperative. The pipe frame can be reused every year, and the netting need be replaced only occasionally. They paid off the initial investment and turned a modest profit the first two years, and the third year was a very good one. In 1975, however, they experienced their first serious setback, for the vines began to yellow and wither in July, just as they had roughly reached the break-even point.

The head of the family was concerned:

I don't know what went wrong. This never happened before, so I went to the Cooperative right away to get their advice. They weren't much help. All they could suggest is that we may have applied too much fertilizer or over-watered. It may be that we were too anxious about the water. Up here ordinary irrigation is usually enough for the vegetables, but there has been so little rain this year that we watered quite a bit by hand.

They cleared the plots and replanted in early August, in hopes of capitalizing on a late harvest. Kurusu's climate is enough cooler than that of the plain, where most of the truck farmers are located, that it is often possible to supply vegetables at high prices in what amounts to the off-season. The whole experience of this family, however, confirms the general view that the farmers need far more help in learning the intricacies of what is for most of them a qualitatively different kind of agricultural enterprise. They are willing to try new crops and techniques, to work hard and to take risks if they are not threatened with a total loss. Indeed, the Agricultural Cooperatives have been sharply criticized in recent years for their alleged abandonment of their classic role as promoters of agricultural production and for a tendency to concern themselves more with procuring rice as agents of the government and as sales agents for consumer goods (Iinuma 1974:348).

Kurusu farmers do not directly market the vegetables they grow, nor have they ever done so. No one uses his automobile to carry produce to town, for the whole operation is controlled by the Agricultural Cooperative. Kurusu is by no means unique in this absence of direct commercial activity, usually designed to eliminate the middleman. Shimpo (1976:53–85) offers extensive documentation of the point for a farm community in northern Japan where considerable diversification of cash crops has occurred. An unusual development that may give a foretaste of the future is cited by Iinuma (1976). It involves the efforts of some housewives to contract directly with individual farmers to supply them with vegetables grown without the aid of chemical fertilizers or pesticides. Over the past several years public concern with the possible dangers of eating produce to be had through normal channels has risen sharply. Unfortunately, Kurusu farmers are located too far from the city to profit from what may develop into a widespread practice, and they lack the experience of dealing directly with the consuming public.

Families with smaller areas of lowland rice fields and more upland paddies have turned to alternatives other than vegetables. One of the first was the raising of flowers and nursery stock, which is reported for the late 1950's. A man in Kurusu was among the early experimenters with this potentially very valuable cash crop, and by 1968 he had committed several of his upland fields entirely to the new undertaking. He became even more seriously involved after the 1973 oil crisis, when he lost his job as a night attendant at a nearby filling station that was forced to curtail its operations. His wife works full-time and has nothing to do with his attempts to develop his nursery business.

In front of their house he has put in some cold frames and has started a small plot of trees suitable for dwarfing as *bonsai* as well as some varieties of plants suitable for flower arrangements. One of their larger upland paddies has been planted in grapes and fruit trees for several years, but he has given up on both and the vineyard and orchard are untended and choked with weeds. Over the years this man has again and again been involved in schemes designed to produce a steady cash income, but so far he has met with limited success. He has no readily marketable skills, like many Kurusu men his age, and is perhaps only less fortunate than most in pursuing goals that all share.

Some families have tried raising domesticated animals as a supplementary source of income. In 1951 there were a few chickens, but few people could afford to feed them and they offered little more than eggs and occasional meat for the family's table. In 1960 the seventeen households responding to the questions of the agricultural census listed their domesticated animals. Eight of them owned a work cow, three kept one goat each, and one family kept two sheep. Chickens were raised by nine families, the two largest flocks twenty-two and thirty birds each, the remaining houses had an average of only six fowl each.

In 1975 there were no domestic animals of any kind. The work cows, of course, have been completely displaced by machines. What the goats and sheep may have represented, I could not find out; there had been none in 1951 certainly. One family remembered there had been some talk of there being money to be made in goat's milk. As for the chickens, a man who had once kept as many as a hundred told us that there had been a time when almost every family in Kurusu had some. But the price of feed, almost all of it imported, kept rising, while the prices of eggs and chickens remained the same. When it became obvious that it was cheaper to buy what eggs and chicken one wanted, they all gave up.

The Difficult Decision: To Hold On or Sell Out

In 1951 it was estimated that the agricultural households of Kurusu derived 80 to 85 percent of their incomes from crops, primarily cereal grains. The rest came from home industry and by-employment. The range of family income in Kurusu was estimated to be from about ¥40,000 to ¥200,000 per year.

For Kurusu families we have the results of the 1960 agricultural census, in which they were asked to estimate what proportion of their incomes came from agriculture. Their replies, though doubtless inaccurate, are nonetheless revealing, for at that early date nine of the seventeen estimated that less than 10 percent of their income came from agriculture; eight estimated that they derived from 10 to 50 percent of all income from farming. Ten households estimated that their total income from agriculture had been less than ¥100,000 in the preceding year, and two set the level at between ¥100,000 and ¥300,000. Five did not reply.

They were also asked what proportion of their agricultural income came from grain sales. Of the ten who responded four said that grain accounted for all such income; three estimated that it accounted for from between 90 and 95 percent, two set the figure at about 60 percent and one said 30 percent. For those who listed other sources of agricultural income the principal ones were vegetables and chickens. Three households said that cut flowers and nursery stock were contributing substantially to their incomes. These figures and others that are available from large-scale surveys give some point to the comment of one man who said to me, "We are even less farmers now than we were when you first came here." The pace of change, clearly, has accelerated.

As we have just seen, rice production yields a modest return by any standard. At the Agricultural Cooperative they estimated that if a family had about two hectares of farm land, an operation inconceivably large by Kurusu standards, they might make a decent living from agriculture alone. Nevertheless, if they put all the land in rice without diversifying at all, they would net at most two million yen a year. For its part the government estimated that in fiscal 1974, for Japan excluding Hokkaido, the average income of farm households was about three million yen, two-thirds of it derived from by-employment.

From the foregoing figures it will be clear that today no family in Kurusu can make a living by farming alone. Yet, deeply involved as they are in outside employment, few people have sold any appreciable amount of agricultural land; some have even purchased additional fields as they became available. In almost every case where a family head has died, furthermore, an heir has been found to take over both house and land. What remains in doubt, and what we shall be concerned with in this section, is whether the children who stand to inherit the land will continue to farm it.

A man in his early fifties who has a large, fairly new house and about as much land as anyone in Kurusu, said:

> When I was growing up it never occurred to me that I'd ever be anything but a farmer because like everybody else I had very little education. I have two sons myself, but I could not possibly urge them to take up farming. It's a life of hard work from dawn to dusk. To spare them that, I did my best to see to it that they got training for other kinds of jobs. My first son works for a big construction company and my second son, who has a good job, too, has been adopted into a family that has very little land. In the old days parents demanded of their children what was in the parents' best interests. All that talk about filial piety was just a cover. I think it's best to let one's children develop as best suits their talents. Still and all, my elder boy will come back and take over here when I'm too old to farm.

Despite these brave sentiments he remains uncertain, as well he might, whether when the time comes his son and his daughter-in-law will really want to return. Perhaps most important of all, there are moments when he wonders if his son actually knows how to farm. He seems to feel that if he can persuade him to come back to Kurusu early, perhaps upon the father's retirement from his present job at the mandatory age of fifty-five, there may yet be time to teach him. If the son stays away until his father's strength fails, then who will show him what needs to be done? On the other hand, he occasionally takes cold comfort in the thought that the timing may not be so crucial after all, for the expertise of older farmers is increasingly irrelevant in the context of the new, mechanized agriculture (Shimpo 1974:488–89).

A Kurusu man in his early thirties touched on some of the same issues:

> There are indeed a lot of old people around here who can't get used to the way things are. But what do they expect us to do? We're not ungrateful, but we don't want to become farmers. No one likes to see grandmothers out in the fields well beyond the age when they ought to be taking it easy. I don't know any young people who think that old women should have to go on working until they can't carry on any longer. But most of them wouldn't stop if they could. I begged my mother to come live with us in the city, and all she could do was worry about being bored with nothing to do. It's true, as she says, that it would be a mistake to sell out. What would we do if I got sick or lost my job and we had no place to go?
>
> Anyway, after a lot of arguing, we came back here. We've tried to get her to

slow down, but she won't, and we can't help her much with the farming now
that we both work. I suppose we'll go on like this as long as she holds out, and
then I'll get someone to cultivate the fields on shares. There's nothing else to
do, but she'll try to pressure me into farming even though she knows perfectly
well that it is economically impossible.

In any event, it is not in this generation but the next that the major
problem will arise (see Chapter Six). In a series appearing in the *Asahi
Shimbun* in 1975, the attitudes of farm fathers and their sons of
middle-school age were contrasted. Few men wanted their sons to become farmers and not many sons indicated any desire to do so. Middle-school graduates, popularly known as "the golden eggs" (Morris
1973), can easily secure jobs which pay a beginning wage larger than
the income of an entire farm family. The author of this piece, in obvious distress, reported that even the rural schools no longer need give
their students two weeks off at the peak agricultural seasons, and that
it is not uncommon to see the parents working in fields close by the
school grounds where their children are engaged in after-hours club
activities and extracurricular sporting events. A boy was quoted as
saying that he had found transplanting a dirty and unpleasant task,
and a teacher reported that things had gone so far that the pupils in
her class who had been asked to bring sickles to clear the weeds from
the schoolgrounds did not know how to use them, and had said that it
would have made more sense to use a herbicide instead.

Certainly the national figures are less than encouraging. The number
of young people finishing middle-school who entered the agricultural
labor force held steady at 400,000 annually from 1868 to 1952, when
it began to drop. In 1975 it was down to 10,000, but the trend has
been offset somewhat by another kind of population movement. In
1974, for example, 93,900 males engaged primarily in agriculture
shifted to other kinds of employment, while 55,000 returned to agriculture from other jobs. The highest return rate was in the age group
thirty-five to fifty-nine (*Nōgyō hakusho* 1976:142).

What might bring a man back to the part-time agriculture of Kurusu? It cannot be the attraction of money, for even a laborer on a
construction job can earn in two or three months what he can make
from ten ares of rice paddy fields in a year. In Kurusu in 1951, when
most houses derived the lion's share of their income from agriculture,

only two families had men working away from the hamlet during the slack seasons. Nowadays, as the current cliché has it, agriculture has become the subsidiary occupation.

From the staff members of the local office of the Agricultural Cooperative to local teenagers, it was said that agriculture has become a deficit operation. This puts the case too strongly, but it is true that the cash outlays for machines and agricultural chemicals have kept income low despite the greatly increased yields (Fukutake 1974:48). As one elderly man put it, trying to indicate how extreme the situation has become, "Even the successor has to take a full-time job."

Even though they realize that agriculture has become a marginal proposition, farmers continue to cultivate the land far longer than might reasonably be expected. As it happens, there are both technical and legal reasons for doing so. Before we consider them in detail, let us review the extraordinary developments in postwar Japan with respect to the price of land of all kinds.

In 1952, although the official price was much lower, ten ares of good paddy land was said to be worth about ¥50,000. All sales were strictly controlled by the national government. In 1975 there was, of course, a market for agricultural land as such, and there were special low-interest government loans available to support its purchase. Nevertheless, in places like Kurusu, buyers are more likely to be interested in converting fields to other uses, especially for housing. Kurusu land is particularly well-suited to this purpose, despite the distance of the hamlet from the city, because it is relatively flat, offers immediate access to the highway, and has a recently installed water system to which new dwellings can easily be connected.

In 1975 dry-field land would have brought about ¥600,000 per ten ares. Locally it was estimated that paddy fields would bring as much as 50 percent more. These prices compare favorably with the average figures for Kagawa Prefecture. In 1974 paddy fields averaged ¥784,000 and dry fields ¥419,688 per ten ares for Kagawa, substantially higher than the national figures, which were ¥571,250 and ¥353,771, respectively. For some perspective on why selling one's land has become an increasingly attractive option, consider the rise in prices over the national figures for 1955, when paddy land sold for ¥116,018 and dry fields for ¥67,694. Land values have more than quintupled in twenty years, but the speculative character of the market is revealed by the 9.2 percent decline in land prices registered in 1974, the first drop since the end of World War II, and the very large acreage left undeveloped after it changed hands.

In view of the inflated value that their farmlands have suddenly acquired, it is worth considering in some detail the legal and technical constraints that we have mentioned above. It is our impression that the legal checks are of prime importance, or at least that they have been until very recently. As we have already seen in Chapter Two, they can be traced back directly to the land reform program of the postwar years and the subsequent legislation designed to protect the interests of agriculturalists. In 1952 the government enacted the Agricultural Land Law which prohibits the annexation of farm land as well as its sale or purchase except under rigidly specified conditions. "While strict enforcement of the law has been moderated by degrees in recent years, there is yet strong adherence to the spirit of the law *whose primary object is to increase the number of landed farmers*" (Kawano 1973:14, emphasis added). Indeed, one of its principal purposes was to encourage the sales of land to its tenants, with the result that by 1965 the 520,000 hectares of tenanted land that had survived the reform measures had been reduced to 270,000 hectares. More important, perhaps, even if farmers "should find it necessary to seek employment in the non-agricultural sector and thus to absent themselves from the village, they must be in a position to leave a family member capable of cultivating the land behind in the village, in order that the title to their farmland property be preserved" (Kawano 1973:17). If they fail to take this precaution they become absentee landlords by definition and will be divested of their holdings if the letter of the law is observed. This is surely one of the major reasons for the slow decline in the number of agricultural households during the period when the agricultural population fell sharply.

Despite the many legal restrictions on renting out agricultural land, however, over the years a substantial number of farmers have entered into tenancy agreements of an informal sort (Dore 1959:196; Shimpo 1976:108–9). The usual agreement is verbal, with no written contract of any kind. The owner agrees to let out his fields to the man who will cultivate it for a price, ordinarily some portion of the rice harvest.

Owners prefer these informal agreements, for contracts in the pre-reform style would give the other party tenancy rights that make it extremely difficult to put the renter off the land. Under the present system the renter has fewer rights than he enjoyed under the old.

Such arrangements have become increasingly common. In 1972, .87 percent of the 5,117,000 farm households in Japan had entrusted all of their farmland, and another 46 percent a portion of their land, to other cultivators. A great many of these people have emigrated to the cities. This amounts to the appearance of a new form of absentee landlordism, of course, under a strict interpretation of the Agricultural Land Law. But the government, now concerned to promote more efficient and larger-scale management, moved to relax the provisions of the law that affect this practice; and beginning in 1976 it undertook measures to permit utilization of lands that would otherwise be left idle because their owners would quit agriculture altogether for want of a successor to take over the operation (Oriental Economist 1976:49–50).

Thus, until quite recently the existence in the countryside of what is often called a residual labor force of women and older men is as much a result of proprietary considerations as any other factor. Furthermore, it should be clear that the non-fluidity of farmland—the tendency of its owners not to sell—arises also from its having become a very valuable and extremely stable asset in a period of steady inflation. The persistence of the small operating unit and the difficulty of consolidation into larger, more efficient units are, then, as much the results of larger legal and economic conditions as they are of considerations of the importance of the household and ancestral property. Fukutake (1974:34) has put it more strongly: "Despite their strong sense of family property, most farm families now regard farmland and mountain land simply as the most dependable kind of property; this is a different attitude from that of an earlier era, when they were regarded as symbols of family status."

There are also, as we have said, some technical reasons why people will try to keep their fields in cultivation even though they expect to make little or no money from the agricultural operation. In 1975 in Kurusu there were some small-holders whose able-bodied family members could not or would not cultivate their land, but who hired others to do so primarily in order to keep the fields in good condition.

In some cases their holdings were so small that they could not justify the purchase of any machinery; in others the reasons were more complicated, usually turning on domestic difficulties that had precluded their getting in the crop at the proper time. For the most part the fields of the former were being cultivated by men with farm equipment who were anxious to expand the area of land they cultivated; in extreme cases the "renter" received 90 percent of the crop.

In such cases, where a family has been unable to put in a crop, the fields are grown over with weeds. Conceivably they could simply let them lie fallow until a buyer comes along, but it is very difficult to restore a plot even after only one growing season has passed. No one is much disturbed when upland fields are abandoned, but it is a very different matter when someone lets a lowland paddy stand idle. One major problem is the spread of weeds and insects from such a neglected field, which damage the crops in neighboring plots. Moreover, the delicate balance of the irrigation system may be thrown off (see Chapter Seven), and a greater economic burden placed on those who must see to the maintenance of that system as long as they continue to farm.

Should a Kurusu family decide to sell its land despite all these considerations, both it and its neighbors would much prefer to sell it to another farmer than to someone who will put it to another use. In part this attitude is a function of the tax laws, but it also has to do with the troubles that arise if the buyer builds a house on his land. The chief problem is that the house shades the neighboring fields, thus reducing yields. This may seem a weak argument at first blush, but down in the suburbanizing towns nearer Takamatsu the shadows that fall on the cultivated fields are only one of the many problems that have been encountered.

One man told us that the many shops that leave some electric lights or illuminated signs on all night pose a serious threat to the crops because the lights attract hordes of insects. These in turn attract birds, especially sparrows, in great numbers. Both do great damage to the rice, especially during the three days it is hung up on racks to dry. The lights also upset the balance between normal daylight and hours of darkness, and yields decline because the growing plants have no time to rest. The non-farm households have their own complaints about the situation, particularly about spraying with insecticides. Although the spraying dates are widely posted, and in some areas advance warning given over loudspeakers, the fine chemical mist penetrates the most tightly shuttered house, causing a variety of respiratory and eye irritations. To compound the difficulties, the increased insect population makes it necessary to spray more often.

Complex questions of equity and comparative advantage have long been dealt with in rural Japan, where the pattern of fields and the nature of the terracing and irrigation systems traditionally mandated differential rents for many different categories of agricultural land. But in the postwar period, clearly, a great many new problems have been faced. They are never very far from the minds of the farmers of Kurusu. A man in his forties explained his decision not to sell out in the following terms:

My nineteen-year-old daughter recently graduated from higher-school and works for a small firm in Takamatsu. Her salary is low—she only gets ¥60,000 a month. With the two bonuses, which have been running about 25 to 30 percent of her salary, she makes about a million yen a year. And the most that I can make from farming at my age is a million and a half!

Why don't I sell out? Well, if I go on farming and the children work outside, then we can make it pretty well. I am not really well trained to do anything else anyway. Of course if I could get *oku* [he used the word, which means one hundred million, in the sense of a great deal of money] for my land, it might be worth selling, but the prices here are in *hyaku-man* [literally, one million]. There's really no point in selling at such a price. For instance, if I could get *oku* I might be able to build some kind of rental property and live off the income from it, but I could never do that if I sold out for *hyaku-man*.

Everyone in Kurusu has heard stories about farmers living near the cities who have sold their land for truly fabulous prices. They are contemptuously referred to by city people as *tochi narikin*—nouveaux riches whose money comes from the sale of their land. The press delights in trying to top earlier stories about the follies of the erstwhile "peasants." Among the favorites are detailed descriptions of their elaborate new residences, said to resemble old-fashioned public bathhouses, snide accounts of the antics of their suddenly moneyed children, and chronicles of their descent into financial ruin. It is not entirely clear to us why these nouveaux riches are so bitterly resented.

Part of the reason, surely, is the failure of the farmers of today to conform to the urbanite's expectations of their proper life-style. In the view of city people, farmers are not *supposed* to drive about in their own automobiles, live in fine homes, dress their wives in fine clothing, and send their children to college. They are supposed to live frugally, but they do not. We have heard city people make genuinely extraordinary statements: "Farmers will no longer do any work that requires them to dirty their hands." "Farmers have too much free time nowadays and spend it all gambling and getting drunk." "Those country kids get into so much trouble because their parents give them far too much spending money." All of these canards are very wide of the mark as far as farmers like those who live in Kurusu are concerned. They are not rich, they do not find time hanging heavy on their hands, and they work very hard indeed at very dirty jobs.

Despite the fact that they still lag far behind most of the rest of the population, rural people today obviously enjoy a standard of living that is far higher than it was in 1951. The irony is that the degree to which their condition of life has improved is related directly to the extent to which they have become committed to non-agricultural employment. It is equally obvious that farmers enjoy no fringe benefits and are inadequately protected against impairment of working ability through injury or illness. The pressures to shift occupation, in whole or in part, are immense.

Non-Agricultural Employment

In 1951 home industries were less important for any high return they yielded than for the fact that they provided some cash income. All of these activities were carried on in the slack season by women, whose production was in many cases entirely for the family's own use rather than for sale. They were not always very skilled at the tasks, at which most had very limited experience. Among the most important of these home industries was the weaving of a kind of mat called *kamasu*. In 1948, 80 percent of the total production of these mats nationally was accounted for by Kagawa Prefecture (*Shikoku chihō . . . 1950:84*). In Kurusu there were four kamasu looms, ranging in cost from ¥4,000 to ¥12,000. Some weaving was done on contract for large suppliers, some for people who brought their own straw for custom orders, and some for the family's own use. Today the production of kamasu seems to have stopped altogether, for people say that when the old ones wore out they were unable to find replacements.

Another home industry was the manufacture of straw rope. A skilled operator of one of Kurusu's eight hand-powered rope-twisting machines, which cost about ¥7,000, could net about ¥100 per day, and it was said that a household engaged in one or another or a combination of these enterprises might take in ¥10,000 annually.

Of far greater economic importance was employment as wage-earners. Four Kurusu people worked full-time at the local sawmill and two part-time. Moreover, six Kurusu men—three family heads and three unmarried dependents—were working on the construction of the Naiba Dam in Shionoe. For all of the unskilled and semi-skilled workers, the daily wage was about ¥200. Some men picked up casual day-labor jobs on road construction in the area, or worked as agricultural laborers for others. Twenty-five years ago, in 1949 and 1950, the daily wage for agricultural laborers in Yasuhara averaged ¥217 plus two or three meals.

The securing of cash income from non-agricultural employment has long been a necessity, but until the late 1950's and the early 1960's, the urban labor market was of such a character that a great many local people with very small holdings chose to concentrate on agriculture, supplementing that income with seasonal employment away from the community rather than giving up completely and selling out.

The pre-reform tenant had nothing to lose if an opportunity occurred to better himself in the towns. The post-reform owner of land, albeit a miserable two or three *tan*, is held back by the strength of his attachment to land which is "his very own," and by the thought that this two or three *tan* at least represents the security of a guaranteed food supply, a security which contrasts with the uncertainties of the urban labor market [Dore 1959:263–64].

Then came the period of labor shortage during Japan's extraordinary economic boom. Two extremely important effects of this unprecedented development should not go unnoticed. Not only did it reduce wage differentials that had always existed between younger and older workers, but it also narrowed the gap between wages paid by small-scale and large-scale enterprises (Ohkawa 1966:150). The double appeal to the farm population—youthful and largely destined to enter small-scale enterprises—was irresistible. Today, it will be recalled, 84 people live in Kurusu, 24 of them in school or of preschool age. Half of the 60 adults (18 men and 12 women) hold full-time jobs outside the community.

"Everybody needs a lot of cash these days." My wife and I were constantly reminded that "in the old days" one needed cash only at the New Year and at *o-bon* in midsummer and could operate on credit the rest of the year. Actually, the people of Kurusu had frequently said exactly the same thing to me in 1951. While their perceptions seem not to have changed very much, the situation has. Now one must have a constant supply of cash for paying the charges for the telephone and television, buying propane gas for heating the bathwater and for cooking, and paying all manner of taxes, an issue that was a sore point in 1951 as well. It also takes a lot of cash for the children's school expenses, particularly, parents say, because children are so wasteful nowadays compared to the children of a generation ago who treasured even a single lead pencil until it was worn to a nub. And, of course, there are the expenses for clothing—Kurusu people now dress very much as city people do—and the payments on furniture, automobiles, motorcycles, and farm machinery, and in a few cases, even mortgage payments on the house. Babies are no longer delivered at home by a grandmother or a midwife, but at the hospital, where in 1975 the cost ran about ¥100,000.

Cash is king, and a young woman with a job has a better chance of finding a husband than one who, as a young woman put it, "sits around the house all day practicing the tea ceremony and arranging flowers." Moreover, young people with degrees from industrial or commercial higher-schools had the best chance of finding jobs.

But in the summer of 1975 everyone was concerned with the continuing negative effects of the economic slump, particularly on the incomes of those employed off the farms. For the first time in four years the gap between high-income and low-income brackets in Japan widened in 1974. The major reason for the depression of the income of the latter groups, defined as those whose average annual income was about ¥1,400,000, was the drop in the amount of overtime work available and a decline in the size of bonuses paid out. Indeed, the average extra income of all brackets actually declined 7 percent in fiscal 1974. The *Asahi Shimbun* of July 9, 1975, reported the results of a survey of 4,000 companies employing thirty or more persons. Between January and March of 1975, 74 percent had cut the volume of overtime work and given part-pay furloughs to some employees; 71 percent had repeated these cuts in the April-June quarter. At the end of the year there were said to be two applicants for every job opening, and all of the companies were warning that they would reduce their spring hiring of college graduates by as much as one-half to four-fifths of their normal intake (Halloran 1976).

One of the most dramatic results of the recession can be seen in figures released by the Ministry of Agriculture and Forestry (Anonymous 1976d:5). While the number of farm households had continued to decline, the number of those engaged in full-time agriculture rose slightly for the first time since the end of World War II. It appeared that farm household members who had lost their jobs or who could not make ends meet without substantial overtime work were returning to agriculture for want of other options.

Just as the lower-income workers were more severely affected by the slump than those earning higher salaries, so did women workers fare less well than men. Despite the public comments of such figures as Iwasa Yoshizane of Keidanren, the Federation of Economic Organizations, to the effect that Japanese enterprises were holding millions of redundant workers because they could not be laid off under local labor practices, by December 1975 unemployment was at a sixteen-year high. According to the government, which uses statistics that give a very misleading impression of the number of *un*employed, by May 1975 there had been a 2 percent drop in the number of employed men and an 11 percent decline in the number of employed women, who made up almost 40 percent of the labor force at the time. And while the average annual income of workers in private industry for 1975 rose 11.5 percent, consumer prices rose 11.8 percent in the same period (Anonymous 1977:8). All of these developments were bad economic news for Kurusu's working people, for they are in the lower-income bracket, have limited education, and generally hold the less skilled jobs.

The reduction of the size of the bonus was almost as serious as the layoffs. Bonuses are paid semi-annually or quarterly by all Japanese employers. In 1975 the summer bonus was up 7.4 percent over that paid in 1974, which may seem an adequate increase, but it must be noted that the summer bonus in 1974 had been 47 percent greater than that of the preceding year. (These figures are for the 271 major enterprises in Japan as reported in the August 12, 1975, *Asahi Shimbun*.) Moreover, the summer bonus was smaller than the preceding winter's bonus had been. Since everyone depends heavily on the bonus for savings and for large expenditures, any reduction in it is felt very keenly. Savings are likely to be especially affected, as is indicated by the results of a survey of 2,000 working young people on vacation north of Tokyo conducted in May of 1975. They reported that they were saving 23 percent of their salaries and 39 percent of their bonuses and other income (*Asahi Shimbun*, July 16, 1975).

We have some partial evidence of the changing financial situation of the people in Kurusu, as reflected in their deposits in one of the major local savings institutions. In July 1975 seventeen families had savings deposits in the local Agricultural Cooperative totaling ¥5,589,804, an average of ¥328,812 per family. The range was enormous—from ¥5,792 to ¥1,235,471. The medium figure of ¥37,615 suggests how unevenly distributed the savings are. Actually, the six largest accounts were all over ¥500,000; the seven smallest were under ¥11,800. It should be noted that July is probably the low-point of savings in the year; accounts are at their highest levels after both grain crops have been sold in December. The Kagawa Agricultural Cooperative reported in 1975 that it had nine million yen in savings deposits, an average of about ¥161,000 per family.

The contrast with the situation in 1951 could hardly be more dramatic. In that year the total savings for Kurusu's twenty-two households was ¥239,913, an average of ¥10,905 per family. The range was from a low of ¥10 to a high of ¥82,000. Again, the distribution was extremely uneven. The top six accounts were all over ¥11,705 and the eleven lowest were all under ¥1,800. Nonetheless the 1951 figures were almost twice as great as they had been in 1948, partly because of the election of a new director whose reputation and abilities had greatly improved the operations of the cooperative, rendering obsolete the standard joke about his predecessor's regime—"the accountant's fingers are always red." In spite of this rapid growth in savings at the cooperative, few families in Kurusu in 1951 could save the ¥50 per month recommended by the Yasuhara Women's Association, and there were probably no more than two or three who were putting aside as much as ¥100 per month on a regular basis.

So, over the past generation, cash income is up sharply and outside employment has become the rule for men if not yet for women. As examples of some of the kinds of jobs that younger persons from Kurusu might qualify for, we have given below selected notices carried in the *Shikoku Shimbun* for July 21, 1975, under the heading "Positions Available":

1. Women. 5.5 hours per day (10:00 A.M.–5:30 P.M.). Base pay ¥37,000 per month plus other compensation. Six days of vacation per month (two Saturdays and four Sundays). Firm has nursery.
2. Women. 5 hours per day (7:00 A.M.–12 noon, or 5:00 P.M.–10:00 P.M.). Waitress, cashier, kitchen helper. ¥35–40,000 per month.
3. Women. Higher-school diploma. Training or experience in bookkeeping and abacus (above third-class competence) required. Age up to 25. Salary from ¥55,000 per month. Apply Kagawa Prefectural Chamber of Commerce.
4. Men and women. Janome Sewing Machines. A large, depression-proof company. Hiring office clerks, shipping and packing personnel, bill collectors, service agents, public-relations specialists, and management personnel. Ages 18 to 55. Monthly salaries from ¥70,000 to ¥150,000. All fringe benefits. Bonuses quarterly.
5. Men and women. Two shifts on alternate days. 8:30 A.M.–4:00 P.M., or 4:00 P.M.–11:00 P.M. Ages from 18 to 35. Men: ¥110,000 and up. Women: ¥100,000 and up. Transportation paid. Bonuses.
6. Men. Full-time position as accounting clerk. Age up to 40 with experience. 8:30 A.M.–5:00 P.M. Salary from ¥79,000.

While younger people might qualify for some of these positions, in reality the outside employment of most people in Kurusu is of other kinds. The job situation in 1975 for men is shown in Table 21. Eighteen men held full-time outside jobs and all but two commuted by automobile. These figures do not include the owner of the local sawmill or the part-time Buddhist priest, both of whom operate out of their homes in the hamlet. Only three male family heads, two of whom are seventy-one years old and one of whom is fifty-seven and had just lost his job, did not hold full-time jobs. All three were engaged in full-time agriculture for want of alternative employment.

For women the proportion of those employed and their places of work were very different (see Table 22). Those who commuted went

TABLE 21
*Place and Kind of Outside Employment of
Kurusu Males, 1975*

Age	Place or kind of work	Location
22	Foundry	Takamatsu
27	Electrical appliance manufacturing company	Yashima
29	Carpenter	not fixed
30	Salesman	Takamatsu
31	Carpenter with construction company	Takamatsu
34	Carpenter	not fixed
34	Foundry	Kōnan Town
39	Bus driver	Marugame City
39	Tray factory	Takamatsu
39	Sawmill	Kōnan Town
40	Sawmill	Kawahigashi
41	Taxi driver	Takamatsu
49	Carpenter	not fixed
53	Office worker	Shionoe Town
58	Delivery van driver (glove factory)	local
59	Construction company	Takamatsu
65	Carpenter	not fixed
67	Barber	local

by bus, with the single exception of a young woman who drove her own car. Twelve women held full-time jobs, two young mothers were temporarily at home with infants but planned to return to work as soon as possible. Two of the three widows who did not work outside Kurusu took in piecework from local factories. Half of the employed women work locally, for the most part in one or another of the factories built in the area since the mid-1960's. Although not all of these establishments have prospered, and some employ no Kurusu people, it will be useful to consider them all here, for as a class they represent the results of concerted efforts on the part of many interested parties to accomplish several aims.

First among these aims is for the town government to provide local jobs in order to stem the outflow of population. We have raised the issue before, but we have not asked why anyone should care if the marginal agricultural lands are abandoned and the farm population declines. There are in fact several reasons for concern. As the number of children of school age drops, the effect on the school system can be disastrous; as the population declines the tax base shrinks and public services must be curtailed, and so on. A major effort was made, therefore, to persuade manufacturing enterprises to move in. From the point of view of the entrepreneurs, the situation appeared to offer the advantage of a work force prepared to settle for wages lower than those paid to urban workers. From the point of view of the local people, the proliferation of such employment opportunities seemed to promise some stabilization of the younger population, which could live at home and work nearby.

As it happens, few of these desired outcomes have materialized. Part of the problem lies with the character of many of the local undertakings: "Unstable small enterprises whose immediate futures are precarious, and others paying nonsubsistence wages, often spring up in rural areas, but they offer no security or adequate benefits. Local farm labor is unable to become fully industrial labor and continues to cling to agriculture" (Fukutake 1974:61).

Before we consider some of the other reasons for the disappointment of so many hopes, let us look at the establishments in and around Kurusu, regardless of whether they actually employ people from the hamlet.

TABLE 22
*Place and Kind of Outside Employment of
Kurusu Females, 1975*

Age	Place or kind of work	Location
19	Office clerk	Takamatsu
28	Sales clerk	Takamatsu
31	Hani pajama factory	local
32	Office clerk	Takamatsu
35	Factory work (office?)	Takamatsu
44	Hani pajama factory	local
48	Fasuto glove factory	local
49	Hani pajama factory	local
50	Agricultural Cooperative	Kawahigashi
57	Hani pajama factory	local
62	Mitsuwa foundry	local
65	Hospital (custodial)	Kagawa Town

Local Industries
Hani Pajama Factory

The Hani (Honey) Pajama Factory is a classic example of an "invited industry" (*yūchi jigyō*). It occupies the site and some of the buildings of the old Yasuhara Middle-School, which was closed with the school-consolidation of 1965. The plant is about a ten-minute walk from Kurusu.

The first Hani enterprise to locate in Shionoe opened in 1963 and promptly failed. A second effort failed before the end of 1965. Both of these early operations had concentrated on production of children's clothing for export, and the Town Office had been sure that the kinds of skills needed were available in the surrounding area and that local women would welcome a stable if modest income. There can be no doubt that these assumptions were entirely accurate. Why, then, did the first two efforts fail? The current explanation is that they simply were unable to meet production and delivery deadlines. Management assumed none of the blame, but tended to place it on the workers instead:

These farm women took off for weddings and funerals, at harvest times, and whenever else they felt like it. They didn't understand the kind of schedule a factory has to operate on. In June and October, production would slow down because they'd just take off for the harvests. Now we lose less time during those months because the agricultural machinery has cut the time they need off almost in half.

The women who are employed there have a very different view of the matter. One from Kurusu said that she neither likes nor dislikes the place, and that its greatest advantage is that it is so close to her home. For about five years she had held a job in Takamatsu, but she always worried about what would happen if there were some emergency at home. When the opportunity came, she applied for the job at Hani, but she actively dislikes the schedule:

In the old days when I was home, I could chat with my neighbors whenever I felt like it or when I wanted to take a break. Now it's a fast "good morning" as I rush off to punch in at eight. When you are doing housework, you can let some chore slide if you don't feel like doing it just then, and you can rest when you are tired or nap when you are sleepy. That's all in the past now, although I still come home and have lunch here because it's cheaper than eating out.

Whatever the truth of the charge that it was the women's fault—one almost hears the overseas manager of some European-owned plant saying, "These natives simply do not . . ."—the enterprise did stabilize after it shifted to the manufacture of men's pajamas for the domestic market. This move has resulted in a far less rigorous production schedule and has had the effect of making loans available on a far more flexible basis than was the case with companies engaged in manufacture for export.

It was in 1969 that the factory became part of Shikoku Hani, owned by an Osaka branch of Nagoya interests. The same company has similar operations in Tottori and Wakayama Prefectures.

In Shionoe Town they employ a large number of people, in three widely scattered hamlets. At Nishitaniguchi 75 people (65 women, 10 men) work in the old middle-school building. At Higashitani 20 people (18 women, 2 men) work in the old primary-school building, which they moved into in 1972. At Kaminishi five or six women work in an old clinic, recently abandoned with the thinning out of population in this hamlet. Over the entire area they offer employment at home to about one hundred women, most of whom do unskilled work such as cutting loose thread ends, or folding and bagging the garments, as one Kurusu woman does in a small room in the storage building adjoining her home. Some of them do simple sewing on machines loaned to them by the company.

Abandoned school buildings and an empty clinic—such quarters sound like a sure recipe for substandard working conditions. In point of fact the buildings of the main establishment have been extensively remodeled and are now air-conditioned and centrally heated. Indeed, one Kurusu woman who works there told us that in summer she finds it too cool for her taste. She thinks that they lower the temperatures to keep the younger workers happy. The workrooms are huge, well-lighted, and open, as they are at the glove factory (the next enterprise to be discussed).

Full-time employees at Hani get six days off a month—two Saturdays and four Sundays. The present management, determined to break the farm women of what it sees as their bad work habits, has instituted a system of cash rewards for consistent attendance. Those who are present for the full complement of workdays in a month are paid a bonus of ¥4,000. Those who miss one day receive ¥3,000, and so on down the scale. By all accounts it has proven a remarkably effective positive incentive, but management nonetheless estimates that about 20 percent of the work force is sufficiently unreliable that it may take off without notice. The workers are usually given four or five days off at the New Year and three days at *o-bon*. In 1975 there were complaints because they were given only two days, since the third day of *o-bon* fell on a Saturday and management decided to count Sunday as one of the three days of the normal holiday. The women from Kurusu felt cheated and said so.

The women, who are paid a daily wage, as is the case at the glove factory as well, earn about ¥70–80,000 per month, but the absolute minimum is either ¥1,500 per day or about ¥36,000 per month for the newest and least skilled workers. For the women of Kurusu this is not a bad wage. Most have a sixth-grade education at best, and few have any marketable skills beyond their considerable competence at domestic and agricultural tasks. Their families have very little land and need outside employment; places of work like Hani are literally in sight of their homes. Conditions of work are not unpleasant, and the work is far from arduous.

For management, despite having hit upon a successful formula on the third try, the outlook is not rosy. It takes the self-congratulatory line that it has succeeded in no small part because it has taught its workers to adhere to a schedule, and it also takes the position that they prefer this kind of work to agriculture. The factory work may be monotonous, but agricultural labor is harder and more tiring, partly because people do not do it every day, they argue. But for all their efforts, management finds its labor force aging. Young women generally will not take this kind of work, preferring to finish higher-school and find a white-collar or sales job in the city. Even those who marry into places like Kurusu continue to work elsewhere if they possibly can. To keep up the operation, the factory owners are considering the likelihood that they may have to build a dormitory and import labor from more benighted rural areas. In this sense, the venture has proved a partial failure from the point of view of the Town Office, and Hani has no plans for expansion, since the local population continues to decline.

Fasuto Glove Factory

The Fasuto (Fast) Ski Glove Factory occupies a large building on the highway across the river from Kurusu, about a five-minute walk away. It is a light and open structure, with air conditioning and central heating, which was being enlarged during the summer of 1975. The owner had started out with a smaller glove factory three or four miles down the highway toward Takamatsu, and had moved to his present location in 1970. He had thought that it would be possible to draw on a more stable labor supply, and it seemed to him that opportunities for expansion were more favorable in Shionoe Town; he professes to be very pleased with his decision. Until 1972 almost all of his gloves went to the United States market, but because they are made of real leather rather than vinyl, business with the United States has all but dried up. He now supplies the European and domestic markets, both of which seem able to bear the premium prices that he must charge for his very handsome product.

Fasuto employs about forty persons, thirty women and ten men, at the factory and about twenty additional women who do piecework at home at about one-third the pay earned by regular workers. The owner praised his employees highly, saying that they were both productive and highly skilled at their work. Only one Kurusu woman works here, and the two daughters of another family do piecework at home. The company supplies them with heavy-duty machines, needles, and thread. One Kurusu man is a driver and delivery man for the company.

Mitsuwa Foundry

This is an Osaka-financed enterprise, established in 1967, which produces cast-iron plumbing fittings for the domestic and foreign markets. The foundry is a short walk south of the Hani Pajama Factory. The manager is a young man who left Shionoe and spent ten years in Osaka. He came back when the Mitsuwa company was invited to establish the plant by the town government. The timing was perfect, for the cities were experiencing a labor shortage, soaring wages, and, as he put it, "all kinds of trouble over pollution."

The company has found it very difficult to get and keep workers, largely because young people much prefer service and white-collar jobs. Middle-school graduates are scarce, for most go on to higher-school and will not take jobs like these. Mitsuwa employs thirty people (equal numbers of men and women), all from the local area. The work is hard and dirty and conditions are unpleasant. The company uses a base-wage system plus a piecework rate. Management estimates that wages here are about two-thirds of what they would have to pay in Osaka. Only one Kurusu resident, a widow, works at Mitsuwa.

The Tea Factory

In 1954 the village government moved a part of the old Yasuhara Primary School building to Kurusu and set it up on village land near the Kangetsu Bridge. This represents one of the early postwar efforts to encourage cultivation of new cash crops in the area, for the structure was made into a small-scale processing plant for tea. A few houses in Yasuhara had raised their own tea on the hilly slopes, but it was not until immediately after World War II that any effort at commercialization was undertaken. The tea factory was transferred to the Agricultural Cooperative by the town in 1960, and since that time it has processed about 10,000 kilograms of tea per season. One or two Kurusu women are employed there in the very short period after the harvest when the plant is in operation.

The Ornamental Marble Goods Factory

Up the narrow road that leads to the east out of Kurusu into the hills stands an abandoned factory building. Built in 1972, it operated on an experimental basis for only six months. The place looks exactly as if it closed down at the end of a working day and no one ever came back. All the machinery, including bandsaws, polishers, and cutters, is still in place, and objects in various degrees of completion lie about inside the building. Outside are blocks of rough-cut marble and a large winch and front-loader. The plan, conceived by an engineer whose work took him into remote areas where he saw deposits of marble, was to ship in the stone from Tokushima Prefecture. At the factory it would be made into vases and table tops for sale in Takamatsu, perhaps in the Osaka-Kobe-Kyoto area as well, and eventually for export. Initially the enterprise concentrated on the Takamatsu market and employed six or seven people, including one woman from Kurusu who now works at the pajama factory.

According to some people, the operation closed down shortly after it started up because of the oil crisis of 1973, but the more likely explanation for its failure is that the products were too heavy to attract the tourist, and too expensive for all but a very limited clientele. A woman who had worked there said that there were also many unsolved technical difficulties; some varieties of marble fractured easily, making for a high proportion of wastage, and the vases often leaked water at the veins in the rock. Others alleged that the entire operation was basically experimental in nature. In any event, in 1975 it seemed to have little future; as one local resident said wistfully, "They keep saying that they'll reopen, but nothing happens."

The Carnation Greenhouse Complex

The development of the carnation-*danchi*, the term by which the greenhouse complex is known locally, is a direct result of the efforts of the town government to attract capital, in this case from Osaka, into the area. Like the pajama factory, it is an "invited industry," brought in under the Second Plan for the Improvement of Agriculture, which provided for the infusion of a great deal of money from the national treasury into schemes to stem or reverse the direction of the rural exodus. The enterprise is owned and operated by outside interests and lacks any cooperative component.

The danchi is laid out on three great terraces on which vast greenhouses are being built. The mountain has been cut back by earthmoving machinery, and even on Sundays the place is a beehive of activity. The facilities cover about 3.5 hectares in an area located up behind Kurusu where there have never been any dwellings, although many Kurusu people own fields and forest plots there. Again, it is the Kangetsu Bridge that has attracted the developers. All the heavy equipment moves across it and over the main road through the community. In order to obtain a subsidy for the construction of the new road that had to be put through from Kurusu up to the danchi, it was designated an agricultural road (*nōdō*). Without the designation, the town would have had to build the road itself and bear the entire cost.

It is wide, but as yet unpaved, and in the summer of 1975 there were some problems with washouts.

It is said that the carnations raised here are of the highest quality; they can no longer be grown near the cities because the air pollution spoils their color. As an indication of their high quality, we were told repeatedly that the flowers from this greenhouse development are regularly supplied to the imperial palace in Tokyo.

Although no one from Kurusu was employed at the carnation-danchi in 1975, the building of the road to the greenhouses, which began in 1974, had serious consequences for relations between the hamlet and the government of Shionoe Town. Some residents of Kurusu were angered and many were made even more suspicious of the government than they had been before. One of the families, which owns a dry field which adjoined some forest land belonging to another Kurusu family, was particularly bitter about the course of events. They rarely visited the upland dry field in winter, but one day in 1974 someone stopped by their house to ask if they knew that there were stakes across their land and the adjoining piece of property belonging to the other Kurusu family. The visitor also reported that some fifty-year-old pine trees had been felled. Neither family had received any advance warning, and when they went at once to the Town Office, they were simply told that the new road was being put through their land. Ultimately, the family in question agreed to give up the field if it was absolutely essential, but they refused to take cash payment for it and demanded an equivalent piece of land elsewhere. After more than a year the issue had not been resolved, and the other family had received no compensation for the lost trees, all of which turned out to be on their land. All the other owners of land needed for construction of the road sold their parcels outright.

Shītake-en, The Mushroom Garden

On the same road that leads to the abandoned marble factory but much closer to Kurusu is a *shītake* (mushroom) growing enterprise. The owners are from Chūtoku and formerly owned a small amusement park called Playland, build about 1970 on an island in the river south of Kurusu. Their principal business is the growing and drying of the mushrooms, and in 1975 they were planning to open a small restaurant on the premises that they hoped would attract weekend tourists. They had put up a modest building for the purpose, but had not yet begun to keep regular hours or to advertise for customers.

Summary

It is by no means certain that the carnation-danchi will be the last enterprise of its kind to be established near Kurusu. Yet one must wonder to what extent such undertakings will be a feature of the next quarter-century. The issue of pollution is now being taken seriously, even though it is frequently exploited by those whose real interests lie elsewhere. The younger members of the labor force have so far shown little interest in local employment, in part because the near universality of automobile ownership has greatly extended their range of employment opportunities. They have become commuters, and since wages and salaries paid by more distant urban employers are higher, there is every reason for them to take full advantage of their newfound mobility. Perhaps today's young women will choose nearby employment when they become the wives of the next generation of family heads, but neither they nor the local entrepreneurs appear to be counting on such a development to occur.

For the men of Kurusu, the future seems to hold only the prospect of continuing to seek employment outside the area. With the educational level now much higher than it has ever been, and with every prospect that it will continue to rise, they will move increasingly into service-related and white-collar jobs. There is no likelihood whatsoever of their returning to agriculture as a major subsistence activity. Some changes are irreversible, and those wrought in agriculture in this last generation are surely among these.

One major effect of all of this outside employment and the mechanization of agriculture has been to alter the daily schedule of everyone. Kurusu people used to rise very early and in peak agricultural seasons most of them consumed four meals in their long workday, and often napped in the early afternoon before resuming work in the fields. Our first inkling as to some of the consequences of what had been happening came, appropriately enough, on the first day we came down to Kurusu by bus and walked across the bridge from the highway into the hamlet. It was mid-morning, but there seemed to be no one about—no one working in the fields or walking on the road, and no one in the dooryards of the houses. To my 1951 eyes, it seemed very peculiar. As it turned out, the maximum daytime population of Kurusu is 27, and they are by and large men and women over sixty years of age and children under the age of four. Almost everyone else leaves early for work or school, and those who work come home in the late afternoon or early evening six days a week. On weekdays there is little visiting between houses, many of which are empty all day in any event, and in the evening after dinner most people settle down to watch a favorite television program before retiring. With so little time devoted to visiting one's neighbors, some people fear that Kurusu is on its way to becoming a settlement of nodding acquaintances.

CHAPTER FIVE

The Changing Domestic World

OUR AIM in this chapter is to discuss some of the qualitative changes that have occurred in the lives of Kurusu's people. We shall deal with topics as seemingly disparate as the dwellings of the hamlet, the clothing and diet of its people, their nearly universal ownership of automobiles, and the household- and community-centered domestic rituals that make up the bulk of their religious lives. We shall find in all of these evidence of marked shifts in such important matters as residence patterns, food preferences and eating habits, travel for work and leisure, and the marking of certain rites and observances.

Kurusu's Dwellings

In Table 23 we summarize the information available on the amount and kind of construction that has occurred in Kurusu since 1952. There are seventeen new buildings of all types in a place that in 1952 had fifty-six structures, and there have been changes in the kinds of building materials used. In 1952, for example, fourteen of the twenty-one dwellings had thatch roofs. Today not one of these is left and none of the new dwellings has such a roof, a situation that represents more than changing tastes. The kinds of straw formerly used for thatching throughout this area are increasingly hard to procure, for the winter grain crops that yield this straw are grown by fewer and fewer farmers; the expense of thatching is prohibitive and few competent specialists are still in the business; and in any event, tile has always enjoyed greater prestige as a roofing material. There have been other changes as well. Many of Kurusu's older homes that no longer

TABLE 23
Building Construction in Kurusu, 1952–74

Type of structure	No.	Floor area (tsubo)		Number of stories			Roof type					
		Total	Average	1	1.5	2	Thatch	Tile	Bark	Iron	Slate	Prefab
Dwelling	7	196.65	28.09	5	2	–	–	5	–	–	1	1
Storage	3	59.00	19.67	1	1	1	–	3	–	–	–	–
Sawmill	1	16.00	16.00	1	–	–	–	–	–	1	–	–
Chicken house	2	12.00	6.00	2	1	–	–	2	–	–	–	–
Garage or storage	2	13.50	6.75	1	–	–	–	1	–	–	1	–
Tobacco-drying shed	2	12.00	6.00	2	–	1	–	2	–	–	–	–
TOTAL	17	309.15		12	4	1	–	13	–	1	2	1

sport thatch roofs have instead a kind that may be a Japanese invention. The old thatch roof, its classic lines preserved, is completely covered over with galvanized iron sheets and painted a dull red, black or blue. The effect is handsome and the maintenance cost low.

Other changes, very noticeable near the towns and cities, have yet to make a heavy impact on Kurusu. The only cinder-block structure here, for example, is a combined garage and storage building put up in 1973. The owner told us that considerations of initial cost and low upkeep had led him to use this durable if unlovely material. All the remaining sixteen new buildings are of wood, as are all the older ones. By far the single most startling structure, by local standards, is a huge (76.86 *tsubo* or 254.4 square meters) prefabricated dwelling manufactured and sold under the name Misawa-hōmu. It stands between and in sharp contrast to the older houses on either side, on the spot where the modest home of a family that has left Kurusu once stood. Its occupants, who moved here from Osaka, are members of the hamlet association but have no land other than their house lot and thus are completely uninvolved in Kurusu's agricultural concerns.

As we have indicated, the Misawa Home is enormous by Kurusu standards. Indeed, in terms of floor space its nearest competitor is the 45-*tsubo* house of the sawmill owner—which, extraordinarily enough, was built in 1943 at the height of World War II. The average floor area of the dwellings in Kurusu in 1952 was 21.4 *tsubo*. The average size of the new houses, excluding the large prefab, is a shade under 20 *tsubo*.

There is a kind of miniature housing development located within Kurusu's boundaries. An outsider purchased a bloc of land that formerly was occupied by a modest older house, its outbuildings, and some adjacent plots. He has created terraced lots and in 1975 had already put up four new houses. One was purchased by an older couple from across the river in Chūtoku and another by a family from a remote area of Shionoe Town. By the summer of 1975 two more lots had been sold and the house going up on one of them was being built by a family moving out from a newly suburbanizing area near Takamatsu.

In addition to the new construction, several older outbuildings have been torn down to make room for new ones that often have living quarters in the second storey. New storage problems have arisen as old uses for outbuildings have disappeared. Stables for the work cows, chicken houses, and tobacco-drying sheds are no longer used for those purposes, if indeed they still stand. Many have been replaced by a few garages and larger sheds for the storage of farm machinery.

Many homes have been substantially renovated and some have been partially rebuilt. Improvements include the metal roof coverings for thatch, aluminum-framed sliding glass doors and windows, wooden flooring in some areas of the house that formerly were covered with mats or were dirt floored, and imitation wood paneling called *decora* for the walls of some rooms. While all of these innovations in domestic construction are expensive, they have a much longer life than their traditional counterparts of thatch roofs, wooden door and window frames, tatami mats, and plaster walls. Not only are the materials more durable, but they also require less upkeep than the old ones did. Unfortunately, they are poorly adapted to the hot and humid summer months, a disadvantage offset by their superior insulating power against the penetrating cold of winter.

The owners of relatively unchanged houses are given to apologizing for their appearance, although they are the very dwellings that the foreigner is likely to value most highly because they represent his understanding of traditional taste. The aesthetic qualities of the old houses do not loom large in the sentiments of the women who must clean them, or the house-owner who knows all about the termites and dry-rot in the sills. Nevertheless, by the testimony of every family head we queried, it is primarily pressure from the young people that leads to the tearing down of most old homes, just as it is said to explain the surge in automobile purchases of the past few years. The children of the family want things to be up-to-date; they prefer chairs, and Western-style toilets (there are at least five in the hamlet now). Beds, increasingly popular nationally—15 percent of families had one in 1965 and 35 percent in 1974—are still uncommon. What young people seek most of all is a domestic atmosphere that is "bright" (*akarui*) rather than one that is "dark" (*kurai*) or "plain" (*jimi*). This notion that agricultural villages have been dark is implied in ubiquitous slogans about building bright ones for the future, and it is a notion that crops up in many contexts that equate traditional with dark and modern with bright.

The young people seem also to have acquired an intense craving for privacy, a desire made the more compelling by their own experience of the intimate communalism of the traditional Japanese dwelling. As a consequence, in some houses sliding paper doors have given way to hinged wooden ones that shut off a room from the sound and sight of others in a way that was not possible before. We shall return to the issue of privacy in our discussion of living arrangements.

Household Appliances and Furnishings

In 1948 only one-third of all households in Kagawa Prefecture had radios (Yabe 1949:3), and no one in Kurusu—and few people in the cities for that matter—possessed any of the appliances that have become so common in the past ten to fifteen years. Rural electrification did reach Kurusu in the 1920's, but the power was used almost exclusively for electric lighting. In 1951 few households used charcoal for heating in ceramic or wooden braziers because of its cost—¥170 to ¥230 per bale. Two families were said to consume from three to five bales a year, but most used only about a half-bale. Cooking and heating of bath water were done with wood fires.

Table 24 gives the national figures for ownership of selected electrical appliances over a fifteen-year period. By 1975 almost every family in Kurusu had a dazzling array of electrical appliances, most of

TABLE 24
Ownership of Household Appliances in Japan,
1960–74
(percent of households owning)

Appliance	1960	1965	1970	1974
Sewing machine	73.1% [a]	77.4%	84.5%	84.2%
Washing machine	40.6	68.5	91.4	97.5
Vacuum cleaner	7.7	32.2	68.3	89.6
Electric fan	34.7 [a]	59.6	83.2	93.3
Electric foot warmer	—	57.8	81.4	91.2
Electric or gas refrigerator	10.1	51.4	89.1	96.5
Stereo set	—	13.5	31.2	47.0
Television set				
Black-and-white	44.7	90.0	90.2	55.7
Color	—	—	26.3	85.9

[a] Figure for 1959.

them quite recent models. The standard inventory included a fan, heating stove, foot-warmer (*kotatsu*), rice cooker, blender, vacuum cleaner, sewing machine, refrigerator, washing machine, and color television set. Electrical appliance stores are scattered all over the countryside, and the one in Chūtoku carries all of the items just listed as well as many others including tempura cookers, stereo systems, and microwave ovens.

There are also one or two electrically powered massage chairs in Kurusu, and what is perhaps the most exotic of all the purely Japanese electrical appliances, a small machine that both polishes rice and pounds glutinous rice. One of these, owned jointly by two neighboring houses, was purchased in the late 1960's for about ¥30,000. All agree that the pounded rice it produces has less flavor than that made in the old stone mortar, pounded with a wooden pestle. The reason for its purchase lies in the character of the remodeling that has been undertaken in many of the older farmhouses, which involves replacing the old earth-floored kitchen work area with raised wooden flooring, which cannot bear the enormous weight of the huge stone mortars. As a result, they have been discarded in favor of the lighter portable electric machines.

A universal feature of most rooms in 1951 was a naked light bulb hanging by a cord from the ceiling. Today these are all covered by elaborate glass shades or have been replaced by three-way fluorescent light fixtures. Reading lamps, formerly unknown, are now very common. In many domestic ancestral altars small electric lamps have replaced candles, which have become very expensive. Radios have long been supplemented by stereos and television sets, and the three treadle-powered sewing machines of 1951 have been displaced by at least ten electric ones.

There are many houses in which new consumer items are used to supplement older devices still in use. Several kitchens that have not been completely remodeled still have both the old wood-burning cooking stove as well as a new propane gas one, for example. In two or three houses bath water is still heated with a wood fire, while propane gas is used for cooking. Three houses still use their old wells to supplement the new piped-in water that was brought in by the town in 1974. This last represents a great improvement and something of a threat, for the new system, which insures a steady supply of drinking water, has opened up formerly water-short Kurusu to the construction of new homes.

It should be said that, while the convenience and efficiency of the new appliances are universally acknowledged, their disadvantages do not go unrecognized. Few people would contend that an electric foot-warmer provides the kind of penetrating warmth that the old charcoal one did. As we have seen, everyone agrees that machine-dried rice prepared in an electric rice-cooker loses much of its flavor, as does gluti-nous rice pounded by machine. But the young people, and many older ones, simply do not care. They like and want the new appliances, and over the past six or seven years the number and kinds of appliances in Kurusu have continued to grow. Shimpo (1976:86–90) offers comparable data from a farming community in northern Japan from the period 1961 to 1971.

Little need be said about other furnishings except to remark that almost all of them are new—a measure of how very limited economic resources were until recent years. Everywhere there are new chests, tables, and cushions, and three houses have bought large new ancestral altars. There is even a piano in Kurusu today, and several young people own at least one musical instrument.

Both changing tastes and new residential patterns are reflected in the selection of household items that form a part of the bride's trousseau. In the old days it was displayed at her home before being sent along by hired truck to her new home at the time of the wedding ceremony. Today the items are usually delivered directly by the shops and stores where they were purchased to the place where the young couple will live. Until a few years ago the three standard household items brought by the bride were *tansu, futon,* and *geta-bako* (chests, bedding, and a "shoe box," a cabinet set inside the front door of the house for storing shoes, which are never worn in the home), but today's urban apart-ments are too small for the first, the second cannot be used on beds, and all apartment houses have a built-in cabinet for shoes. One house in Kurusu provides dramatic evidence of the seriousness of the space problem in city housing: its main room is almost half filled with chests and boxes, a substantial part of the first son's bride's trousseau that was delivered in two trucks; but the young couple lives in an apartment in town in which there literally is not enough room for all the items. Preferred trousseau gifts are now electrical appliances—labor-saving devices for the new wife, who is expected to have a full-time job—or what were until recently high-prestige items known as "the three C's," color television, cooler, and car.

In every house there is a speaker of the broadcast relay system installed in 1960 by the town government. Weather forecasts and farm news are carried regularly, and the announcer will read notices for anyone who writes them out and brings them to the Town Office. One Kurusu man was so offended by the incessant chatter of the speaker, which can be lowered in volume but not turned off, that he had moved the instrument out into his derelict chicken house, where he cannot hear it. Most people listen for the up-to-date weather reports, and do not seem to mind it otherwise.

In 1951 only the sawmill in Kurusu had a telephone, which was used primarily for business purposes. In 1972 almost every house in Shionoe Town acquired one, and the system was made fully automatic in 1974. We observed that the telephone is used rather casually by all age groups for all kinds of purposes, a development worth remarking on only because it represents a significant change from customary usage. In the recent past most people in this area and many city people conducted formal business in person if it was at all possible, it being considered poor form to use the impersonal telephone for such purposes. With its universal adoption, apparently, considerations of speed and efficiency have won out over earlier views of propriety. One afternoon, for example, while we were visiting a Kurusu house, there were four telephone calls. Three were for the grandmother and involved invitations, arrangements for an appointment at the Town Office just across the river, and the like. The fourth was for her nine-year-old grandson. She asked the caller to wait and went out to find the boy. It was a classmate of his who wanted to arrange to meet at the bus-stop and go to the middle-school for *kendō* practice.

The principal of the nursery school system provided us with another insight into a newly perceived advantage of the telephone, which he uses to consult with the parents of his charges: "It is very convenient because I can raise problems that I could never bring up at the PTA meetings when other parents are present. Before we got telephones I used to have to go to people's houses two or three times before I found them at home. It's been a real help."

Living Arrangements

Nowhere are the changes in attitudes toward the household, family, and individual more apparent than in the living arrangements of Kurusu families. The two basic issues are whether senior and junior married couples will share a dwelling, and whether they will prepare and eat meals together. There are four possible arrangements. The two couples may live together as in the past; or they may maintain separate dwellings but share meals; or they may live and cook separately; or they may live in separate dwellings and the wife of the senior couple may prepare somewhat different foods for the two families.

Thirteen of Kurusu's families do not face the problem of selecting one of these options, for they consist of only one married couple with or without children of their own. The remaining ten stem families have reached the following solutions: in four the couples live and eat together; in five they live and eat separately; and in one case they live separately but the older wife cooks for both. This classification does obscure another kind of change having to do with the new desire for privacy. There are three cases where the second storey of a new storage building contains living quarters. In two of the cases the widowed grandmother and one of the nearly grown children have separate rooms there, while the junior couple and the remaining children occupy the main dwelling. In the third case, the grandchildren are assigned the supplementary living space, leaving the main house to the adults.

In a curious way the new pattern of separate housing for successors and their families amounts to a reversal of an older residential pattern common to many rural areas but formerly beyond the means of Kurusu families. In the past, the ideal was that upon attaining the age of 61 or at some time later in life the head of the house and his wife would retire and pass on the headship to the eldest son and his wife. The retired couple, freed of the burden of responsibility for management of the household and the agricultural operation, would set aside a room in the house for their own use, add a room or two at one end of the house for the same purpose, or build a small dwelling in the compound and move into it (Chang 1970). These small residences for the retired were called *inkyo-ya*. The successor, the *ato-tori*, and his family took over the main house. Up to 1951 no Kurusu family had ever built an inkyo-ya, and there are none in the community today. Instead, separate quarters are provided for the successor's family and for the senior couple, but the new dwelling is put up for the successor's family and the senior couple remains in the main house undisturbed. These new residences are not called *ato-tori-ya*, although they might well be; indeed, there is no term for the practice or the new dwellings. Nevertheless, their chief function is the familiar one of putting some distance between the senior and junior couples in order to reduce the potential for conflict between them. The separation serves also to give recognition to their differing responsibilities and, increasingly, to their very different tastes and life-styles.

An excellent example of the complex considerations surrounding the decision to build a new house is afforded by the case of a dwelling we saw put up in the summer of 1975. The builder had found a house in a nearby hamlet that had never been occupied; he bought it, had it dismantled, and moved it to Kurusu. During the months of July and August it was being erected between his main dwelling and a small outbuilding, on a piece of land almost exactly the width of the new house, where an old outbuilding had stood. It was generally thought that the builder had got the house cheap, and that with so many carpenters in the hamlet he would have no great difficulty in getting it up before the harvest. In fact, the project involved a great deal of work by the builder and his wife, who sorted, labeled, bundled, and stacked the various wooden elements of the structure. In the later stages of construction their grown children helped, but they did much of the work themselves. As for the cost, the family head estimated that it would probably run about 5.4 million yen, roughly ¥250,000 per *tsubo* for the 21 *tsubo* (69.51 square meters), two-storey structure. Even places like Kurusu have not been immune from the staggering rise in the cost of housing in Japan. In 1952, when prices were thought to be very high, it was estimated that a tile-roofed house would cost about ¥20,000 per *tsubo*, and a thatched-roof house about ¥15,000. In

1935 one of the medium-sized houses in the community had been built for a total cost of about ¥1,000.

On Sunday, July 20, work had progressed far enough to permit the holding of the ceremony for setting up the framework of a house (*mune-age-shiki*). The head carpenter consulted his almanac and set the time for the start of the ceremony at 2:56 P.M., the moment at which the tide was at its lowest ebb on that day. The association is obvious; the tide, like the fortunes of the house, would begin to rise from that moment. The man who was building the house explained that he had decided to hold the ceremony, which he regards as being very expensive, because it was a rare chance to show his children a traditional observance rather than just telling them about it. "How often does one build a house, after all?" he asked, "I don't know if my sons will carry on traditions like this—that doesn't concern me particularly—but they should know how it has always been done." As if to answer the implied question, the head carpenter later remarked that he is never asked to conduct the ceremony when he builds a house in the city, and that not all rural people request it.

Sometimes a Shinto priest is called in, but on this occasion the head carpenter was asked to officiate. For the ceremony a wooden platform large enough for five persons to kneel on is built just below the roof timbers. On it are placed a set of offerings: a bottle of *sake*, a cooked sea bream (*tai*)—which cost an exorbitant ¥10,000 in 1975 because the heavy pollution of the coastal waters had greatly reduced the catch of this most auspicious of fish—a small tray of washed uncooked rice, a kind of seaweed (*kombu*), dried cuttlefish (*surume*), and a dish of salt. There were also two large wooden boxes, bearing the family's name, filled with glutinous rice cakes (*o-mochi*), and a blue plastic bucket filled with an old-fashioned form of a kind of cake called *o-manjū*, with the red character *iwau* (felicitations) on the face of each. This latter item is one that is always used on such occasions in his native village in Tokushima, he told us. At each of the four corners of the roof timbers were placed two very large glutinous rice cakes of the kind called *kagami-mochi*, which are the standard offerings to the Shinto gods.

Promptly at the tide's lowest ebb, the head carpenter, the man building the house, and his two sons who had been helping, mounted a ladder to the platform. They knelt and exchanged cups of *sake*; the carpenter recited Shinto prayers, and all clapped their hands sharply to invoke the deity. Meanwhile, the other carpenters and those who had been helping out gathered down below, where they were joined by two grandmothers from nearby houses who had brought their small grandchildren with them. At the conclusion of the ritual on the platform the men threw the rice cakes and *o-manjū* down to the people below, who laughed and scrambled to catch them as they fell. The old women and their charges all got some and went back home. Although the entire community knew all about the ceremony, no one else came.

The remaining offerings were lowered carefully to the ground and set up on a small low table by the new house. While the men washed up, the women, who had been preparing food most of the day, set out an elaborate meal in the main room of the old house. They had previously served a snack of watermelon, ice-candy on a stick, rice crackers, and soft drinks. The main meal, for twelve people, consisted of octopus and cucumber salad, *sashimi* (raw fish), *tamago-yaki* (an egg dish), glutinous rice with red beans (*sekihan*, obligatory for auspicious occasions), *o-manjū*, beer and *sake*. The serving dishes belonged to the family itself; they did not borrow the hamlet's community dishes, which are kept in the meeting house. It was obviously a very costly occasion, and the family members were proud of having done it properly.

The participants in the *mune-age* ceremony were the five professional carpenters and ten male helpers. The helpers included the builder himself, two of his three sons (one is married and came up from Takamatsu where he lives, the other lives at home), and two men from Kurusu with whom the builder jointly owns some farm machinery. The other three men were kinsmen of the builder and his wife (his elder brother, his niece's husband, and one of her cousins), all from outside the hamlet. In the kitchen were his wife and unmarried daughter, who lives at home, his son's wife, the wives of the two Kurusu men, and the wives of the three kinsmen. They served the food and all ate in an adjoining room near the kitchen. The occasion was very festive. The older men dominated the conversation in the main room, just as they would have done a generation ago. The women were having a fine time, and there was much talk and laughter. Had they eaten in the same room with the men, the women would have been required to be far more decorous.

The house was being put up for the successor, not the first son, who works and lives near Takamatsu. It was generally assumed that he would be married in the fall and move into the new house with his bride. The finishing touches were still being put on the house when my wife and I left in August. One hot Sunday afternoon we stopped by to see how the work was coming. All three sons were helping their father. Their mother, one of the Kurusu women who has a full-time job in a nearby town, was out in the fields. The wife of the eldest son, who had come up from Takamatsu ostensibly to help with the cooking, was sitting in the house watching television.

Clothing and Food

The shift to Western-style clothing, except for certain work gar-ments, is virtually complete, and the people of Kurusu—who in 1951 spent about ¥10,000 annually on clothing for a family of five—now dress very much as city people do. Kimonos are worn on very few occasions other than weddings and funerals, and then only by women. Everyone agrees that kimonos are far less convenient and far more expensive than Western dress, and a few young people have never worn Japanese dress at all. We observed one dramatic example of how far the trend has gone. A young woman in her early twenties who is employed as a shop clerk in Takamatsu borrowed her grandmother's thonged sandals to join us on an afternoon stroll. When we returned, she was teased by her grandmother when she complained of having raised a blister, and we could not resist telling her that that style of sandal is now popular around the world; she said that she had not worn a pair since she was a little girl.

More astonishing is the change in diet and food preferences. In 1955 the per capita daily caloric intake of the Japanese was 2,217, com-posed of 74.1 percent starch, 6.1 percent animal protein, 5.8 percent sugar, and 3 percent fats and oils. In 1973 the caloric intake had risen to 2,526, and starch was down to 52 percent, animal protein up to 13.7 percent, sugar up to 11.8 percent, and fats and oils up to 10.7 percent (Anonymous 1975:3). Similar shifts have occurred in Kurusu, and people frequently remarked on how extensive the changes in diet have been. "The really big difference between now and the old days is that today the members of the family eat the same food we serve to guests. Everybody eats fish and meat." In 1951 meat was rarely eaten by family members and only very occasionally served to guests. It was not even stocked by the shops in Chūtoku during the hot summer months because they lacked refrigeration. An ordinary meal, prepared in haste by the women of the house, consisted of a soup, vegetable, pickles and relish, rice, and tea. Fruits in season were sometimes served. Twenty-five years later, a middle-aged man said, "We eat better now than the domain lords ever did, and when I want a cold drink I just get some ice from the refrigerator."

Most houses still make their own pickles and relishes, but almost none makes soy sauce, bean paste, dried radish, and the like, all of which may be purchased at the shops across the river in Chūtoku. Some families have even given up growing their own vegetables, finding it much easier to ask a daughter or daughter-in-law who works in the city to buy the next day's vegetables at the market on her way home. It is much easier and the selection much greater, people say, but older people in particular often remark on the lack of flavor of the store-bought produce.

The few food vendors who came through this area in 1951 traveled by bicycle. Nowadays the occasional fruit and vegetable seller comes in a pickup or panel truck; the most colorful one we encountered was a hearty man who advertised his "Aomori apples" over a loudspeaker mounted on the cab of his truck while his wife handled the transactions out the back. But most garden produce and fruits are sold at shops in Chūtoku, and both fresh and frozen meat and fish are readily available. There were complaints that the cheaper fish had disappeared from the shops because there was too little profit in them for the merchants, and one of the unexpected results of the frightful pollution of the coastal fishing grounds was that fish sold in the stores was so expensive that many people preferred to buy the cheaper meat.

It may well be, as many people claimed, that the major change since 1951 is that villagers now eat the same food they serve their guests. Certainly all meals have become far more elaborate. The menu for a meal shared by a family and its guests is given here for the interest it will have for those who knew the old countryside and for others who may read this long after meals of this kind have ceased to be common.

A large bonito (*managatsuo*) provided the materials for three of the dishes: raw fish (*sashimi*), boiled fish (*nīzakana*), and roe for the soup, which was spiced with a home-grown herb called *sanshō*. Eggplant was served boiled. Cucumber, like the eggplant taken from the garden, appeared in two dishes, an octopus and cucumber salad, and in shredded form with the raw fish. There were home-made noodles (*udon*), a specialty of the region, with a garnish of ginger and another fresh spice called *aojiso*. The meal ended with boiled white rice, of course, and pickles and relish. Three beverages, beer, *sake*, and plum wine (*umeshu*), were served throughout the meal. Perhaps the most remarkable feature of the feast, which contained items and quantities of food that simply were not to be had in Kurusu in 1951, is that so many of the vegetables and spices were home-grown and that so many of the ingredients were homemade. The grandmother of this house still supervises the making of soy sauce and bean paste, for example, although she herself is too old to undertake the actual preparation of the items. The only things that came from the store were the seafood, beer, and *sake*.

The greater variety of foods is by no means the whole story of dietary change. The Japanese consumption of rice, the staple food whose name is synonymous with "a meal," has been declining steadily for years, as we have seen. In 1951 the average person in Kurusu consumed about five *gō* (0.9 liter) of rice per day. Twenty-five years later it was generally agreed that in agricultural households the consumption has dropped to about two *gō* and to about one *gō* in nonagricultural households where people do less physical labor. A man from another community who owns some land near Kurusu told us that he no longer cultivates the paddy fields left to his family after the land reform. "I pay a man to farm them and give him most of the crop. We don't eat much rice anyway, not nowadays, and it's not worth my while to raise it for sale."

The other central issue in the matter of diet is the considerable difference between the food preferences of the older and younger generations, a development that has made the preparation of meals a real problem for the older women of Kurusu. The change in eating habits among the young has been so great that women in their fifties and sixties find it very difficult to cook for the whole family. In some households, as we have seen, the divergence in taste is so great that the older and younger couples actually eat as well as live separately. An elderly woman spoke of these matters:

It is so hard to cook to everyone's taste. The young people like oily foods and eat a lot of bread instead of rice. But they're not the only problem. Everyone has become so choosy. They leave food on their plates, make a big fuss about what they like and don't like, and won't even let me cook perfectly good things like radish greens. The younger ones don't even know about seasonal foods any more. Most things are available year round, even if they don't have any flavor, and they have no idea what it's like to eat *hatsumono* ("first things," the first of any food item to come on the market or to ripen).

What has brought about the conversion of the younger generation to "oily foods and bread?" Without question a major factor has been the school lunch programs, which for years have been designed to offer maximum nutritional value. Lunches are served at the nursery school, as well as at primary and middle-schools. Only higher-school pupils carry their own. "And what a battle that is," the same old woman said. "When we were kids we carried leftovers and cold rice in our lunch boxes, and for picnics we took a *hinomaru-bentō* (literally a "rising sun lunch," an extremely low-cost and not very nutritious meal of red pickled plum on white rice, which looks a bit like the design of the Japanese national flag), while today's kids must have something fancy like *sushi*."

We were talking to the woman who cooks for the Yasuhara nursery school one day. She said:

Every child brings a *shō* of rice a month and the town supplies free milk. It is very difficult to cook for the children because they won't eat Japanese food and are always asking for things like "omelette rice" (*ōmu raisu*) or "curry rice" (*karē raisu*)—things like that. Nowadays even farm children are used to delicious food. The worst of it is, if one of them won't eat, they all refuse to touch their lunches.

We should inform the unwary that omelette rice and curry rice belong to that great class of dishes served in Japan which have no counterparts in the West, but which are thought of by rural people—and many urbanites—as being foreign in origin. The clue is that the loanword "rice" is used rather than the word for cooked rice (*gohan*) that is used for all Japanese dishes. "Rice" dishes are eaten with a spoon or a fork, never with chopsticks, and are served with water rather than tea. There also has been an explosion of the prepared-foods industry, which now produces practically every variety of both Japanese and foreign dishes and ingredients for them. Takamatsu has a very large number of eating places, including a McDonald's, that serve what may safely be described as non-traditional foods.

Across the river from Kurusu, not far from where several of the hamlet women were employed in one or another of the local factories, there is a restaurant run by the Tanioka family. It was there in 1951, and was going strong in 1975. Indeed, it was with reference to this eating place that an eighty-year-old grandmother from Kurusu made an immortal remark. We asked her if she had ever eaten at Tanioka's, where we often had our evening meal. She said that she had not, but added, "The food must be good. All the truck drivers stop there."

The food is good, and the menu is varied by the standards of twenty-five years ago. Live eel and a fish called *amego* are kept in a tank and there are sweetfish in the freezer. Many other varieties of seafood are brought up from Takamatsu; young Tanioka drives down to the market very early every morning to buy fresh fish for the day's menu. Young people who work in the offices of the town government are regular customers, as are the truck drivers and traveling salesmen who are on the road between Takamatsu and Tokushima. Tanioka's is not a fancy eating-place like those farther up the highway toward Shionoe which have fewer customers; but the mere fact of its having refrigeration, an air conditioner, a television set, and a varied menu removes it very far beyond the most that its founder could possibly have hoped for it twenty-five years ago.

Getting Around: The Coming of the Automobile

In 1951 the people who made the eleven-mile trip to Takamatsu went infrequently. Young people sometimes went to see a film there, but most of them visited Takamatsu no more than seven or eight times a year. The hour-long bus ride, which cost ¥40, was made the more tiring by the roughness of the gravel road, then unpaved from the outskirts of Takamatsu to the bus terminal in Shionoe, the village on the southern border of Yasuhara Village. There were many complaints about the service. The buses, which made twelve runs a day in each direction, seemed always to be overcrowded.

Like much else about life in the rural areas in those days, this situation marked a considerable decline in the standard of living. Everyone compared the bus service unfavorably to that provided by the gasoline-powered railway, built in 1929, which once covered the same route. This line, called the *gasorin-michi*, had offered more efficient service at lower cost, and trips to town could be made rapidly and in comfort. Although there were few direct relationships between the rail-line and Kurusu, which had one of the small stations, there had been advantages to Yasuhara Village generally. In the days when the railway flourished there were many more shops in Chūtoku and a taxi company which took wealthy tourists up into the high hills for cherry-blossom and maple-leaf viewing. The farmers of Kurusu found the line extremely useful for travel, but they sold nothing to its passengers and produced no handicrafts of any kind that could conceivably represent forerunners of the current boom in the souvenir business elsewhere.

In any event, the rail-line was dismantled and sold piecemeal when the company failed in 1941. The tracks were taken up and sold to the Taiwan Sugar Company; the cars went to the municipal transportation company of Mukden, the largest city in Manchuria. The right-of-way is still easily picked out on any map and many of the bridge pilings still remain in the riverbed.

For a time the only buses that could negotiate the wretched mountain roads were very small, carrying ten passengers. In 1951 they were full-sized and sometimes packed in as many as fifty or sixty people. The only other way of getting around was to catch a ride on a passing truck, hire a car (completely beyond the means of everyone in the village), or go by bicycle. Bicycling to Takamatsu was no great feat, for it is literally downhill for the entire distance, but the return trip was far too arduous for any but the most vigorous. In those days, moreover, the few bicycles owned by Kurusu families were old and had no gear-shifts.

By 1975 the two-lane highway was paved all the way from Taka-matsu to the border of Tokushima Prefecture. The buses on one of the two lines serving Kurusu are now air conditioned, and the doughty bus-girls of twenty-five years ago have been replaced by cassette tapes that call out the name of the next stop. The trip from Takamatsu still takes about an hour, although the buses could make much better time if it were not for the heavy traffic. The local companies, like all bus firms throughout the country, were in deep financial trouble. The

Asahi Shimbun reported on August 4, 1975, that in fiscal 1974 fully 87 percent of 207 companies had operating deficits because of a drop in transport efficiency owing to traffic congestion, the increase in the number of private automobiles, the granting of a series of very large wage increases, and the skyrocketing cost of fuel.

Twenty-five years ago people looking out across Kurusu's fields to the highway used to remark on the passage of a large truck and occasional passenger car, for there were few of either. Indeed, in 1951 the total number of passenger cars, taxis, and cars for hire in Kagawa Prefecture was 1,639, and in all of Japan only 157,312. By 1973 the figures were 86,338 and 11.6 million, respectively. As has been the case with farm machinery, the increase had not been a steady, gradual build-up; in 1960 there were about 440,000 cars in Japan, and in 1965 there were 1.8 million. Between 1965 and 1974 the percentage of families owning their own automobiles rose from 9.1 to 39.8.

Now there is a constant stream of traffic of all kinds of vehicles in both directions—trucks hauling freight, lumber, produce, and machinery, private automobiles, service vehicles, charter buses, and motorcycles. Only a few bicycles are to be seen along the road, and the pedestrian runs an unacceptable risk the whole length of the highway. Fatalities continue to occur at an alarming rate—acquaintances could recall twelve deaths along the road between Chūtoku and Shionoe, a distance of only a few kilometers—the result of the combined innocence of the pedestrian and lack of skill and caution on the part of the multitude of new drivers. Pedestrians suffer the further disadvantage of being unwary, for they are largely drawn from the non-driving age groups of the elderly and the very young. Periodic public educational campaigns have done little to reduce the slaughter in the rural areas, although the accident rates have declined sharply in the major cities.

At the end of World War II only two of Kurusu's sixteen households owned bicycles. By 1950 thirteen of the twenty-two families had acquired one machine, and two households owned two machines each. There were still several bicycles in the hamlet in 1975, for the most part owned by families with children, for they are now almost never used by adults for transportation. In 1975 eleven households of the twenty-three had one automobile each, five had two cars, and one family had three, a total of twenty-four privately owned automobiles in a community of eighty-four people. As with the national figures for automobile ownership given above, this astonishing situation is not the result of a slow build-up over the years; almost all of the vehicles have been purchased since the late 1960's. It was only in 1970 that the rate of automobile ownership in rural areas surpassed that of urban workers.

One man told us that he had finally given in and bought their two automobiles only about four years before, "when our boys got old enough to insist. That's the way it usually happens." This does seem to represent a pattern, for many people said that when a boy graduates from high school he wants a car so that he can commute to his place of work. Girls and young women, it turned out, are more likely to have to commute by bus. At first the farmers of Kurusu bought second-hand vehicles, but now almost all of the cars owned by hamlet people are purchased new. They are primarily small models, such as Subaru, Daihatsu, Isuzu, and Suzuki, although there are two or three larger Toyotas and Datsuns. There are no real farm trucks, but one family uses what looks like a junked Datsun sedan to haul sand and gravel and for getting to and from its more distant fields.

In 1953 I wrote: "Villagers do not ride in automobiles, for taxis are too expensive and there are no private cars in the community" (R. Smith 1953:43). In the spring of 1952, thinking to return a number of favors, I borrowed the Jeep station wagon belonging to the University of Michigan Center for Japanese Studies in Okayama and treated myself and some residents of Kurusu to trips here and there in the immediate area. In 1975 I was introduced to a young man visiting the hamlet by his aunt as "the American who gave you that car ride you talked about so much when you were a child." As it turned out, he did not remember me, but he did remember the ride. I realized that there had been a revolution of sorts one day when we were waiting by a bus stop in a light rain. A small car pulled up and a man from Kurusu put his head out the window to ask if he could give us a lift.

Most of the automobiles in Kurusu are used primarily for commuting to and from work in the Takamatsu-Yashima area, and very few people share rides—because of uncertain schedules, they say. On weekends, principally Sundays, young people often drive to visit friends or for recreation, greatly increasing the likelihood that their parents are not sure where they are or when to expect them back. This affords an entirely new kind of independence of parental control, for a generation ago it would have been almost inconceivable that the whereabouts of any family member should be in doubt. The family Sunday drive is now routine—a young couple and their small child, perhaps accompanied by grandmother, may drive up to a hot-springs town in the mountains to the south or go to visit a nearby temple or shrine of renown.

The bus is now used freely by those who cannot drive or who do not have access to automobiles. Even young children may ride it a few stops up or down the highway to get to a baseball game or to a sports practice session at one of the nearby schools. Formerly the fare alone would have been a major deterrent to such travel, but nowadays it is apparently taken for granted that the children should be given the pocket money required and allowed to go off on their own.

A few young men in their late teens and early twenties have motor-cycles, which simultaneously widen their worlds of experience and friendship and greatly increase the likelihood of their being injured or killed in traffic accidents. What the Japanese called the Thunder Tribe (*kaminari zoku*) have been on the scene far longer than private cars, and today no head turns at the sight of a young man and woman (both helmeted) flashing past the hamlet on a big Kawasaki machine. Nonetheless, some parents told us that they breathe easily in the evening only when the last of their motorcycle-riding children is safely home.

Domestic and Communal Rites

In 1951 most rest days and festivals were still scheduled by the old lunar calendar, while national holidays, which were of very little interest to the villagers of Yasuhara, were all reckoned by the new calendar. The ceremonial calendar as it existed in 1951 (R. Smith 1953:278–92) did not differ in any major way from the annual rites and festivals described by Embree (1939:263–98), Norbeck (1954:142–59), and Beardsley, Hall, and Ward (1959:188–94). Sugiyama (1972) analyzes changes in agrarian rites in a northeastern village that may usefully be compared to the situation in Kurusu today.

There can be no doubt that religion in its various public and private manifestations has continued the decline that was already evident in 1951. The victory of the seven-day week is almost total, and Sunday has become the ceremonial day both for shrine festivals and for the scheduling of household memorial services for the dead. Yet the attenuation of religious observances so marked in Kurusu is not a universal phenomenon. Just up the highway in a hamlet called Nakamura there has been a revival of the celebration of *o-bon*, centering especially on the participation of children. What Kurusu lacks perhaps, is anyone with the drive of the woman who single-handedly has organized the Nakamura observances. When we described them to a man in Kurusu, he remarked that in the early 1930's when he was small the children of Kurusu had done something similar, but at the July 23 Jizō festival rather than at *o-bon*. He thought that they had given it up some time before World War II.

The general decline in religious life is nowhere more apparent than in the virtual absence of any local interest in the syncretic sects called the New Religions. A modest effort to propagate the doctrine of Tenri-kyō in a neighboring hamlet had already faded by 1951. One older woman in Kurusu became a member of the Sōka Gakkai in the mid-1960's when her health began to fail, but she remains the sole convert. Today, as in 1951, one villager remains a devoted follower of the teachings of the founder of the ethical system called Moralogy (*moraroji*), but no one else has followed his lead. He was converted by the president of an Osaka company where he worked for some years after finishing middle-school. He subscribes to the Moralogy periodical and occasionally embarks on another unsuccessful campaign to convert others.

People say, rather vaguely, that there are some converts to Reiyūkai up in Shionoe, and that over in Kōnan Town Seichō-no-Ie has been fairly successful. But in the immediate area the old established religions have so far escaped serious challenge by the new sects. A priest of one local temple estimates that of the approximately 450 families who are its parishioners perhaps 15 percent have at one time or another converted to one or another of the New Religions. Of these, about half have returned, usually when a death occurs in the family. "Then," he said, "they tend to revert to the customs of the household," a somewhat oblique way of saying that they call on the priest of the temple to which their ancestors belonged to officiate at the funeral and memorial services for the deceased.

"Shinto"

The dismantling of the national system called State Shinto was one of the early objectives of the American Occupation forces. A variety of orders terminated the teaching of mythology as history in the schools, eliminated the subsidies paid to shrines by the central government, and forbade the holding of Shinto rites in schools and other governmental contexts. None of this had any marked effect at the local level, where the rites and ceremonies had continued to center around the agricultural calendar, the veneration of the tutelary deities, and certain points in the life-cycle of the individual.

In 1951 all of Kurusu's houses but one had a domestic god-shelf (*kamidana*) enshrining either Izumo-daijin (Daikoku) or Tenshō-daijin (Amaterasu, the imperial ancestress). On most of them were to be found amulets, talismans, and a variety of souvenirs from famous shrines, as well as small unglazed ceramic offertory vessels. Daily offerings were made to the gods and to the ancestors in the domestic Buddhist altar. A small dish of the first rice of the harvest was offered the gods, and at the New Year glutinous rice cakes and an evergreen called *sakaki* were placed on the god-shelf. In many homes freshly cut flowers or grasses were regularly placed in a small vase next to the altar.

Twenty-five years later, no one has removed the god-shelf from his house, but few families make any offerings there except at New Year's, when the domestic ritual is almost exclusively Shinto. In one re-modeled old house there is a very large new shelf. The owner told us that he had installed it because no house would be complete without both the god-shelf and the ancestral altar; since he had renovated the dwelling, he had purchased new examples of both. Two of the newly constructed houses have small god-shelves, put there by the older family heads who had built the dwellings for their successors. Neither elderly man expressed much confidence that the young couple would be concerned to make the appropriate offerings to the deities, however.

Buddhism

In 1951 every household in Kurusu had a domestic Buddhist altar (*butsudan*) in which were kept the memorial tablets of the ancestors.

Indeed, in some homes the altar was by far the most expensive item of furniture, but size and quality varied greatly, reflecting the financial circumstances of the family at the time of its purchase rather than any variation in religious sentiment. The largest and most expensive altar was in the home of the Buddhist priest, and although many new ones had been purchased in the intervening years, it remained the most elaborate in Kurusu in 1975. On Buddhist festival days and at all of the periodic memorial services for the dead, lights were burned on the altar. Candles were the most widely used illumination, but in 1951 the altars of the priest and sawmill owner had been electrified.

Buddhism has long been primarily a household religion, and its priesthood was generally supported by the income earned through participation in funerals and memorial services for the dead. Every household in Japan has had at least a nominal affiliation with a specific temple since the seventeenth century (R. Smith 1974:20–21), and in 1951 the seventeen households of Kurusu for which I have information were parishioners of six different temples. Twelve households were registered in one or another of the temples located in Yasuhara Village—seven of the Shinshū sect and five Shingon. The remaining five households were parishioners of three temples located in other villages—three Shinshū and two Shingon. The affiliations of these last five families suggest that they were the most recent arrivals in Kurusu, for people are slow to change temple registration after they change residence. In any event, all three temples in question were located only a few miles from Kurusu.

It could hardly be said that the local temples and priesthood were flourishing in 1975. Their incomes were down, not only because the rural exodus has sharply reduced the number of families that they serve, but also because people now require more modest services when they do call on them. The priest in Kurusu, for example, has never been attached to a temple, but operates out of his home as his father did until his death in 1970. This man remains largely committed to agriculture, and over the years has experimented with many cash crops in an effort to supplement his family's income. Another local priest has a full-time job at the Town Office and yet another runs an electrical appliance store. The implications are obvious; like farmers, priests can survive only if they pursue other occupations.

In many respects, however, the overall condition of Buddhism in the rural areas was not very different in 1951 and 1975, in that few priests make any effort to become involved in activities other than the mortuary rites. One local exception is a fortyish Shingon priest who is a university graduate. He commented that while Buddhism stresses the development of the priest, it neglects the religious education of the layman. He has thought this its weakest point ever since as a college student he attended a Christian church service and heard first-hand the sermons and the hymns. As for religious education in the home, he said that it is usually nothing more than training the child in *kafū* ("the ways of the house"). That is, the child is taught only that he must pray to the buddhas in one way and to the gods in another. Few people come to the priest with their troubles, and children are not taught the meaning of what they are doing when they participate in domestic rites.

Shikoku is the locus of one of the best-known pilgrimage routes in Japan, the circuit of the eighty-eight temples allegedly built by Kōbo Daishi, founder of the Shingon sect. The nearest of these, the eighty-eighth, is about an hour's drive by automobile, but the recent boom in the combined pilgrimage-tour has not touched Kurusu directly. One of my 1951 photographs shows two pilgrims standing in front of a Kurusu house, but it was agreed that such travelers never come this way now. "Even then," said one woman, "they were more like beggars than pilgrims."

Funerals and Memorial Services for the Dead

Unlike many other religious occasions, funerals are still scheduled with proper regard for the traditional constraints of the ceremonial calendar. It is not entirely clear what the attitude of the layman is, but no priest will approve the holding of a funeral on a day of *tomobiki*, an almanac designation that puns to "pulling another along." If necessary, the corpse will be packed in dry ice to permit postponement of the rite to a less ominous day. Memorial services are another matter, however, for although they should be held on the actual anniversary of death, they have for the past few years been almost universally rescheduled to Sundays. The trimming of the ritual calendar has gone even further; as one man said, "Yes, memorial services are usually held on Sundays nowadays, but most people don't hold them at all in the summertime. It's too hot then, and so many people are away on holiday that it's hard to get relatives and friends together." In 1951 some memorial services were already being rescheduled to Sunday, but those who did so said that it was because of the work-schedules of their urban kinsmen.

One consequence of the shift of memorial services to Sundays is, of course, that the priests are hard-pressed to put in an appearance at all of the houses that require their services. This unfortunate situation has done little to improve their reputation, which was never terribly high in any event. "The memorial services are almost all held on weekends, so the priests rush from place to place, recite a prayer at each, eat, pocket ¥5,000, and dash off. The sponsor of the rite even has to pay the taxi fare." Under the circumstances, this seems a rather ungenerous attitude, for the priests really have no option but to rush from ceremony to ceremony when there is a particularly heavy demand for their services over the wide area that they must cover.

According to priest and layman alike, most people remain punctilious in the matter of holding the ancestral rites. Almost all request the shortest service—which is one day in length, to be sure—but most houses are careful to observe the memorial dates for adults up to the sixty-first anniversary of death. They are, one priest said, as faithful in observing early memorial services for deceased children as they are for adults. This man estimates that about one-third of his parishioners observe the full schedule of the seven seventh-day rites that follow the funeral, and then the hundredth day and the first year. Most of the others observe only the seventh, forty-ninth, and hundredth days and the first year. Contrary to popular impression, he asserted that it is not that older people are more faithful in such matters and younger people less so. He had been very impressed recently when two young couples came to him to ask exactly what they should do for the souls of their dead infants. They were, he thought, very sincere in their desire to take proper care of their spirits, and both asked for his recommendation of an appropriate sutra to recite before the memorial tablet.

Although not everyone is very strict in the observances of these matters any more, most families will have only vegetarian food at the family's first meal after the funeral. As conspicuous consumption has won out over dietary restrictions, however, raw fish is sometimes served. Broiled fish is never served, for even the insensitive will recognize an untoward reminder of the act of cremation. A peculiarly intimate aspect of the interaction between living and dead in the context of memorial services is the offering of foods of which the deceased was especially fond during his life. Elsewhere we have remarked on the very considerable changes in food preferences over the past several years, and it seemed to us worth inquiring if these have been reflected in an easing of the restrictions on what may be offered at the Buddhist altar. Lest the point be missed, let us remind the reader that the foods offered at altars on the occasions of memorial services for the dead were formerly the foods ordinarily consumed by a vegetarian— because Buddhist—population. At the very least, the Japanese ate no flesh of four-footed animals.

No priest we interviewed could remember ever having seen fish or meat offered as a favorite food. Indeed, they all seemed mildly shocked at the mere suggestion, but one did volunteer the odd opinion that chicken might be offered because it has been raised to be eaten (so are beef cattle), but he doubted that anyone would actually do so. Yet all agreed that it is only in recent years that *sake* has come to be offered at the Buddhist altars, and then chiefly at the memorial service for people who were fond of tippling in life.

Another issue linking the living and the dead is that of the portrait of the deceased, now universally found at funerals and the early memorial services. A priest told us that it is very difficult to find just the right photograph for use in the altar. When the elderly grandfather of a family in Chūtoku was killed on the highway, his family found that the only suitable picture they had of him was one that I had taken in 1951. They remarked that they never did find a good one of his wife, whose first o-*bon* they were about to celebrate. An acquaintance remarked to me that his family had been unable to locate an appropriate picture of his mother. "She died at seventy-five, and all the good pictures of her were taken when she was much younger. You had better take a good one of me while you're here!" This problem has not escaped the attention of a professional photographer in Shionoe. The glass-covered display case in front of his shop shows two examples of what can be done to salvage the situation. On display are two snapshots, one of a man and one of a woman, both wearing everyday clothing and standing against some ordinary, everyday background. From these snapshots the photographer has made two large funerary portraits, with backgrounds wiped clean and garments transformed into formal black kimono.

Kurusu people do not visit graves on a fixed schedule, but go when it is convenient or when a relative has stopped by. It may be, therefore, that the shift of memorial services to Sundays is not so serious a concession as it first appeared to be. Although the last death-day observance is the thirty-third or fiftieth anniversary in one sect of Buddhism and the sixty-first in another, the priest is called on to go to the grave only during the first three years of death, usually in connection with the memorial services and when the individual's name is put on the family stone, formerly when the individual's own stone was put up.

The high point of summer is the three-day observance of *o-bon*, the Festival of the Dead. Like the New Year celebrations, it has for centuries been an occasion when it is hoped that scattered family members can come back to the countryside, visit the graves of the ancestral dead, and share in a joyous reunion. Increasingly, it is a precious time for the old people and a kind of holiday for the young. A great many people did come back to Kurusu in 1975, and on the middle day of *o-bon* there seemed to be children everywhere, and there were two or three automobiles parked at most of Kurusu's houses. The license plates were from as far away as Tokyo, Hiroshima, Osaka, and Okayama. No one was out in the fields in the morning, but by early afternoon a few older people had drifted back to the paddies and many of the visitors had gone off for a drive to the mountains or the beach.

Sennichi-sama, Cleaning the Graves

In 1975, August 10 fell on a Sunday. This is the date called *sennichi-sama* (no one is sure what the word means), on which the people of this district clean their family graves in preparation for *o-bon*, the Festival of the Dead, on August 13–15. There are no large cemeteries here. Each household has its own plot, sometimes located quite close to the dwelling, but usually higher up on a hillside, partially screened from view by shrubs and grasses. There has been a recent tendency to move the family's graves closer to the house in those cases where the sites are a considerable distance from the settlement. A good case in point is a very large stone that represents a consolidated grave for the several people whose individual markers were formerly located a good twenty-minute walk into the hills.

All around the area large new family gravestones dot the landscape. One belonging to a Kurusu family is located very near the gateway to the shrine of Jichin-san, in such close proximity that it surely would have occasioned a protest twenty-five years ago. Someone would have raised the question of propriety then, given the reluctance to contaminate the places sacred to the Shinto gods with the paraphernalia or symbols of death, the ultimately polluting condition. It is a mark of the utter unconcern of many people with such matters now that no objection seems to have been raised.

Most of the handsome new family stones had been erected only a few years before. Some people feel strongly that the old stones should have been kept as well, but most of them were for individuals and the recently favored style is a single large monolith inscribed *X ke ie dai dai* (the generations of the X house), with a smaller stone to the side bearing the names of all the individuals whose ashes are placed in the grave. While agreeing that it is much easier to clean the graves that have been consolidated and moved nearer the settlement, one of the local priests urges people to collect all the old gravestones in the new spot and give them care too, so as to avoid the danger of wandering ghosts (*muen-botoke* or *muen-butsu*) who may harm the living if they are neglected.

The graves belonging to one of the former landowners of Kurusu are located on a narrow shelf high up above the community. The large family stone is bigger and obviously much older than any other in Kurusu. There are also a number of individual markers, ranging from small natural rocks to statues of Jizō, the protector of children. At *o-bon* all of these are cleaned and offerings of fresh flowers and incense made. Further up the slope is an even larger collection of old gravestones, containing everything from a very contemporary granite monolith to natural boulders with no inscriptions at all. There are also some graves here that are marked only by bamboo or plastic flower-holders, and many uncleared stones bearing surnames that are no longer found in the Yasuhara area.

Not everyone has been comfortable with all the moving about of graves and old markers. A woman in her fifties told us that when the Ikeda family had moved their graves down to the area near the road and put up a new family stone, their six-year-old son had contracted blood-poisoning and died. Her tone of voice indicated that only one conclusion was possible. An elderly man had gone to one of the local priests to ask about the geomantic orientation of the spot where his family was planning to put its relocated graves, and had been told that it would be all right if the priest came and corrected it through ritual. They had paid him a small fee to set matters right. For the most part, however, the people of Kurusu regard such concerns as surviving superstitions, and young people are completely unpersuaded of the necessity for any expression of concern or remedial action.

On the side road not far from Kangetsu Bridge there are two groups of graves. On the early morning of sennichi-sama both were the scene of considerable activity. At eight o'clock in the morning there were already several people at the cluster of graves of the Watanabe household, for people say that it is better to finish up with the cleaning of the graves before the intense heat of the afternoon. A very old man was praying at the largest marker, while a couple in their forties was washing the other smaller stones, several of them obviously dating from the early nineteenth century, and pulling weeds and grass. They had a plastic pail and metal dipper, some hand tools, and a bucket of flowers and evergreen branches. The base of the second family stone, for the members of a branch of the household, held an almost unweathered wooden memorial tablet for an infant, who had died in a home accident the year before, and offerings of incense and a small gaily colored box of candies of the sort sold at any shop that caters to children.

About nine o'clock the adopted son of one of the households came along, and was followed shortly by the young wife of the son of the Chūtoku branch who lives in a new house in Kurusu, carrying their new baby. A little later the adopted son's foster mother came down the road carrying a pair of clippers and a bucket filled with flowers and greenery. Candles and incense were lighted at the two large stones and flowers were placed in the vases attached to their bases. Each small gravestone was given one blossom each, in a section of bamboo that holds water. Everyone present at the time of the lighting of the incense participated at the prayers at the graves, and then drifted away back toward their houses.

The second scene at the other of these gravesites began about nine o'clock, when four women, the wife and her three daughters, from the Furuta household came down the road. The Furuta graves are by far the most imposing in Kurusu and the most idiosyncratic, for not long before he died the old man of the house commissioned the making of a very large family stone and two highly unusual lantern-stones. The plot, which is basically a narrow ledge up the very steep slope, is quite long. In addition to the new *Furuta ke ie dai dai* stone, there are five other stones grouped nearby. They include the graves of an aunt of the family head; when her family left the area for Tokyo, they had asked permission to have the stone moved here. Another is that of a man, not a kinsman at all, who asked the Furutas if they would take care of it after he died. One of the five bears the simple inscription *namu amida butsu*, the mantra much favored by the Shinshū sect of Buddhism, and may be only a votive stone. On the side and slightly down the slope is a second group of much older markers, and all of people who are unknown to the family. Often old grave-markers were simply small boulders, as are some of these, but there are also some carved ones, including a statue of Jizō, the deity whose special responsibility it is to see the souls of children into the other world. As long as anyone remembers, no one else has ever come to care for these graves, so the Furuta family does so.

The women did a very thorough job of cleaning and decorating the graves. They had with them several large bamboo flower-holders that had been cut earlier in the morning by the head of the family. (Most other families use commercial gray plastic holders instead.) Cleaning the graves is hard work. The women clipped overhanging branches from the bushes and trees, swept up the year's accumulation of fallen leaves and twigs, and pulled weeds and grass. The gravestones all were washed with powdered soap and a scrub-brush and rinsed thoroughly. The bamboo flower-holders were hammered into the ground, incense was lit, and the two openings in the face of the stone lantern papered over.

While the mother did the heaviest work, the eldest daughter was quite busy, too. There was a great deal of chatter, some mild bickering

among the sisters, and some joking: "Grandpa will be angry if you
do that," "He'll be pleased because everything looks so nice," and
perhaps most telling, some half-serious comments on the future, in
which not they but their brother would be the beneficiary of this service, because they would marry into other families. At length the job
was done; they put the flowers in the holders, lit the candles and incense, and prayed.

Where were the rest of the family? The father was off to a memorial
service for the dead far up in the mountains to the south in the
Kaminishi area. He had left the house before eight in the morning and
returned after three in the afternoon. Grandmother, who is now too
feeble to do such hard work, was back at the house making some
foods that are characteristic of the o-bon season. And the son, as ever,
was off somewhere with friends. All three did visit the graves much
later in the day.

O-Bon, The Festival of the Dead

The cake shop in Shionoe lays up a substantial stock of ceremonial
offerings for o-bon. The proprietress, who said that they are very busy
at this season, showed us a large box containing a number of lotus-
shaped cakes, larger individual cakes in three tiers (pad, cup, and bud)
wrapped in clear plastic and tied with black and white ribbon. People
usually offer one of these to a small domestic altar, two to a large one.
The shop also stocks a special paper in which cakes for o-bon are cus-
tomarily wrapped, with a single black line and an embossed lotus on
the white ground.

On the thirteenth of August some people take white paper lanterns
to the graves, but observation suggests that the custom is far more
popular in the cities than in rural areas. In the cities the graves are in
large cemeteries and people seem to be more concerned about the
opinion of others. In Shionoe Town, gravesites are more scattered and
isolated and less easily seen by others (see Suenari 1972:80–81).

Few people go to the temples at o-bon, unless they have left ashes
there to be cared for rather than keeping them at the family grave. The
priests here do not make the rounds of the houses of parishioners, nor
was it ever their custom to do so at o-bon. There are too many houses
to cover in a three-day period, and in any event the occasion is defined

so thoroughly as a domestic affair that priests will go to houses at *o-bon* only on request. The Shingon priests make the rounds of their parishioners' houses in the spring—the birthdate of Kōbo-daishi, founder of the sect, is April 21—when the visits can be spread over a whole month.

On August 11, just two days before the start of *o-bon*, the elder brother of Furuta's wife died. They had prepared a large quantity of holiday foods in anticipation of visits from three or four families from Takamatsu. With the death, however, the house would receive no visitors save kinsmen. Throughout *o-bon* the Furuta ancestral altar remained closed, and on August 13 had before it a box of fresh peaches, a large bunch of bananas, and several boxes of cake and rice crackers. Our box of lotus-shaped cakes, made especially for the festival by the shop in Shionoe, was placed with the other offerings without ceremony. The grandmother of the house fixed a tray of sweets laid on lotus leaves brought in from the garden by one of her granddaughters and placed it in the altar, again without ceremony. Subsequently we were all served a portion of the same sweets from the kitchen.

Relations with some of the local industries were not of the most cordial at *o-bon* in 1975. The dates August 13, 14, and 15 fell on Thursday, Friday, and Saturday. Seeing their chance to save a day's work, the companies had closed only Friday and Saturday, counting Sunday into the standard three-day holiday for *o-bon*. Nevertheless, on Thursday there were many people in the fields and along the highway with small groups of people with bucket, dipper and flowers, obviously just getting around to cleaning the family graves. One such latecomer in Kurusu was the son of a family that had moved away several years before. Their house is empty, but he had driven up from Takamatsu the night before and opened it up. On the afternoon of the thirteenth he was napping on a folding cot he had brought along, his Subaru parked on the side of the road.

In one house the family was observing the "first bon" (*hatsubon*) for the spirit of its grandmother, who had died within the year. On either side of the sizable domestic altar were two large white lanterns, and a smaller one to be carried to the grave was hanging out under the eaves. In the alcove beside the altar were two large photographs of the deceased and her husband, who had died some years before. In front of the altar were several boxes of cakes and other offerings. A priest had been called in—this is the chief occasion on which they are invited to the houses of their parishioners at o-bon—and while he recited a sutra all the family members sat quietly. When he was done the housewife brought out fruit, soft drinks, tea, and cakes, including some special ones taken down from the altar for the guests. Everyone then walked across the highway and up a bit of a slope behind the family's store. The family head put up the smaller white lattern, lit a candle for it, and all stood by while the priest again recited a sutra. Each family member prayed briefly and all returned to the house. Except for the roar of the traffic in the background, and the clothing of the mourners, the scene could easily have been duplicated a generation before.

Jizō

In addition to the shrine of the tutelary deity, there are two statues of Jizō in Kurusu. Both are regarded as vaguely protective of the hamlet's residents, but only one is the object of any special observances. In some communities located on the highways of Japan, these little stone statues have disappeared completely, many taken by tourists or dealers in antiquities in whose city shops they are often found for sale, the place-name chiseled away. But Kurusu is just slightly off the beaten track, and both statues remain where they were in 1951.

One of the Jizō, whose image bears the date 1763, had a new shelter of cinderblock, put up by the hamlet in a day's time a few years ago to replace the decrepit one that had housed it in 1951. The feast-day of Jizō, formerly the 23rd day of the sixth lunar month, is now marked on August 21. Twenty-five years ago one could see occasional offerings of fresh flowers and small prayer-strips tied to the limbs of the bushes that grew near the spot. People say that this Jizō represents the spirit of a mountain-priest of the area who, because of the great benefits he had brought the people, was deified upon his death. Another more romantic and generally favored identification makes him a fallen warrior of the period of the great struggle between the Minamoto and the Taira. The power of the Taira was finally destroyed in 1185 and the remnants of their routed armies are said to have fled to the mountains of the islands bordering the Inland Sea, where they are commonly claimed as founding ancestors of descent lines. Before

World War II, older people say, they used to make *sekihan* (glutinous rice with red beans) and *udon* (noodles) and buy sweets for the children on Jizō's day. Now the housewife of the family who lives near the spot where the statue stands still makes a special dish for that day, but there is no more elaborate observance.

Summary

The domestic lives of the people of Kurusu have changed in manifold ways in the past quarter-century. But it is only fair to observe that so have the lives of people in small communities almost everywhere in the world. The cities drain off the young and many of the old as the character of agriculture and the labor market changes. The coming of the automobile, television, and the whole panoply of consumer goods, coupled with the ready availability of wage and salaried work, has everywhere conspired to alter social relationships within the family and the community.

Would a Japanese ethnographer who had lived in a small midwest American farming town in 1951 be less surprised by what he finds there today than I at what I found in Kurusu? It is unlikely. But surely, one insists, there must be at least differences in degree if not in kind. Perhaps so, but the death of American small-town life was swift and the changes in agriculture massive. We forget how much is gone and how quickly it went, perhaps, simply because we have an uninterrupted experience of the changes in our own society. Coming back to a place after so long an absence may artificially heighten our sense of the profound nature of the alterations that have occurred. Yet the people who live in Kurusu now constantly comment on the radical changes in their lives, and they tend to phrase the differences between then and now most clearly when they discuss the disparity between the generations. In the next chapter we shall try to show how both young and old perceive these differences and how they attempt to cope with them.

1951. *Top*: A bride, in elaborate headdress and kimono, drinks ceremonial *sake* during her introduction [to] the women of Kurusu. The groom's mother is to her right; her nurse is to her left. See p. 212. *Bottom, [le]ft*: The fishmonger who periodically bicycled up from the coast weighs out an order for a Kurusu [w]oman. See p. 144. *Bottom, right*: A woman rolls out dough for *udon*, noodles prepared for guests and [on] special occasions.

1951. *Top*: A farmer spreads unhulled rice on mats to dry in the sun. *Bottom, left*: A woman in typical work clothes of the time strips rice stalks on a treadle machine. *Bottom, right*: A woman strips heads from barley stalks with an old-fashioned device that even then had largely been displaced by treadle machines. See pp. 79–80.

1952. *Top, left*: A man and woman, helped by a boy out of school for the harvest season, thresh barley with what was then a new kerosene-powered machine. See p. 80. *Top, right*: Women transplant rice seedlings with the aid of a wooden frame to mark out rows. See p. 79. *Bottom*: A man from a neighboring hamlet carries barley straw home from Kurusu on a pole. Such carrying poles are little used today.

1952. *Top, left*: Mother and daughter in everyday clothes. Both wear *geta* (wooden clogs), which are now seldom seen. *Top, right*: A young family in holiday attire on New Year's Day (lunar calendar). The small boy standing is the young man on the left of the picture at the bottom of the facing page. *Bottom*: 1963. The Takao family dressed to receive visitors. The man on the left is Takao Hōen, to whom this book is dedicated.

1975. *Top, left*: A brother and sister. The boy's "Charlie Brown" shirt was purchased at a shop in Takamatsu. *Top, right*: Three girls on their way home from primary school. They wear the uniforms required by all schools. *Bottom*: Young people of Kurusu. The girl second from right is the little girl in the center of the Takao family portrait opposite.

1975. *Top*: One of the main buildings of the Hani Pajama Factory, formerly the Yasuhara Middle School. See pp. 122–24. *Bottom*: A large workroom inside the Fasuto Glove Factory. Roomy, well-lighted, and cool in summer, it is a prime example of the good working conditions provided by local factories. See p. 125.

75. *Top, left*: The proprietress of the Mushroom Garden displays the lengths of hardwood on which *shiitake* are grown. The entire crop is grown under transparent vinyl. See pp. 128–29. *Top, right*: A Kurusu farmer inspects his power tiller. *Bottom*: The Misawa-hōmu, the only prefabricated dwelling, and the largest house, in Kurusu. The family that lives there left the city for the quiet of the countryside. See p. 133.

1975. August 10, *Sennichi-sama*. Two sisters of the Takao family in jeans and T-shirts wash a graveston in the family plot not far from their house. In the Takao family portrait, they are the girl standing on th right and the baby. See pp. 158–62.

CHAPTER SIX

The Generations

ON AUGUST 15, 1975, Japan observed the thirtieth anniversary of her surrender to the Allied powers at the end of World War II. In 1951 the people of Kurusu talked a great deal about the war, which had ended only six years before. They had had very little direct experience of the Occupation forces, whose most obvious manifestation was the occasional military vehicle that passed along the highway across the river, but they had had a great deal of direct experience of the war itself. Twenty men from Kurusu were in military service; five other persons had gone to other parts of the empire and returned as destitute repatriates; and scores of evacuees from the burned-out cities had packed into the houses of Kurusu for stays of several weeks to several years. Of Kurusu's men who between 1937 and 1945 went out to Korea, Manchuria, Taiwan, China, the South Pacific, Malaya, Burma, and New Guinea, eight did not return. They were the first men from the hamlet to die in any of Japan's modern wars. Takao Hōen, to whom this book is dedicated, wrote the following *waka*, which sum up the mood of the times admirably. The occasion for their composition was Kurusu's first memorial service for the war dead, held in September 1946.

Asanake ni	Giving our all from morning
uchiteshi yaman to	to night, fighting without
mi o kona shi	ceasing, we protected our
hone o kudakite	country.
kuni o mamorinu	

Mi o kona shi   Giving our all, even unto
hone o kudakite   death, our country was
chirinu tomo   defeated. There is no
kuni wa yaburete   way to repay our debt.
mukuyu subenashi

Haisen no   Defeat. Sadly, before the
kono kanashimi o   spirits of the war dead,
eirei no   we apologize. Our sleeves
mae ni wabitsutsu   are wet with tears.
sode shigure shite

Eirei no   Under the protection of the
gokago o ukete   spirits of the war dead,
atarashī   we will build a new
yamato no kuni o   Yamato.
taten to zo omou

Both the vocabulary and the sentiment would seem anachronistic to today's young people. As it happens, on the thirtieth anniversary of the surrender, the government reported that of Japan's roughly 111 million people, almost half were born after August 15, 1945. If we add to that figure all those who were not yet of school age on that date, then almost 60 percent of all living Japanese have only the vaguest recollection of the war, or none at all. Even the parents of most primary school pupils remember little about the Pacific War or its immediate aftermath. The generations are worlds apart in terms of their life experiences. It is another question whether they are so far apart in other ways as well.

The Japanese are at least as given to categorizing persons by age or generation as are other peoples, and their talk is full of references to "Meiji men and women," meaning those born in the reign of the Emperor Meiji from 1868 to 1912; the "Taishō-born," after the Emperor Taishō who reigned from 1912 to 1926; the "early-Shōwa type," born in the first twenty years of the reign of the present Emperor; and the "late-Shōwa type," born since the end of World War II. A more general distinction between prewar and postwar kinds of persons, which formerly served as a rough division of the population into the old and the young, does so no longer. Instead, it has come to carry a complicated load of meaning. When a "prewar" person uses the terms, he is likely to intend to draw a distinction between the hard-working, frugal, moral, ethical, and patriotic (us) on the one hand, and their polar opposites (them) on the other. Used by a "postwar" person, the distinction is probably between the narrow-minded, conservative, rigid, and hopelessly traditional (them) and the new breed of Japanese (us). I know of no more poignant statement of the dilemma of the prewar male than that offered by Plath (1977:363):

> They are the Last Confucians, the last cohort born and raised in the prewar era with its ethos of dedication to the family, community, and emperor. They were thrust into adult roles just at the moment that Imperial Japan was thrust into a situation of defeat and devastation. Without ever leaving home, they became Displaced Persons, because all that they were trained to revere and to strive for was now in public disrepute.
>
> Some men say flatly, "I died on August 15, 1945." They go on to explain that of course they have married, raised children, supported their families, pursued ordinary occupations. But they have had to struggle to find an outlet for the idioms of pure action and sincerity instilled by their earlier training. Those idioms were embedded in the institutions of nationalism and militarism. Defeat muddied the institutions and left the idioms in limbo. And the chief postwar alternatives—idioms of entrepreneurship and enjoyment—are what ... the prewar generation ... were taught were the source of industrial Japan's human malaise.

It goes without saying that parents of the prewar group are in considerable doubt about how to raise their postwar children, as parents usually are. In Kurusu some of these stereotypes loom large, as we shall see, while others are of little consequence.

The educational system is perhaps the chief institutional context in which adults can most directly express their concerns about the quality and character of the training given to the young. The children of Kurusu families are in school for many more years than their parents were, and today most of them hope to secure better opportunities by completing some level of training beyond middle-school. In 1951 the people of Kurusu were confronted with an imperfectly understood educational system only recently subjected to a thoroughgoing overhaul at the direction of the Occupation forces. Not only had the reforms produced a 6–3–3 coeducational system, but textbooks and the curriculum they had known as school children had been extensively revised in the course of the effort to eliminate nationalistic and militaristic content. It is true that in 1951 not many people offered to comment on all of these issues, "although an occasional middle-aged person expresses regret that the children are no longer taught Japanese history as it was given in pre-surrender education. It seems to them unnatural that a child does not know of Amaterasu-ō-mikami, the Sun Goddess, and it is surprising even to the foreigner to realize that a whole generation of children is almost wholly ignorant of its country's mythology" (R. Smith 1953:182).

Far more likely to excite the passions of the middle-aged parents in those days was the issue of the quality of the "new education," as it was called.

The principal complaint . . . is that children learn nothing much at all in school today. This lamentable situation is blamed on several factors, most important of which is the relaxing of the severity of examinations for passage into mid-dle- or higher-schools. Parents say that in primary school the children do nothing but play, quite unlike the days when even in primary school pupils worked hard to go on to middle-school if they could possibly afford it. Lax discipline is laid to the inexperience of new teachers. . . . While the villagers feel generally that the shift away from the pre-surrender emphasis on long hours of study and extremely severe competition for entrance to higher-schools has been beneficial to the health of the children, they suggest that it should not be necessary to lower standards to the point that children no longer feel constrained to study at all [R. Smith 1953:182–83].

The Yasuhara PTA, also an Occupation-inspired development, was quite active in 1951; it was estimated that its monthly meeting commanded a 50 percent attendance rate. Educational issues and fund-raising were its major preoccupations, and the school staff were at some pains to tout the advantages of introducing more vocational courses into the curriculum, so that the middle-school graduates who were not to be successors to family headships would have a better chance of finding work. One major issue, taken up again and again by the PTA, was the high cost of textbooks, estimated at ¥800 a year for primary school children and ¥1,000 for those in middle-school. To send a child to the nearest higher-school, about eight miles north of Kurusu, would have involved a considerable outlay for transportation, clothing, and lunch money, and about ¥2,000 for textbooks. The cost of attending the Takamatsu Higher-School, by far the best in the area,

would have run at least double that amount. Yet it was less the expense of higher-school education than the consequences of the loss of
earning power for the family that kept Kurusu families from educating
their children beyond the compulsory level.

Today, however, almost every young person goes on to some kind
of educational institution after completing the compulsory nine years
of schooling. Higher-school graduates actually command about the
same starting wage and salary levels as do the graduates of minor universities, a situation tending to dampen the enthusiasm of some young
people for continuing their education. Nevertheless, because it is generally recognized that college graduates can anticipate long-range salary advantages as well as more rapid and higher advancement than
can the graduates of higher-schools, many parents would like to send
their children, especially their sons, on to college, and most of them
would like to go. Prohibitive cost is usually given as the major obsta-
cle. One man who had sent his son to the university of a neighboring
prefecture estimated that it cost him at least ¥300,000 a year. In 1974
the cost of sending a child to one of the prestigious universities in the
Tokyo area ran to ¥500–700,000 annually, up more than 45 percent over 1972, according to the Ministry of Education survey cited in
the *Asahi Shimbun* of August 1, 1975. Such sums are entirely beyond
the means of any Kurusu family.

In 1975 many people were anxious to talk about the schools, and
most of them were at some pains to make clear just how thoroughly
they disapproved of the whole situation. One man told us about a long
debate within the PTA that my wife and I have come to think of as a
story of Ninomiya Sontoku and the Three-Legged Race:

Do you remember the statue of Ninomiya Sontoku at the primary-school—the
one of him walking along reading a book, carrying a bundle of firewood on his
back? Well, it's gone now. It's been replaced by a statue of a little boy and girl
running a three-legged race. Yes . . . a three-legged race. It was the teachers'
idea. When the plan was first brought up we all said that Ninomiya's ideas had
been excellent guides for us, but they said that his teachings were not up-to-
date. Today's children don't need to develop their bodies, they said. They have
to develop their minds, and that being the case, it makes no sense to have a
statue of a child carrying firewood. And as for reading a book while walking
along, one teacher said that any child who did that on his way to school today

would most likely be run down by a truck. The three-legged race is supposed to mean that you can only attain your goal through cooperation.

Here was food for thought. In 1951 the story of Ninomiya Sontoku (Ishiguro 1955; Armstrong 1912; Yoshimoto 1912) was known to every Japanese school child. Orphaned at sixteen, the boy, then called Kinjirō, had been sent to live with an uncle. He worked very hard for very long hours, but was determined not to remain ignorant and so read the Confucian classics late at night after his work was done. Chided by his uncle for burning oil which he had not produced himself, Kinjirō planted rape on some wasteland and raised a crop of seed of his own to exchange for oil. But his uncle was displeased by his resumption of his studies and demanded instead that he make sandals and weave mats after his day's agricultural chores were completed. At length Kinjirō made his own rice crop by transplanting surplus seedlings discarded by the farmers and using this as his stake was able to return to his father's house. There he reclaimed wastelands where he could find them and was admired by all for his thrift and industry. It should be noted that he was renowned for having achieved all his worldly success by his fiercely independent actions. The classic statue of the youthful Kinjirō is intended to reveal his love of learning and willingness to perform the essential labor of the farmer. Although he gained fame later in life as a rural reformer, in Meiji educational materials he serves as the prime example of the self-made man, motivated by the Confucian virtues of love and sincerity, and practitioner of frugality and self-discipline.

That this paragon of the traditional virtues had been displaced by two roly-poly children running a three-legged race seemed unlikely, but it was true. The statue embodying the new morality shows a boy and a girl—the coeducational system imposed by the American occupation is blamed by many parents for everything from lazy children to teenage pregnancies—engaged in an activity that is a staple event in every school athletic meet. Thus its message, far less complex than that of Ninomiya, is clear to every school child from his personal experience, for indeed the only way to reach the goal in a three-legged race is to coordinate the efforts of the two runners.

This is not the outcome that we should have expected. In the Japan of the late nineteenth and early twentieth centuries through World

War II, might not the two-runners-as-one have been the more apposite symbol for primary school children? Of course, both children would have had to be boys, but no other adjustments would have been required. And might not the self-made man as boy have been an elegant symbol for the children of today—with perhaps slightly less emphasis on frugality? Is the confusion ours, or do the two statues and the debate over them reflect some of the continuing confusions of the postwar educational system? Our strong impression is that they do, and we will take up some of these issues below.

The subject of morals and ethics (*dōtoku*) was reintroduced into the primary and middle-schools by the Ministry of Education in 1959, and into the higher-schools in the mid-1960's. Because of the political perils involved in offering the course, the Ministry offers special training in methods of teaching the subject. Most of these precautions are occasioned by the determined opposition to the reintroduction of the subject by the nationally powerful left-wing Japan Teacher's Union. The union is very weak in Kagawa Prefecture, however, and only three teachers in Shionoe schools are members. The general opinion is that they are very quiet because the conservative parents would object at the first sign of any political activity.

As far as the parents of Shionoe Town are concerned, then, the Ministry of Education's worries are misdirected, for they regard the present educational system as too permissive, just as *their* parents did in 1951:

It's so bad these days that teachers can no longer punish students. They have to *please* them, if you can believe it. If a teacher can't discipline his pupils as he would discipline his own children, how can he give them an education? Oh, yes, they put the morals courses back in a few years ago, but they are nothing like our old ethics courses. What can they be thinking of? After all, morality and ethics (*dōtoku*) are the basis for religion (*shūkyō*) and you cannot expect children to have the one if you don't teach them the other in school.

These sentiments persist despite all the efforts of educational authorities to persuade parents that training (*shitsuke*) in morals and ethics is not primarily the responsibility of the schools. They try to draw distinctions between three kinds of education: "education in the school," "education for society," and "education in the home." A major component of "education for society" is sports, and every effort is made to emphasize the point that athletic activity is more for improvement of health than competition for prizes. Under this rubric fall the Children's Sports Club and the Children's Club. In the old days teachers were completely in charge of such activities, but nowadays there is much emphasis on self-government in student groups like the Children's Club, with some guidance provided by parents and older children. There have also been efforts to make the schoolgrounds available to the whole community, rather than the children alone, in line with Ministry of Education's policy of "open campuses" and "cradle-to-grave instruction," but both programs have met with limited success in Shionoe Town.

Since the 1973 oil crisis, there has been a revival of efforts to teach both the children and their mothers conservation. The primary school organized an exhibition of old homemade toys, children were shown how to sharpen pencils with a knife rather than with the electric pencil-sharpeners found in all schools, and how to make use of and re-use old things, as they had routinely done in 1951. "Maybe the programs will have some effect. There is a saying that if the Japanese are told 'Right face!' they face right," said one man who had been lamenting the irresponsibility of the young.

The nursery school is officially open to children from three to five years of age, but since the principal criterion for admission is that they be toilet trained, there are some two-year-olds as well. In 1953, when it first opened, Kurusu people sent their children there because the women were so busy with agricultural work. In 1975 they sent them because so many mothers were employed full-time outside the community. A survey of the employment picture of the 44 mothers whose children were enrolled revealed that 25 of them were "at home"—16 being in agriculture, and 9 serving as housewives—whereas 19 were employed outside the communities in which they lived. All 9 housewives were temporarily out of the labor market caring for infants.

School hours are from 9:00 A.M. to 3:30 P.M., but because many parents leave for work very early, some children are dropped off at seven. A woman who lives in the small house beside the school is on hand to look after them until the two teachers arrive; she is also the cook. When the schoolbus drops off the children at their homes in the afternoon, they all will find someone, usually a grandmother, waiting for them. There are no "key children," an expression widely used in the cities, referring to the house key a child wears on a string around his neck, with which he is expected to let himself in when he gets home. All the nursery-school pupils—even those who live in Kurusu— are taken home by bus, because none of the parents is free to come to pick up his child at the school when classes are over.

The school year begins in April and there is a two-week summer vacation when the older siblings are on holiday and can help look after the children who are home all day. Where there are no older children in the family, grandmother is expected to serve as full-time babysitter. The curriculum is not demanding. The four-year-olds are taught a little reading, but no writing. In the hot summer months they are taken by bus once a week up to Kaminishi to wade and swim in the river there, where the water is not polluted. There is a PTA, and although it is said to be more and more difficult to schedule meetings in the afternoon, the three or four meetings a year are attended by most of the mothers. The parents expect the nursery school staff to teach the children elementary manners, and are quite critical when they feel that a poor job is being done. The teachers complain that so much of their time is spent trying to bring order out of chaos that they can do little more than train the children to wash their hands before eating and after going to the toilet.

The teachers say that their charges are not at all like children of a generation ago. Some approve the change; others lament it. One woman, no longer actively teaching, said: "Because they have few siblings or none at all, they are selfish, willful, impetuous, and spoiled. When they first come to nursery school, they do not know how to get along with other children at all. They snatch toys from each other and instead of sitting and waiting for everyone to begin to eat they start right away and even grab food from the teachers." Another said that it takes about a month to teach them not to do these things. Girls, she thought, are likely to understand more quickly and are more compliant than boys, who are generally mischievous and obstreperous. The children in their third year often serve as group leaders and are said to be a great help to the staff. Any grandmother in Kurusu would concur in this assessment of the basic differences between the temperaments of the sexes, and would surely approve of the kindergarten's policy of training little girls to responsible and nurturant behavior while little boys are allowed to shirk responsibility and receive indulgent care.

For all the continuities at this level, no study undertaken in 1975 could possibly ignore the issue of the "generation gap," and it was not at all difficult to elicit comments on the problem. Perhaps the opinion most commonly expressed by older people is that, compared to them, the young of today have never known real hardship. In all fairness, it should be remarked that the claim is entirely justified, for the parents and grandparents did experience the stern austerities of the prewar years and the extreme deprivation of the war and immediate postwar period. Many of the men and some of the women of Kurusu survived the debacle of Japan's military collapse overseas, were imprisoned in China and Korea, and fled on foot from the advancing enemy armies or from the burning cities of the home islands. At the end, after all the privation and sacrifice, they awaited the arrival of the Allied armies with apprehension and despair.

No parent or grandparent in Kurusu wishes that their children or grandchildren had gone through any of this. What they do yearn for is some recognition by the young of the extent of their suffering. In this hope they are doomed to disappointment, for talk about World War II has, for a Japanese teenager, all the charm and interest of a discussion of the imperial succession crises of the Heian Period. One woman, now in her sixties, put it bitterly:

Today's young people don't know anything about suffering, and they don't care what we went through. I was in Takamatsu when the Americans bombed it on the night of July 3, 1945, just a few weeks before the war ended. As the fires started to spread I gathered up what I could carry, strapped the baby to my back, and walked all the way here. I'd stop from time to time to catch my breath and look back. The city was a carpet of fire. As dawn came I could see that the whole plain was covered by a pall of smoke. The road was jammed with people, but no one said very much. Now I'm sorry I came back to Kurusu. I thought it would be better to come to the country, where I could at least grow my own food. But now it's obvious that it would have been better to take my chances in the city. City people have done a lot better than we have. But one of the big reasons for coming back was so the children would be safe and have enough to eat. When I try to tell them about those days, they look bored or change the subject.

There is more to the matter, of course; older people firmly believe that they are the better for the travail they endured. They worry that because their offspring have not been tested and tempered by adversity, they will not develop the moral fiber they will need to succeed in this competitive world.

Young people are also often accused of having no understanding of or much respect for tradition. It may well be that the older members of any society inevitably take this line, and with considerable justification in the case of Japan. Yet not all old beliefs and customs have been relegated to the dustbin of superstition. Weddings are still the occasion for the activation of much traditional behavior. The date, invariably an auspicious day by the almanac, is selected by the parents or grandparents of the bride and groom. Old people are consulted about which entrance of the house the bride should use, what kinds of ritual objects are required, and the like. One young man said, "We don't know much about these things, but weddings and funerals don't take place very often, and it's better to do them right in any case."

The lack of knowledge of the young concerning the proper usage on occasions such as weddings is often pointed to by older persons, who represent it as a lamentable new development. In this connection we cannot resist quoting from a letter written in the autumn of 1955 by a young man who was about to get married:

There are many things I have to take care of, such as making arrangements for offering the betrothal gift, for a place to live, and a job for my wife. I find that I do not have enough knowledge about marriage arrangements, or perhaps I have forgotten many of them. For example, when offering the betrothal gift we wrap the money in *noshigami*, and whatever the amount involved, we add five yen to it. The pronunciation of "five yen" is *go-en*, which means fortunate connection. In the old days five yen had a proper value, but now it's worthless as money, though it still keeps the value of superstition.

I had planned to have the wedding around the end of March of the coming year. When I told my parents, they and the parents of my fiancee all objected, saying that according to the *eto* (sexagenary cycle) next year is the year of the monkey (*saru*), which sounds like another word *saru* that means leaving or parting, and by implication, divorce. Since my engagement I have had to spend most of my time adjusting and coordinating the discrepancies arising between the younger and older generations, and found it absolutely impossible to make them understand how meaningless all this superstition really is. Japan is not only not yet democratized, it isn't even civilized! And even now I do not know when my own wedding is to be. I can only guess that it will be some day in the early part of January, before the New Year's Day by the lunar calendar, so as to avoid *saru*. In my case, my younger sister and her husband are taking the role of go-betweens and they are presenting the betrothal gift to my fiancee's family today because it is *dai an* by the almanac—a day of good luck and happy fortune—although I feel neither lucky nor fortunate.

Not everyone is so impatient with tradition. For example, one young man told us that when his first child was born he consulted a diviner in the city in order to get advice on a felicitous given name, one that would "fit" the surname. He also took both of his children to the Shinto shrine on the one hundredth day after birth. "Surely it would be a mistake not to take every precaution." This wary approach to tradition may be seen among youth on all hands, and they have even added a few variations of their own. An example is to be found in the selection and rejection of certain combinations of license plate numbers. In general the number four (pronounced *shi*, homonymous with "death") is avoided, though one young man had asked for and got a plate with the number 4747 (*shi-nana-shi-nana*, which by a slight shift can be made to sound like *shina-nai shina-nai*, "won't die, won't die").

Yet much of the vital community-centered ritual and ceremonial life that still existed in 1951 is now gone. Let it be noted that the older residents of Kurusu could easily have maintained much of it without the participation of their children. They failed to do so, and they tend to place the blame on the young. A schoolteacher in her thirties, for example, asked: "Why can't we keep the good things while at the same time improving our standard of living? These children have absolutely no sense of the seasons—flowers, fruits, and vegetables all come from greenhouses the year round. It seems odd to think of coming generations of Japan not caring about such things that were so important to us." Again, it is not the *children* who decorate the playground at the Shionoe Hot Springs Hotel with plastic cherry blossoms twelve months of the year.

Of far greater concern to older people than all of this, however, is the continuity of the house and the continuation of the agricultural operation. Most are agreed that the kinds of work available outside the hamlet are much easier than farming, especially in the case of jobs for women. One afternoon we were talking to a young man in his twenties who has a full-time job in Takamatsu. The discussion turned to the boom in ownership of agricultural machinery and how much easier it made farming. He made a wry face and said, "It's made it easier, maybe, but it will never be as easy as other kinds of work." He volunteered the information that most of the males in his age group had left Kurusu long before, and I have the strong impression that he envied them.

Despite the overall record of success to date in finding a successor and heir, no one in Kurusu takes it for granted that when the time comes he will be able to do so. Bernstein (1976:47–48) reports from a village in neighboring Ehime Prefecture:

It is the generation of rural Japanese in their early forties for whom this problem is most pressing. They are the first members of their family to be educated in high school under the new democratic curriculum. Reluctant to impose strict discipline on their youngsters, eager to further their children's economic earning power through education, and inclined to encourage greater independence than they themselves had, middle-aged parents today sympathize with their offsprings' feelings of alienation from the land and their attraction to urban lifestyles. Witnesses to the declining rural population and sensitive to their children's aspirations, this transitional generation of Japanese in the countryside today view with a mixture of relief and regret the prospect of becoming their family's last generation of farmers.

Throughout rural Japan parents have made concessions to their children that were undreamed of a generation ago, in part because most couples want and have only two children these days, which greatly limits the number of options they can exercise in the selection of the successor and heir. In Kurusu there is even one adopted husband who would not take his wife's surname and who was given a house lot on which he has put up a separate dwelling in order to avoid having to live with his wife's parents.

Most of the young married couples living in Kurusu have very little to do with farming. School-age children, including the teenagers, were not in the fields much in 1951 either, except during the peak agricultural seasons, and it was generally felt that they were too busy with their studies to be counted on at other times. Unmarried young people who had completed their schooling were expected to help out, but today they rarely do so because they hold full-time jobs outside Kurusu. On any number of occasions we observed that the people who were out in the rice fields, the vegetable plots, or in the wastelands cutting grass, were either women over forty or old men. In the nearly two months of the summer of 1975 that my wife and I were there, we never saw anyone in his early twenties engaged in any agricultural activity whatsoever. On a Sunday afternoon, for example, we came across a sixty-three year-old grandmother hoeing a vegetable patch while her son and his wife were inside the house watching television with their children. Just down the path at another house the husband and wife, both in their late forties, were out in the fields and the grandmother was in the garden tending her melons. The two girls of the family, both in their teens, were in the house, and their younger brother, it turned out, had gone to Takamatsu with some friends from school. Most remarkably, his sisters knew where he had gone, but his mother did not.

On another occasion we visited this same house and found only the eldest daughter at home. She served the obligatory cakes and chilled soft drinks, while conversing with considerably more poise than any girl of her age would have been able to muster twenty-five years before. But when her father and mother returned to the house and joined us, she fell silent except for an occasional response to a comment or question. When her mother was telling us about how active the girl had been in her high-school band, for example, she said that she had been so busy that she never had any time to help with the housework. The girl wrinkled her nose and shot back, "Why are you always bringing that up?" Her grandmother, who has spent at least sixty of her eighty-odd years at hard work in the fields and garden, chuckled indulgently.

Given these conditions it might appear that today's young people will under no circumstances farm the land when they inherit it. But we were struck by an emphatic comment made by a young man in his mid-twenties: "When the time comes for a boy to do what a man does, he *does* what a man does." Nonetheless, many older people expressed grave doubts about the likelihood that anyone will ever again work as hard as they did to raise rice because, "They have none of our experience of struggling to grow enough rice just to feed our families and satisfy the landlords." What is more, one man commented, "No one eats much rice anymore anyway." When asked, the young respond that they have not thought much about it, but that if a situation arose in their families that required them to work in the fields, they would of course do so.

Most younger people will tell you that they are too busy to help much with farming, but several remarked that in many families the members of the junior generation in their thirties do in fact help out a great deal. The point is, of course, that the parents of children in their late teens and twenties, the group that has completed its education but is not yet married, are not only unlikely to have any readily marketable skills, but are also quite capable of carrying out agricultural tasks, especially since the farm machinery came in.

Like their elders, young people seem to take a conservative position on the issue of selling land. They are perfectly well aware that agriculture hardly yields a handsome return, and they see the apparent contradiction in the decision made by so many people to take full-time outside employment, partly in order to earn the cash with which to make the payments on the agricultural machinery that enables them to remain part-time farmers. Even so, they see none of this as indicating that it would be a good idea to sell out. They have, after all, heard it said all of their lives that if a family holds onto its farmland it will be able to get by no matter how bad things become. This sentiment is apparently quite widespread among the young, and there are some people in their thirties who buy land when it comes on the market. We talked with many in their twenties who said that they too would like to buy land, but that somehow their bonuses seemed always to be spent even before they came in. They took a surprisingly dim view of those who do sell out. Given their attitudes toward the household, which are discussed below, we did not expect to hear them say that one should try to keep the land passed down by one's ancestors. And indeed, while they registered no such opinion, they were quite firm in the belief that when a family sells land it is a sure sign that it is in serious trouble. "Why would anyone sell land," they asked, "unless he had to?"

However much their attitudes may coincide, however, the parents and children of Kurusu obviously feel that they rarely understand one another. We were told a story that speaks volumes for the character of the relationship between them today. A father, now in his mid-fifties, said that on the preceding Sunday he and his wife were scheduled to cut green fertilizer for the fields and spray insecticide *and* then to work on the new house they were building for their successor. Their son had got up unusually early for a Sunday and asked his mother to fix him a lunch to take to a beach picnic he had planned with his friends.

I could hardly believe it. He knew how much work there was to do. As he was leaving I asked him how a son I had raised to be twenty-four years old could possibly fail so thoroughly to understand my wishes. He looked me right in the eye and said that *he* could not understand how a father who had raised him to be twenty-four could fail so thoroughly to understand *his* wishes.

This is a new world for older people, and they confront it with highly varied attitudes. In 1972, when we were back in Kurusu for a short visit, a widow had told us:

All of my children were away at one time, but now one of my sons and his wife, who were living in Takamatsu, have come back here to live with me. They both commute to their jobs and their daughter attends primary school there. My first son and his family live in Osaka, and my daughter married and moved away. I've always said that young people ought to do as they wished, but there are a lot of old people around here who are bitter and unhappy because they cannot accept the fact that things are different now. A lot of them blame it all on the Americans, but however that may be it is obvious that the household (*ie*) is gone and nothing is going to bring it back.

As one young woman put it, "You must understand that a lot has changed. Succession nowadays has nothing to do with the *household*. It has to do with the *family*. The only issue is which of the children will take on responsibility for the parents when they get old." Matsumoto (1962:68) made much the same point several years ago in his study of primogeniture in Japan, and Befu (1962:35) cites a survey of 277 rural communities which revealed that one-third of all first sons between twelve and eighteen years of age who finished school between 1929 and 1933 left their native villages and thus did not take up the headship of the household.

One of the chief issues on which specialists in the study of the generation gap in Japan concentrate is whether or not the old and the
young have the same expectations with respect to co-residence, and
whether parents plan to depend on their children's support in their old
age. In comparable national surveys in 1950 and 1971, the proportion
of parents who said that they planned to depend on their children
dropped from 55 to 26 percent. Yet in a 1974 survey of 700 persons
between eighteen and twenty-four and 300 parents with children in
that age group, 70 percent of the respondents said that children should
live with their aged parents (*Asahi Shimbun*, July 12, 1975). And in a
1974 survey of 8,000 men and women between the ages of thirty and
fifty-five, it was found that 66 percent said that they expected no
financial aid from their children after they retired, yet 45 percent
wanted to live with a married child. Of those who said that they
wanted some financial assistance from their children, 65 percent said
that they wanted to live with them as well (Anonymous 1976a:8).

We would argue that in Kurusu older people simply want one married child to be close by, even if they plan to be financially independent. The issue is an important one because the rural population is
aging rapidly; at the national level the percentage of persons over
sixty-five rose from 5.3 in 1955 to 7.9 in 1974, when almost 14 percent of the farm population was over sixty-five.

Today, as there has always been, there is a great deal of talk among
young people about marriage, having children, and living arrangements. Perhaps the classic formulation of the ideal is one given us by
another young woman:

It's best for a young couple and the husband's parents to live separately—but
not too far apart—until the first baby comes. Then the young couple can move
in with the parents. I think the trend to living separately went too far. Now the
generations are moving closer together and both children and parents are
more willing to adjust and make compromises than they were until recently.

Not only have many young couples found it hard to manage in the
city, especially when both work and the first baby is born, but since the
1973 oil crisis the level of affluence has declined somewhat and they
now see the economic advantages of co-residence in the rural areas.

Clearly, when the parents build a new house for a married child they are offering the young couple one of the most valuable of all conceivable gifts. They are also providing an arrangement that very nearly meets the requirements of a saying, purportedly an old English proverb, that was very popular in 1975: "Parents and married children should live close enough that the soup won't get cold when carried between the two houses, but not so close that it's too hot to drink." One of the major considerations in all of this is the attitudes of young women concerning the traditional role of the bride in the farm family. It is no wonder that they seek to avoid the situation as I described it in 1951:

The girl has almost no contact with her own family following her marriage. The bride of the eldest son takes up her duties as the newest and lowliest member of her husband's family, and devotes much of her time to coping with her mother-in-law. Nothing that she does is quite right; she is made to work longer and harder hours than the other women, and her tasks are hard and menial. In all this she finds little support from her husband, for as resident heir to the household he concerns himself seldom with the women's world [R. Smith 1953:222].

Young people maintain that though the old style of arranged marriage (*miai kekkon*) has vanished completely, true "love marriage" (*ren'ai kekkon*) is not at all common as yet. Older people are more inclined to estimate that about half of all marriages are one variation or another on older patterns of arranged marriage. According to the young, what happens is that a young man and woman are introduced by a friend or acquaintance. If they like each other they may decide to pursue their relationship, which either of them may break off at any time. They may decide to get married, but this is not love marriage at all, in their view. Indeed, as we have seen, a common form of the new marriage is called work-place marriage, and some of Kurusu's younger brides are young women from quite distant parts of the country who met their husbands at their place of work.

Our impression is that the young people are right in their assessment of the current situation. The second son of one Kurusu family had not yet settled on a bride, although he was expecting to marry later in the year. His younger sister was also unmarried. The young man had been approached by friends and acquaintances who had suggestions for possible mates, and her father told us that several offers had been made to him concerning his daughter's marriage, but that they have all come from too-distant places like Hokkaido and Kyushu. He and his wife said that they hoped to find her a husband from Kagawa Prefecture, so that she would not be so far away that they could see her only rarely. Neither the boy nor the girl had a candidate in mind.

However a young person in Kurusu finds a prospective bride or groom, the new affluence is reflected in the expense of the wedding ceremonies, which require a considerable outlay on the part of both families. In 1952 a wedding cost the groom's parents between ¥40,000 and ¥65,000, an enormous sum for the time. This included the betrothal payment (*yuinō*) by the groom, amounting to some ¥10–15,000; the go-between's fee, usually 10 percent of the betrothal payment; meals for helpers (¥500 each), relatives (¥1,000 each), and women of the hamlet (¥350 each); and all other direct expenses. The bride's family was responsible for her dowry, perhaps three or four times the amount of the yuinō, but it was estimated that the total cost to them was about half of that borne by the family of the groom.

While we lack reliable estimates of the average cost of weddings in 1975, partly because as the number of possible expenses has greatly increased so has the variability of cost, we can offer some comparative figures for some items. It is clear that weddings have become even more expensive affairs relative to income. In one case we know that the yuinō alone was ¥500,000, and that the bride's dowry had been at least four or five times as large, probably somewhere in the neighborhood of ¥2,000,000. The ratio between the two is not fixed, but is one of the issues negotiated by a go-between whether the marriage is arranged or a "love-match." An older woman in Kurusu estimated that the absolute minimum for a yuinō in 1975 would be about ¥300,000, more than twenty times greater than it was twenty-five years before. It was her opinion that the dowry could be as large as the bride's parents chose to make it, and she knew of cases where no go-between had been involved at all. As for the go-between's fee, once fairly rigidly set at 10 percent, she said, "Few people would make much of a fuss about the figure today and would probably accept whatever they are offered."

For young people who are still unmarried, there is the Shionoe Youth Club, which meets three times a week when its directorate is active, much less often when those in charge offer less vigorous leadership. Ideally, there is a weekday meeting for males only, and coeducational meetings on Friday and Saturday. Only twenty persons are formally enrolled in the club. Since 1974 the Youth Club has organized the Bon Dance on the grounds of the middle-school, and they have a folk-singing group, but those who had hoped that the club would revive the lion dance and perhaps even Kagawa Prefecture's only unique folk dance (called *tatara odori* and mimicking the operation of the bellows used in the now-vanished bell-casting foundries) have been disappointed. The cynical say that both are too difficult and require more practice than the members of the club are willing to devote to them. One activity in which the members are eager participants is the annual summer field day, in which many clubs from all over the prefecture compete. Above all, the organization provides an approved context for social interaction between unmarried men and women.

There was a Youth Club in Yasuhara in 1951 as well, and the young people of Kurusu had tried with limited success to organize a branch of their own. All in all its purposes were very different. The village-wide club sponsored an annual oratorical contest and the Bon Dance. Its members also carried the god's palanquin in the fall festival of the Hachiman Shrine. For a brief period they showed monthly movies at the middle-school, charging an admission fee of ¥40 in an effort to raise money to support their other activities, but the films—mostly old Westerns and Japanese costume pictures—were not very well attended and the scheme was abandoned. The Kurusu club had obtained copies of a new middle-school text entitled *Democracy*, which they had met to discuss on at least three occasions. They were also studying a number of agricultural bulletins with a view to learning new methods of plant-disease and pest control.

Today's young people engage in many leisure-time recreational activities, and can pick from a variety undreamed of only a few years ago. They may go to a movie in Takamatsu, as their parents did in their youth, or they may join the family in watching television at home. Every house in Kurusu has television, seventeen of them color sets. But what most directly determines the recreational patterns of the young is the automobile. Since most either have their own or can use the family's, their geographical range is greatly expanded. For a while—up to 1972 or thereabouts—there was a national craze for bowling, reflected in the surge in the number of bowling alleys from 254 in 1966 to more than 3,000 in 1972 (Bureau of Statistics 1975). The Takamatsu area is never very far behind the fashion, and there were at least twenty bowling alleys within easy driving range of Kurusu. At the height of the bowling fever, the charge was a modest ¥350 per game, and waits of two to three hours were not uncommon. But as the number of establishments grew and the fad faded, the fee dropped to ¥50 and all but one or two of the largest and best-run bowling alleys closed their doors.

In 1975 *pachinko*, the durable postwar pin-ball machine, was all the rage. Its popularity had even grown with the economic slump following the 1973 oil crisis, which had put some people out of work and cut down on the amount of overtime work available. "You have to get there early to get a machine," said one young man, who was something of a celebrity for having once won ¥10,000 in three hours of uninterrupted play.

Recreational travel is now undertaken by everyone much more casually than was the case in 1951, when many school-age children in Kurusu could not even afford to go on the semiannual school excursions to nearby places; today, travel, whether for pleasure or business, is accepted as routine. Whether it has proved broadening for all is hard to say, but in the homes of Kurusu one now finds souvenirs of such places as Okinawa and Hokkaido, either purchased by a traveler or brought back by a family member, friend, or kinsman. People are also given nowadays to driving off for part of the day—staying overnight anywhere is considered an extravagance—to visit a relative, to see a famous shrine or temple, to swim and picnic at the beach or in the mountains, or to attend a sporting or entertainment event. The young people go off by car or bus to meet their school friends or shop in Takamatsu. We were constantly surprised at how often their parents were unsure where they were or when they would be back.

The degree of independence of the young can be exaggerated, of course, for while almost all of the unmarried men and women who have finished their schooling are employed, their incomes are not sufficient to make them self-supporting. They are obliged to live at home, but almost none of them contribute directly to the finances of the household. They may purchase their own clothing, pay for their own transportation, and meet many of their other expenses, but they tend to put nothing into the household accounts.

Yet there is much evidence to suggest that the gap between the generations in Japan may not be as wide as it is often perceived to be:

The change in Japanese values, attitudes and beliefs has often been discussed in terms of the pre-war and post-war generations. In such discussions some frequent themes on change run as follows: change from work-orientation to leisure or pleasure-orientation, from 'wet' (rather emotional and traditional human relationship) to 'dry' (individualistic and sometimes egocentric human relationship), from *'risshin-shusse'* (literally, to erect one's body and embark into the world) to 'my-home-ism.' Although people often speak with one of these characteristics in mind, the above changes are seldom validated by research. One reason for this is the lack of pre-war data comparable to present data; we do not have an adequate method of investigating the change in values and attitudes without cumulative or longitudinal data. This is always a problem when one tries to study change. In the absence of such data, one of the most commonly used methods of investigation of generational differences in values and attitudes is by comparing the views of the older and younger generations, assuming that those held by the older generation represent former values, attitudes and beliefs, while those held by the younger generation represent current or newly emerging views. Since most "generational difference" approaches deal with the generations in the same social, cultural and historical settings, two further assumptions may be made. Firstly, basic attitudes and beliefs are acquired at a relatively early stage in life, and, secondly, after their acquisition they persist more or less unchanged. But the real situation is not quite so simple, and it is easy to find examples of changing attitudes and values in a man's lifetime as well as instances of stable values [Kato 1971:415–16].

Kato conducted a small survey of college students and their fathers, and with all the cautions mentioned above nonetheless concluded that there were two major differences between the two groups. There did seem to have been a shift from a work orientation to a leisure orientation, and a contrast between the ideal of self-development and that of concentration on the development of a happy family life with children, a car, and a home of one's own. Yet even in these differences, he found much evidence to suggest that the values of the fathers had shifted over time in the directions of the values held by their sons.

Another interesting set of results is reported from a survey conducted in a relatively urbanized provincial city about 120 kilometers from Tokyo. The sample was of a prewar group, aged forty to seventy-nine, and a postwar group of seventeen- and eighteen-year-olds.

The two generations do not diverge as widely as anticipated. They share . . . the same moral orientation, judging by the responses of the majority. Divergences showed up in minority responses. . . . We might conclude that the two generations are continuous in dominant patterns and discontinuous in more extreme orientations. This statement does not contradict the prevailing keen sense of a generation gap, because it is extreme patterns that draw observers' attention and because only difference, not sameness, conveys messages. Moreover, what appeared to be a gap often turned out to be a complementary difference attributable to different life stages [Lebra 1974:271].

What kind of view do the young have of their past? It is probably no more or less distorted than that of any other group of similar age, and they were fascinated by the photographs I had taken twenty-five years before. Since cameras, now so common, were rather rare in those days, they had never seen photographs of their parents when they were young. They exhibited what must be universal amazement at being presented with irrefutable evidence that twenty-five years before their mothers had been straight-backed and smooth-skinned and their fathers' faces had been less lined and their eyes clearer. They were also struck by the material changes in Kurusu, especially the interior shots of houses that then held none of the consumer goods they now take for granted, and the agricultural technology. This last was a source of amazement, for many of them had never even seen some of the old implements, or remembered them only as they were being discarded during the clearing-out of outbuildings to make way for the cultivators and transplanters of the new era.

The old are everywhere the new problem of the industrial age. In the sections on welfare we have dealt with some of the efforts to afford them some dignity and minimal levels of financial support when they are distressed. In Shionoe Town there were 440 people over seventy years of age in 1975. The oldest was 102. All were automatically enrolled as members of the Ekisō-kai, the old people's club. Twice a year the town arranges trips to nearby hot-springs or to a temple, usually in the spring or fall when the weather is comfortable. Everyone is expected to bring his own lunch, but the transportation by town-owned small bus is provided free. September 15 is a national holiday,

Keirō-no-hi (Old People's Day), but in Shionoe Town its observance is put off until October 2, when it is cooler. The old people of the town are invited to the school, where the Women's Association prepares lunch for them and the children put on entertainment.

None of this is nearly enough, of course, for most of the old are lonely and apprehensive about the future. They dislike many of the new things that have entered their lives, and frequently compare the present unfavorably with the past. One morning we fell to talking with a woman in her eighties about some of the changes she has seen:

O-bon used to be such a big thing here, but people don't do much nowadays. It's like everything else. Life is a lot less fun than it used to be and people seem unwilling to develop close relationships. Why, so many people commute to work by car that most people get up and leave early and come late in the afternoon or even in the early evening. They just don't have a chance to get to know their neighbors well. Their friends and acquaintances are all from the places they work or those they go to for recreation.

Now it is possible that these sentiments are attributable to the normal contraction of the older person's social world, but we would suggest that there is much more to it than that.

It is dangerous to try to project one's self into the position of people so briefly and in so many ways superficially known, but we cannot leave the people of Kurusu without asking whether, given the choice, they would opt for the life of 1951 or 1975. The answers will probably depend a great deal on whether the person is male or female, young, middle-aged, or old. All in all, the new Japan has dealt its older citizens a very mixed bag of blessings and keen disappointments.

Many men are worried about what the future holds for them when they can no longer do hard physical labor or after they are forced to retire from their present jobs. For most who have regular employment, as opposed to those in the construction trades, for example, the retirement age is fifty-five or sixty. One man who holds such a job, a man in his early fifties, said, "Of course I'm concerned. I've managed to get an extra year, fortunately, but I'll be fifty-six soon and will have to quit. I don't really want to look for another job, and I absolutely refuse to leave Kurusu for the city where our married son and his wife live. We have built a small new house for another of our sons and we can only hope that he will come back after he marries."

The older men of Kurusu do not retire voluntarily. Even men over seventy still actively seek part-time or casual work outside the hamlet and they continue to carry primary responsibility for the agricultural enterprise. In their desire to keep on working they are not very different from the majority of their countrymen. The Prime Minister's Office (Anonymous 1976b:8) reported that almost 64 percent of 8,000 men and women interviewed in 1976 said that they wanted to find continuing employment after their mandated retirements at either fifty-five or sixty, largely for economic reasons. Pension plans are not common in Japan, where most retirees receive only a lump-sum severance payment of a few months' salary. That few can survive on the amount they are given is reflected in the fact that less than 10 percent said that they wanted to retire completely. Like many of the older men of Kurusu, they probably will be frustrated in this hope.

One Sunday afternoon in July 1975, my wife and I went to call on a family, our first such visit since arriving. The house itself had not changed much, but at the edge of the large compound there was a small new house. What had formerly been a footpath had been widened considerably—to accommodate automobile traffic, it turned out. Only the head of the family, now seventy-one, was at home, and he asked us in. After we were seated he disappeared into the back of the house; there was the sound of a refrigerator door being opened and shut, and the rattling of bottles and ice cubes. He came back with a tray of soft drinks, glasses and ice, which he served us and then sat down, turning a huge electric fan in our direction to cool us. He and his wife now live alone in the old house. The new one was built in 1970 for their second son and his wife and children. Today, all of them had gone in the son's car to a nearby temple on a Sunday outing. Our host seemed to have nothing much to do and we talked until the rest of the family came back, fairly late in the afternoon.

There are several things about this scene that need to be interpreted. Except for the first three days of the New Year, when men used to serve visitors because the women were free to go out calling at the houses of their friends, I had never before been served anything by a man in Kurusu, except for tea at the priest's house. Moreover, to find the head of the family alone in those days would have been extraordinary, for usually a woman or a child would be left to watch the house while the rest of the family was away. It is still the case that if a man and woman (their relationship is immaterial) are in the house when a caller comes it is invariably the woman who serves the visitor. In the old days, she would also have fanned him, but now she will switch on the electric fan that every household owns.

Our host, as we have said, seemed to have plenty of time for conversation, and seemed far more at loose ends than even very old people were before. Perhaps it trivializes their contribution to agriculture, which is after all largely dependent on their physical labor, but our strong impression is that many of them were just puttering about. "Puttering" is a word or a concept I would never have applied to the activities of the old people twenty-five years ago. When we rather gingerly raised the question of age and involvement in things, he snorted:

Oh they take good care of us all right, but it's all gone flat. I even get a little money from the government [he used the word *o-kami*, an old term meaning roughly "from on high," which I had never thought to hear again]. It's just about enough to keep me in cigarettes. What I'd really like is a job, but nobody hires a man of my years any more. I guess they're worried that I can't do the work, but I can. They just won't let me try.

The older women in Kurusu are in many ways in an even less enviable position. The new conditions have given them even fewer alternatives than the old men now enjoy. Women in their fifties and early sixties can find work in nearby factories, and as we have seen, many of them are so employed. They also do agricultural work and tend the house and garden (see Bernstein 1976). The involvement of women in agriculture has been so great in recent years that several adjustments have been made to their real or imagined inability to match the men in physical strength. The most engaging of these, perhaps, is that the old rice bale of 60 kilograms no longer exists, having been replaced by a vinyl bag with a 30-kilogram capacity, "that even a woman can lift," one farm woman said somewhat sardonically. In any event, older women do not so easily find outside work, and their position in the household is progressively weakened by the growing irrelevancy of their skills.

These older women lead lonely lives, and the government programs designed to brighten their days are minimally effective. Their children, and even the successor, are often gone, and even if these persons still

live in Kurusu they are likely to be away at work all day six days a
week. Some of the grandmothers have become babysitters of their
preschool and primary school grandchildren. In a few houses where
there is a newborn baby, the infant's mother is at home, having
stopped work temporarily until the child is old enough to be left in its
grandmother's care. These young women all want to return to work,
for the unattractive alternatives are housework and agricultural labor,
and their salaries are essential contributions to the family income.

We were visiting a woman one afternoon when her four-year-old
granddaughter came home from nursery school. In the house at the
time were she and her husband's ninety-year-old mother. Her husband
and their son and his wife were all away at work. She got out a snack
for the little girl and we all settled down to watch a program on the
color television set until she began to prepare dinner about 5:30 P.M.
No one else stopped by. It seemed an odd and lonely life for a woman
as vigorous and sociable as she had once been.

The future has never belonged to the old, however, and their position in a community serves more to remind us of changes that have
occurred than to suggest what the future holds. In the next two chap-
ters we shall try to show what Kurusu has become and what its present
condition portends.

CHAPTER SEVEN

The Hamlet as Community

WHEN I FIRST went to Kurusu in 1951, the agricultural hamlet was generally regarded as the basic social building block in the edifice of Japanese society. In those years a great deal of social science research was directed at the hamlet level of organization (Beardsley, Hall, and Ward 1959; Cornell and Smith 1956; Dore 1959; Norbeck 1954), for it was in hamlets that the vast majority of the population of Japan then lived. The hamlet was above all a functioning corporate entity, based at the least on a strong conception of territorial integrity and at the most on a sense of kinship, real or imagined. It was "the most important focus of the farmer's loyalty, the framework for his most important social and economic relations, and the source of the most intense social pressures to which he is subjected" (Dore 1959:351).

The hamlet was also the place where some of the most important consequences of the pattern of Japanese agriculture were reflected in the forms of community life. While each farm operation in the hamlet was essentially an independent family enterprise, as had been the case for centuries, the community served as a kind of labor pool that could be drawn on at peak seasons. For most of the agricultural year, every family did its own work without assistance of any kind (Ogura 1967:36). Nevertheless, bound up with the technology of Japanese agriculture as it existed up to the 1960's was a style of social relationship extending from the periodic sharing of labor for minor tasks to hamlet-centered ceremonial and ritual. If asked to single out the one feature that best exemplified the character of rural communities in the early 1950's, most observers would have pointed to the complex patterns of cooperation and mutual aid.

In the case of Kurusu, there were many such groups. The membership of some included all Kurusu households but no outsiders. Others were composed of all the agricultural households of Kurusu plus some households from outside who cultivated fields within the boundaries of the hamlet. In still others the members were a mixture of hamlet households and outsiders; and some consisted of a small number of Kurusu families with no outsiders included. Thus for certain purposes and on certain occasions, Kurusu was defined as an exclusive grouping. For many other purposes, some but not all of its residents were involved in cooperative activities and mutual aid, often in collaboration with people who did not live in the hamlet (R. Smith 1952).

The joint planting of rice seedbeds, transplanting, and harvesting were all occasions for organizing work on the basis of labor-exchange (*temagae*). Unlike many analogous groups described in an earlier period for another part of rural Japan (Embree 1939: 132–38), the composition of the groups in Kurusu changed from time to time and even from season to season. Repayment of labor received was expected to be made in precise equivalents, even though no formal records were kept. People said that anyone who was known to have failed to return labor would have great difficulty in finding anyone to help him again unless he paid them in cash or in kind. It was widely remarked in those days that with the introduction of cash and machines, the exchange system was in trouble and would fade rapidly. It did just that.

Before we turn to the issue of which kinds of communal activities have survived and try to deal with the question of why others have faded, it is important to point out that the Kurusu of a generation ago presented a far less complex picture of cooperative endeavor than that reported by Embree (1939: 118–57). A few older people remembered a time when there had been cooperative credit associations of the type called *kō*, reported on extensively by Embree (1939: 138–53), but they had apparently disappeared sometime in the 1920's. Other vanished groupings were two Buddhist prayer groups—one composed of adherents of the Shingon sect, the other of Shinshū—which until World War II had met once a month. The meetings were discontinued

during the war because there was no electricity at night, and they were
never revived. I wrote of Kurusu in 1951:

Although the forms of cooperation are decreasing in number and although
rituals and ceremonies tend to become simpler and less costly, it is evident that
the community still places much value on the cooperative spirit and that it
regards itself as a distinctive social unit. . . . Kurusu takes some pride in pointing out that they have an especially strong community spirit (*danketsu-shin*) in
contrast to many of their neighboring *buraku*. . . . Whether or not they will be
able to maintain this close in-group feeling in the face of increasing mobility
and the growth of a commercial cash economy has already begun to occupy
the thoughts of some of them [R. Smith 1953:271–75].

Since these words were written Kurusu has come partly unstuck.
There are many ways in which this can happen to a community. In
Japan in recent years a not-uncommon phenomenon has been simple
attrition of population. In some places the exodus has siphoned off a
substantial proportion of the families that make up the community; in
others, most of the young people have left. In either case, cooperative
endeavor and mutual aid beyond those of the most basic kinds can no
longer be maintained for want of adequate personnel to man the
enterprises.

But Kurusu has come unstuck in a very different way, for while the
population has declined, the number of households is about the same.
Rather than attrition of membership there has been a partial disintegration of links between the households of the community. The integration was never perfect, of course, for personal likes and dislikes,
particulars of past associations between two families and so on, all
conspired to make one's relations with some people very close and
with others very distant. Nevertheless, the dominant sentiment was
that all important issues should be settled within the community itself.
Kurusu people did disagree with their neighbors on occasion, and
some of them were malicious gossips. Some men and women were
respected, while others were dismissed as weak reeds who could not be
counted on in an emergency. But care was taken to preserve the appearance of unity, or to put it more positively, much energy was devoted to the securing of hamlet-wide endorsement of decisions and
policies.

In making qualitative assessments of the degree of decline, decrease, disintegration, and other manifestations of the alienation of Kurusu households from one another, I shall of course be using as a baseline my perception of conditions there in 1951. Before we turn to a detailed consideration of the ways in which Kurusu now operates, it is important to reemphasize that in many respects it remains a corporate community, self-defined in part and administratively defined as such by many outside groups and agencies. In this section we shall discuss some of the activities that define the place internally.

From Dōgyō to Jichikai

In 1951 all households within the geographical limits of Kurusu were members of what is called the Kurusu *dōgyō*, a word written with the characters *onaji* and *yuku*. Meaning roughly "to go together," this is the motto of the Buddhist pilgrims of the Shingon sect, and originally implied that each person "goes with" Kōbo-daishi, founder of the sect, as he makes the circuit of the eighty-eight temples of Shikoku. Ordinarily the hamlet and the *dōgyō* would have been coterminous, but in 1951 the special circumstances of two households that lay outside its boundaries had led the people of Kurusu to call a meeting of the hamlet council at which it was unanimously agreed that they should be included, for both were in need of assistance of many kinds.

The *dōgyō* functioned on seven major occasions: admitting a new member household, births, weddings, funerals, hamlet festivals to the tutelary deity Jichin-san, road repair, and the autumn festival of the village deity Hachiman. Of these, the first five involved only the residents of Kurusu, and the last two tied the hamlet as an entity into larger groupings of communities. The *dōgyō* owned equipment that could be used by any member household. In one small building was kept the paraphernalia used at funerals, and in a storage building belonging to one of the families of Kurusu were kept the twenty sets of dishes, trays, and small tables to be used for serving guests at weddings and mourners at funerals, and at the festivities for the tutelary deity. No fee was charged for their use, but the borrower was obliged to replace damaged or broken items.

Kurusu is far too small to be divided into neighborhood groups, which in many larger communities in Japan have taken on many of the functions once performed by the entire hamlet. Nonetheless there is a sense in which Kurusu is perceived by many of its residents as being divided into roughly two areas of differential interaction. The break is at the small bridge in the approximate center of the hamlet, but the division of houses is far from equal. There are only eight houses in the area to the south of the bridge, the area often referred to as *oku* (back, distant, remote) by the people who live in the northern end of the settlement. The last house to the south in Kurusu bears the house-name *sora*, meaning "sky" or by implication "horizon." It is also called *shimo* (lower, the end, the last), because it is furthest from the entrance to the hamlet. Paradoxically, it is also the house from which the rotation of hamlet offices is reckoned, a role that one might have predicted would be taken by the first house, called *kami* (upper, the head, the first). In any event, informal neighborly interaction is more intense within the two areas than between them, but there are no occasions on which they are formally recognized, nor has there ever been such a time.

The word *dōgyō* is not much heard in Kurusu these days. Now almost everyone refers to the *jichikai* (self-governing association) of Kurusu and its *membā* (members), a loan word that I never heard used in 1951. The transition from *dōgyō* to *jichikai* is one of declining affectivity, and *membā* is an excellent example of the kind of neutral term to which the Japanese regularly resort when they wish to indicate that a relationship is no longer characterized by implicit or explicit ranking of any kind. The members of a self-governing association are equals; the households of a hamlet were not necessarily so.

There has been a change with respect to Kurusu's communal property as well. The small storehouses in which both sets of items were kept are gone. The hamlet no longer has need of funeral paraphernalia of any kind, and the dishes and trays that can be used by any household entertaining large numbers of visitors are now kept in the small house at the edge of the settlement that has been the Jichikai's meeting-place since 1972. It has a large room, a kitchen, and ample storage space. On the wall is a framed certificate, signed by the mayor of Yasuhara Village, awarded to the hamlet for its outstanding performance in collecting taxes in 1949.

The seven "offices" of the Kurusu Jichikai rotate on an annual basis in theory, starting with the last house at the southern extreme of the settlement. The offices are: head of the self-governing association (*jichikai-chō*), formerly the *buraku-chō* or hamlet head; the tax-collection agent (*nōzei kumiai chō*), formerly the *zeikin-gakari*; the agricultural practices representative (*nōgyō jikkō iin chō*); sponsor (*tōya*) with the sponsoring group (*tōgumi*) of the autumn festival of the Hachiman Shrine; and sponsors of the Jichin-san spring and autumn festivals. Only the head of a family can hold office and, again in theory, every meeting of the Jichikai should be attended by the family heads or their representatives. As we shall see, it has become harder and harder to get people to turn out for these occasions. The rule, nevertheless, is that the senior male of the family attends. In a house with two married couples the order of precedence would be the senior male, then the senior female, and last the junior male. The junior female would attend only under the most extraordinary circumstances.

The system of rotating offices dates from the end of World War II; until then, as one of them put it, "we old men ran the place." There appears to have been a major struggle over the decision to break the old pattern of dominance by Kurusu's larger landholders and institute a new one of equal responsibility. Another man said: "It was done not long after the end of the war. There was a big fight between the former tenants and the former landowners, and the ex-tenants finally got the more democratic system they wanted."

The word "democracy" and the barbarism "democratization" were on everyone's lips during the Occupation period, when a great many power struggles in a great many contexts were settled by adoption of what were almost invariably called anti-feudal democratic reforms. In discussing these issues with Americans, the Japanese tended to stress that changes of a fundamental nature had been wrought. I find it remarkable, therefore, that in the hundreds of hours I spent talking to Kurusu residents in 1951 and 1952 no mention at all was made of the revision of the system of assignment of offices in the association, which were generally represented as being elective in character. One reason for their silence on the matter, I suspect, is that I tended to ask how the system worked, but did not think to inquire if it had always worked that way. Another may be that they were simply concealing a recent unpleasantness from me, as for a time they were to do a quarter of a century later.

Although it is firmly established in principle, the rotation system has not always been rigidly adhered to. Two considerations may lead to deviation from the routine passage of an office around the hamlet. One man, for example, has been the agricultural practices representative for three or four years because he has more education than most men of his age, and because he has a great deal of free time at his place of work. Most people agreed, however, that the headship of the Jichikai would never be handled in this way.

The other possibility is that a house will be passed over, usually at its own request. A widow, for example, may ask that she be spared the extra burden of holding a position, especially if she has minor children to care for and little help with her work in the house and fields. A family that has only recently been admitted to the Jichikai may ask or even be requested to pass if the headship reaches their house very soon after they have been admitted, on the grounds that they do not know enough about the community, its customs, and the idiosyncrasies of its inhabitants.

This last point deserves some elaboration, for there are in effect two kinds of "new" family heads. One is the outsider who has recently built a house and moved into Kurusu. The other is the native of the place who has had a try at employment in the city and for one reason or another has returned to live in Kurusu. He is likely to know more about the place than the newcomer does, but he may share very few of the concerns of its long-term residents, especially since he is not likely to be heavily involved in agricultural pursuits.

A widow said of her situation: "My son isn't very much interested in Kurusu affairs because he was away so long. When our turn comes to be head of the Jichikai we will probably take it, though, and I will go along to the meetings with him to pour the tea for everyone. Older people don't go much anymore because the young people—they are so verbal—always take over the discussion." This is an exceedingly disingenuous remark, for the speaker's interest in Kurusu affairs is matched in intensity only by her outspokenness at association meetings.

The head of the Jichikai is paid a very small fee, but by Kurusu custom he uses it to defray expenses of the regular meetings of the association rather than keeping it for himself. He has a great many duties, including the circulation of official and unofficial notices to all the member families by means of a portable notice-board which he takes to the house at the southernmost end of the settlement from where it is passed on from house to house until all have seen it.

The Jichikai ordinarily meets at least once or twice a year, when there is some business or a problem to discuss. It is the responsibility of the Jichikai head to schedule the meetings, set the agenda, and guide the discussion.

In the old days we used to argue a lot, but we always reached consensus. Now people don't even want to attend the meetings. They say that they're too busy, which in many cases is true, but some just can't bear to miss their favorite evening television programs. Why, I remember one meeting just after the war which was called to discuss the government's grain requisition program—so many people crowded into our house that one corner of the floor gave way! Even when we quarreled it was always fun and meetings sometimes went on for hours and hours. These days people try to speed things up and get the business out of the way as quickly as they can. Mostly only the older men go, although an older woman might represent her family if her husband is away or if she is widowed. Young people? They never consider anything from the point of view of the hamlet and its interests. They are not really that much concerned one way or the other.

The other offices can be disposed of briefly. The principal task of the tax collection agent is to make a monthly collection of payments on various taxes and the national health insurance, which he deposits to the individual family accounts in the Agricultural Cooperative. If all the member families pay up early, the Jichikai receives a certificate and a nominal cash award; it is likely to be the holder of the office rather than the families of a community who decides to try for such recognition of community spirit.

The agricultural practices representative collects the dues from member households of the Agricultural Cooperative and was formerly responsible for circulating notices from the cooperative and the Town Office dealing with agricultural practices, new techniques, and so on. The installation of the broadcast relay system in 1960 has greatly reduced his responsibilities, since general information on agricultural matters as well as specific dates for the spraying of insecticides, prices of grain and delivery dates, and so on, are now usually broadcast to all households. For some years he arranged for bulk purchases of staple foods and basic consumer goods for member houses. This program, a function of the Women's Section of the Agricultural Cooperative, became a source of conflict within the hamlet. Not every family wanted to participate, particularly after living conditions began to improve, and some houses were not much interested because their non-agricultural activities produced such items as sugar, Aji-no-moto, salt, and the like, in the form of gifts or as partial payment for services rendered. Their withdrawal from the program drew the charge by other families that they were selfishly denying potential savings to others. However that may be, today only the more isolated hamlets still make use of it, and supermarkets, which offer greater variety and better prices, are cutting sharply into the retail services of the Agricultural Cooperative.

Entering the Dōgyō

It used to be that when a new household was taken into Kurusu, a simple ceremony called *dōgyō-iri* (entering the *dōgyō*) was held. It was essentially a welcoming party held at the house of the newcomers, who provided food for the representatives of member households who attended. The newcomers received no gifts, and paid an initiation fee of ¥50, accepting the privileges and acknowledging the responsibilities of membership.

Today the occasion is marked even less elaborately, but admission is neither automatic nor meaningless, as the following comment reveals:

We don't have a general meeting when members are taken in any more. What happens is that after they have been here a while the head of the family goes to the Jichikai head and asks to be admitted to membership. It's always discussed at a meeting, but there is hardly ever any question about it, especially if it's a request from a family who has built a house here. The Jichikai still has to approve, though. The family pays somewhere around ¥3–5,000 as an entrance fee, which is deposited to the association's account. Some Sunday, then, the head of the family makes the rounds of the hamlet accompanied by the head of the Jichikai. He is introduced at every house and usually leaves a present of a towel (*tenugui*) or small wrapping-cloth (*furoshiki*)—just a token. We admit new members formally because Kurusu owns some forest land and we feel that the people who live here deserve a share in that land and the eventual proceeds from the sale of timber from it.

Such generosity may not last, and it appears to be absent from many places closer to the city. By all accounts it is far more difficult for newcomers to secure hamlet membership in the suburbanizing areas outside Takamatsu. So many commuters have moved into these for mer agricultural villages that in some hamlets the population of white-collar workers is about the same as that of the local farmers. The resulting conflict has been so great that in some communities each group has formed its own Jichikai. This has not happened in Kurusu, where the head of every member household will take his turn as head of the Jichikai and will assume most of the other offices as they rotate through the hamlet.

Birth

In 1951, when a birth occurred in Kurusu, word was spread by the hamlet head and the head of the Kurusu Women's Association, who made the rounds of hamlet houses and collected ¥30 from each to make up a gift to the family. No party was held, but every donor received a box of five cakes of a kind called *o-manjū* on the child's naming day.

Some years ago the amount of money collected from each household was raised to ¥100 and the wife of the head of the Jichikai was assigned the task of making the rounds. Most people feel that even the new assessment is so small that they must supplement it with an additional gift. The cakes received in return today are store-bought, attractively boxed, and bear the character *kotobuki* (good fortune). Those who give an extra ¥1,000 or so on their own usually make the gesture when the child is born to close neighbors with whom daily interaction is likely to be fairly intense. A woman told us that she tends to give the extra sum to those families who live on her side of the small bridge in the middle of Kurusu; those who live to the south of it seem to her more remote socially as well as physically.

Sending Off the Bride

When a hamlet woman was to be married, and thus leave Kurusu, women from all the houses were invited to a sending-off party, variously called *o-mitate* or *o-yorokobi*, held at her home shortly before the date set for the wedding. Similar parties were held for young men marrying out of the community as adopted husbands; the guests were the men of Kurusu on such occasions.

In 1975 it was still the custom for most houses to hold the sending-off parties for their children who are leaving Kurusu to be married. These occasions are almost universally observed on Sundays nowadays, so that as many working women or men as possible can attend. By all accounts the parties have become more and more elaborate, just as weddings and funerals have.

Weddings

At weddings the *dōgyō* figured in a very central way. Inasmuch as intra-hamlet marriage was extremely rare, a wedding was the occasion on which either the bride or the adopted husband entered the community as a new member of the *dōgyō*. The wedding ceremony was held in the house of the groom in the case of regular marriages, and before the arrival of the bride the *dōgyō* women assembled there for a meal and to meet her. Every household sent its oldest still-married woman (widows were ruled out as patently inauspicious to the occasion), who brought with her one *shō* of rice. After they had all gathered they were served a meal, and as they were finishing eating, the bride was brought into the room and introduced to them. She exchanged ceremonial greetings with the women's representative, by Kurusu custom the oldest member of the group. The bride then withdrew, leaving the women to chat for a while, gather up their gifts and unconsumed food, by Japanese usage always wrapped up to be taken home, and return to their houses. These occasions were extremely festive, and there were one or two women noted for their high good humor who could be counted on to sing or tell a good story. When the marriage was uxorilocal the same sequence was observed, but the ceremony was held at the bride's house and the men of Kurusu came to meet the adopted husband.

Weddings are today the occasion for both the affirmation of residual hamlet solidarity and the drawing of a clear distinction between kinsmen and neighbors. The major change in wedding practices has been the introduction of the wedding hall, an institution unknown to villagers in 1951. Kurusu people do not go as far as Takamatsu's big establishments, preferring their somewhat more modest and certainly less expensive counterparts in the satellite towns that lie between Kurusu and the city. In the opposite direction, toward the south, the Shionoe Hot Springs Hotel offers what the staff referred to as "a nice wedding" for about ¥10,000 per person. This 1975 fee included a fixed meal, a small gift for each guest, transportation in hotel-owned cars for the bride and groom, and the use of the banquet room. This figure represents a great deal of money to any Kurusu family, no matter how well off it might be, for rural weddings routinely involve invitations to from thirty to fifty guests.

In recent years, weddings have come to take three forms. The first is the formerly universal one, in which the entire ceremony is conducted at the house of the groom. The sequence is much as it was twenty-five years ago. In the second, the ceremony is split into two parts; the first is held at the house of the groom, the second at the wedding hall. The final form is that in which the entire ceremony takes place at the wedding hall. Bearing in mind that the ceremony serves the dual purpose of recruiting a new member into the hamlet as well as into one family, let us consider the three forms of the wedding ceremony as they are opted for in Kurusu.

It is generally felt that the child who is most likely to be the successor, whether or not it is the first son, should be married in the family's house. Such a wedding gives the bride maximum exposure in surroundings that most hamlet women find congenial, and it meets one other important requirement. Since the successor and his bride at some point in their lives will be taking over the main house, the bride must be introduced to the ancestors and pay her respects to them. Thus holding the entire ceremony in the groom's house continues to serve the dual purpose of inducting the bride into her husband's household and into the hamlet in the manner now regarded as traditional.

Of the two newer kinds of wedding ceremonies, the more common is that held in two parts, the first at the groom's house and the second at the wedding hall. Although the women assemble at the house of the groom where they meet the bride, and although the bride pays her respects to the ancestors there, this form of wedding is not favored for first sons and those already designated alternate successors. Among the many negative comments that we heard about it, most dealt with the summary treatment accorded the women of the hamlet. They come to the house and are served a full-course meal, and when they are almost finished eating the bride is brought in and introduced to them by the groom's mother. Mother-in-law and daughter-in-law do not stay long, however, but after a perfunctory greeting withdraw to go to the wedding hall, which runs on a tight schedule on the favored auspicious dates for weddings. It seems a cool and impersonal affair by contrast to the old days: "No one much likes this new way of doing things. It's really flat and a lot less fun than it used to be."

The most extreme break with custom, the ceremony that is held entirely at the wedding hall, is usually chosen under one of two conditions. A small family that lacks nearby kinsmen to help out at home will resort to it for want of an alternative. More commonly, however, such weddings are given for non-successors: "Our second son was married at a wedding hall, rather than here at home, because he is not the successor and was going to live in a new house, where there were no ancestors to whom his bride had to pay her respects. We still had the Kurusu women bussed down to the hall to present her to them, rather than going to all the trouble of having them here." In these cases the wedding hall sends a small bus to pick up the hamlet women and take them to the establishment where they will meet the bride. This is widely regarded as being the least enjoyable version of this part of the ceremony, for it leaves the women stranded in a strange place until the bus is available to bring them back to Kurusu.

It is said that until some time before World War II weddings were three-day affairs, but by 1951 they lasted only one day, as they do now. A man who had recently served as a go-between for a couple said that he would never do it again: "Weddings used to be great occasions, with lots of *sake* and lots of gaiety. But this wedding! It was at an expensive hall and was very grand, but just as I was getting warmed up the couple rushed off to catch a plane for their honeymoon in Hokkaido, leaving all of the guests behind. Who feels like drinking when you've been run out on like that?"

It is not only the convivial drinker who laments the passing of the old-fashioned wedding. A woman in her forties told us:

When the entire ceremony is held at the wedding hall, they put the women of the hamlet in one room and the relatives in another. The bride and her mother-in-law pop in and pop right out again, and that's that. Even when the bride is presented to the group at the groom's house, the bride and the wedding party leave them high and dry, saying, "Please enjoy yourselves." Nobody does.

The meal served the hamlet women is quite elaborate—soup, *sushi* (vinegared rice), *sekihan* (glutinous rice with red beans), and noodles (*udon*), but never the buckwheat noodles called *soba*. *Udon* is a thick noodle made of wheat flour; *soba*, which is thinner and breaks more easily, is considered highly inauspicious to the occasion. In 1951 all of the food was prepared in the kitchen of the house, but by 1975 the custom was to have such feasts catered, preparing only the soup at home. The expense is not inconsiderable, since, as one woman put it, "You can't serve anything but a full-course meal nowadays."

One woman who was telling us about all of this observed that most families are obliged to give only one big wedding, that of their first sons or successors.

But we had the bad luck to have to give two, for both of our sons. When our eldest son got married, it was understood that he and his wife would be living in Nagoya, but you have to do your first son's wedding right. So we held it here in this house because you never know when a first son might come back, and if his bride has not been properly introduced to the hamlet women, she couldn't look people in the eye. It had been decided that our second son would be the successor and live here, so naturally we gave another big wedding. He and his wife moved out six months later, after she had a miscarriage.

The two weddings cost a lot of money, but after all it turned out that we did the right thing because our first son and his family have moved back from Nagoya and they live here now. He and his wife work in Takamatsu. In the old days, we'd not have had such a big wedding for our second son because there would have been no chance of his becoming the successor.

In this last comment she is quite wrong. Then as now, succession plans often changed because the first son failed to assume the headship of the family (see Chapter Two).

Funerals

It was at funerals that the *dōgyō* assumed the greatest variety of responsibilities. When the head of the hamlet was notified of the death of a hamlet resident, he and others, usually volunteers, undertook to notify relatives of the deceased who lived elsewhere. There being almost no telephones in 1951, they went on foot or by bicycle; telegrams were sent to those who lived in more distant places. The older women prepared the funeral shroud, which was delivered at once to the house of the deceased. On the day after the death, one woman from each household went to help prepare food for the funeral feast, and one group of men made ready the funeral paraphernalia, cleaning and repairing it before carrying it all to the house where the ceremony was to be held. A second group of men, carrying wood, straw, and charcoal, went to the hamlet cremation-ground and prepared the spot for the funeral pyre. Others went to the house of the deceased to help look after the arriving mourners. Every house sent a contribution of one *shō* of rice.

Following the first part of the funeral service, conducted in the main room of the house by the Buddhist priest and attended only by members of the family and intimate friends of the deceased, men of the *dōgyō* carried out the coffin and placed it in the palanquin which they carried in the procession, led by the priest and followed by all the other members of the *dōgyō* who were present. At a spot somewhere between the house and the cremation-ground, the procession stopped and the hamlet people took leave of the deceased, returning to his house to clean up, wash the dishes, and return them to the community storehouse. A small group of men of the *dōgyō*, accompanied by the immediate kin and the priest, carried the coffin on up to the cremation-ground, lit the pyre, and supervised the lengthy process of reducing the body to a small pile of bones and ashes by the following morning when the members of the family would come to collect them.

Although the conduct of funerals has changed greatly over the past quarter-century, the *dōgyō* still performs crucial functions. The older women gather and sew the shroud, and on the day of the funeral the hamlet people cook for the family of the deceased and their relatives. As we have seen, the funeral service formerly had three distinct parts, and in all three stages of the ceremony, the Buddhist priest played an important role. He still has a central role, but the structure of the ceremony now involves him less and the undertaker—a specialist known only by reputation in 1951—has taken up a position at stage center. Even the town government has come to play a vital role.

Today, with rare exceptions, the procession and parting ceremony have been dispensed with completely, and the funeral proper is held entirely in the house of the deceased. The altar and its decorations are all rented from the mortuary, as is the brocade covering for the coffin, the artificial flowers, lanterns, and candles. All of this costs money, of course, and many other expensive items have been introduced in the intervening years. It has long been the custom for large wreaths of artificial flowers to be placed beside the altar and outside the house where a funeral is being held. Formerly they were invariably black and white, the colors of death and mourning since early times, and some families still request that only these austere wreaths be sent. They are more often multicolored, reminding one man of the kinds of floral tributes sent to the owner of a newly opened business: "A house where there is a funeral looks like a new pinball parlor on opening day."

When the conclusion of the rites at the house, the coffin is taken to the crematorium in a hearse, which is followed by the mourners riding in automobiles. The town provides the hearse and in 1960 built the crematorium, which is electric with an oil-furnace back-up. Everyone in Shionoe Town now takes advantage of these new facilities, which have had a dramatic impact on funeral customs. Not only have the old hamlet cremation-grounds been abandoned, but the centralizing of cremation has led directly to the abandonment of the procession and the farewell ceremony, since one could not possibly walk to the new crematorium from most places in Shionoe Town. The traditional procession still survives in places nearer Takamatsu, where the distance between any house in the community and the old cremation spots is not very great. Further changes related to the distances involved include the growing tendency for the priest not to attend the cremation as he formerly did. One priest estimated that in about half of the funerals in which he had participated in recent years he had skipped the cremation ceremony, either because he was too busy or because the family preferred to save the fee that they would otherwise have had to pay for his rather perfunctory performance there.

Finally, the new crematorium has entailed abandonment of the style of coffin that has been used in Kurusu since the oldest people can remember. It was a cask of the kind in which the corpse was seated in a flexed position, but neither the hearse nor the furnace door of the crematorium can accommodate a coffin of such height. As a consequence the dead now lie in oblong boxes, aptly called "sleeping coffins," and are committed to the furnace clothed in the traditional white shroud, flat on their backs.

When a person dies it is usually members of the family who contact friends and relatives rather than the Jichikai head. This formerly very complicated task has been much simplified by the nearly universal accessibility of the telephone. A member of the family notifies the Jichikai head, however, who must still be sure to inform all households in Kurusu. He will also select or accept the volunteered services of one or two people to go to the house of the deceased as representatives of the *dōgyō*. They pay a formal call to express condolences, and all member-households begin to plan for cooking and otherwise assisting the bereaved household. On the day of the funeral, in addition to all the helpers from the hamlet who are at work in the kitchen, at least one member of every family attends the ceremony itself, offering incense and prayers at the altar on which the coffin rests. The event is considered of sufficient importance that people readily take time off from work for the occasion.

After the funeral services the relatives of the deceased go on to the crematorium while the *dōgyō* members stay at the house and clean up the kitchen and wash the dishes. When the relatives return with the ashes, they in turn serve a meal to the members of the *dōgyō* who have helped with the funeral. In Kurusu this is now done all in one day, although until a few years ago most families chose to serve the return meal to the *dōgyō* members on the day following the funeral or on the seventh day after the cremation. There are two reasons for serving the return meal on the same day as the funeral. The first is that the cremation is now completed in very short order; when the old cremation grounds were still in use, the pyre was lighted in the afternoon but the ashes could not be collected until the morning of the following day. The second is that with so many people working full-time, it is considered preferable to dispose of all the requirements on the day that many will have taken off from work. Nevertheless, in some nearby hamlets, the member households still bring cooked food to the bereaved family for the first seven days, when all are polluted by death in the house and are in theory forbidden to use fire, and are only then served the return meal by the family.

Spring and Autumn Festivals of the Tutelary Deity

There is a small Shinto shrine in Kurusu that houses the hamlet's tutelary deity. A small stone gateway stands at the bottom of a short flight of rustic stone steps that lead up to a pedestal on which rests a large boulder representing Jichin-san, Protector of the Land. Many people refer to this deity as Ushi-gami-sama, the Cow God, and until some time around the turn of the century small straw figures of cows were offered here on festival days. In 1951 only one of the oldest men in Kurusu still observed the custom, usually in the company of his small grandson.

Because it represents an important example of the many ways in which over the years the central government has attempted to manipulate and redirect local religious sentiment (Fridell 1973), the history of Kurusu's shrine is of considerable interest. Prior to 1916 it was one of the important lesser shrines of the area, and a small wooden building housing the deity stood at the top of the flight of stairs. In 1915 the Nishitani Hachiman Shrine of Yasuhara was elevated from the rank of village shrine (*sonsha*) to that of county shrine (*gōsha*), and in short order the small shrines of all thirty-seven of Yasuhara's hamlets were physically removed there as a step in the government's campaign to consolidate both sentiment and loyalty on a village-wide basis.

The government failed to anticipate or chose to ignore the principal effect of this administrative coup, which was to leave the hamlets, territorial units par excellence, bereft of their tutelary deities. As was to happen in many such small communities throughout the country, sentiment soon developed in Kurusu to rectify an intolerable situation. Since there was no possibility of actually retrieving the original shrine and its gateway, the hamlet people erected the present gateway and the stone pedestal on the old site of Kurusu Shrine, and it is there that the spring and fall festivals to Jichin-san are observed. The major observances of New Year's and the autumn festival are held at the Hachiman Shrine itself, and many Kurusu people make a special point of visiting the original shrine building there on those two occasions.

A system of rotating sponsorship was used for the festivals of Jichin-san, held on the middle days of the vernal and autumnal equinoxes. All households participated regardless of whether they were agricultural, for Jichin-san is the hamlet's patron, not the deity of farmers alone. In 1952 each farming household gave one *shō* of mugi and each non-farming household the rough equivalent in cash to the sponsor, who could count on the assistance of the two houses on either side of his in preparing for the festival. Up to some time before World

War II—no one was really sure when the decline set in—it was the custom to avoid entering the fields on Jichin-san's festival days, and people called at the sponsor's house to receive festival foods and *sake*. In 1952, the Shinto priest arrived in the afternoon of the day of the festival, and accompanied by the sponsor, a large number of children, and a handful of older people, went to the shrine for a brief ceremony. When it was over the cakes from the altar were distributed among the children and everyone went home. There were no other observances, in sharp contrast to the days before the merger of the hamlet shrines, when at Jichin-san's autumn festival there were night-time *sumō* wrestling matches and other contests of strength among the young men.

The two festivals are still sponsored in rotation by all the houses of Kurusu. Most of our inquiries about the shrine—which appeared to be untended between the festivals, just as had been the case twenty-five years before—brought comments like "No one worships there any more," but in fact the ceremonies have been held annually without interruption. Indeed, they are almost the only rituals that are still observed on the proper days (*ataru hi*) indicated by the ceremonial calendar, instead of on the more convenient Sunday. Some people thought that this was the case because no one attended the ceremonies anyway, and a man who remembered going with me to the Kurusu Shrine in 1952 said: "The festivals have changed a lot. No one pays any attention these days. Why, taking up a collection for *sake* is just a waste. A one-*shō* bottle would be too much for those old women and their grandchildren who show up." As we have seen, however, in this instance the memories of the people of Kurusu have betrayed them; almost no one went to the shrine twenty-five years ago either.

When the sponsor makes his rounds of the hamlet households to collect the money used to pay the priest and buy the *sake* and offerings—now ¥200 from each family—he informs everyone of the date of the festival, and is likely to remind everyone again a few days before it occurs. Otherwise, he is required only to arrange for the Shinto priest to come, and it is still the custom that the priest first stops at the house of the sponsor to worship the gods who are there.

I had to ask several people in order to find out who was to be the sponsor of the upcoming autumn festival. This situation was so intriguingly different from that of 1951, when anyone could have told me who it was, that I asked an older man what would happen if some year the family whose turn it was to take the sponsorship simply failed to arrange for the observance. He was rightly offended: "It may be a lot simpler than it used to be, but that doesn't mean that it's not important."

Sponsorship of the Autumn Festival of the Hachiman Shrine

The sponsorship of the autumn festival of the Nishitani Hachiman Shrine is also handled on a rotating basis. Until 1943 the sponsoring group (*tōgumi*) in a given year was one of the nine hamlets in Yasuhara Village, or one of the three big landlords of the village. Following a series of complicated changes just after the war, Kurusu was designated one of the ten parishioner-hamlets which bore the responsibility for serving as sponsoring group in its turn. Within the sponsoring hamlet the head of one household, chosen by lot, was responsible for coordinating the activities of the group. His duties were considered very onerous, both financially and in terms of the demands on his time. When Kurusu's turn had come a few years before my first stay there, all the residents of the place had contributed ¥30 a month for three full years to make up a fund of about ¥20,000 for festival expenses, an enormous sum for the time. The man who had served as sponsor on that occasion told me that he had very little difficulty in securing regular contributions because the prestige and reputation of the hamlet were at stake.

Among the many duties of the sponsoring group was the training of the young men of the hamlet who were to perform the lion dances that were an indispensible part of any major Shinto festival of the time. On the festival day, the lion-dancers made the rounds of all the hamlets, collecting cash donations and consuming considerable quantities of *sake* as rewards for their amusing and exciting antics. The cash thus collected was usually spent on a party for the young men and the musicians who accompanied them on their rounds.

On October 14, about two weeks before the rice harvest in this area, the god was brought down the steps of his shrine by the men of the sponsoring hamlet and carried about the vicinity of the shrine to survey the crops. Vendors set up stalls all along the road and the paths near the shrine, and in 1951 there were throngs of people, including what seemed to be every child in Yasuhara. Nonetheless, older people complained even then that the festivals lacked the color and spark they once had. On October 15 the residents of the hamlet all came to the house of the sponsor for a party to celebrate the end of their duties until their turn in the cycle came around again.

Kurusu is now one of eight hamlets in the jurisdiction of the shrine that must assume the sponsorship. In recent years the ceremonial schedule of the major Shinto establishment of the area has been completely rearranged with a view to producing even a modest turnout of its parishioners. The spring and autumn festivals (formerly held on April 20 and October 14) are now held on the Sundays nearest those dates, and beginning in the early 1970's the summer festival has been held on August 14, the middle day of the Buddhist festival of the dead. The implications of this seemingly innocuous shift are stunning. Locally, Shinto has fallen to such low estate that the best hope of getting some people to come to the shrine is to have its festival coincide with the great Buddhist festival, when people are visiting their native places. In 1975 the observance of Hachiman's summer festival was wiped out by a major typhoon, a development that might have given pause to those responsible for rescheduling this festival for a god of growth, purity, and light to coincide with the observance of rites that stress darkness and death.

None of the concessions made to the new employment patterns of rural residents has had the desired effect. Old people complain that the Hachiman festivities are no longer fun, no matter when they are held, or that they are bleak or dull, especially since the lion dances have been given up. There simply are not enough young men with sufficient interest and time to practice them, and attempts to revive this colorful aspect of the celebrations have proved only sporadically successful. An older man commented unfavorably on the transformation of the festival market into a string of stalls chiefly selling cheap toys for the children. Far more important, the agricultural implications of the festival have dimmed, as is shown in one small way, as in so many large ones: the sponsor formerly collected first-fruits of rice and mugi from every family to offer to the shrine; now they each contribute ¥500 in cash instead.

Road Repair (Michi-tsukuri)

Road repair, once organized on a village-wide basis by the village office, was scheduled for a day shortly before the autumn festival of Hachiman. Each hamlet was responsible for cleaning and repairing the roads and paths within its borders, and every household sent one adult member of either sex to join in the work. People gathered in the mid-morning, decided how to organize the work, and set about it with much joking and laughter. The work was not really strenuous, and the occasion was particularly joyful because it marked the approach of the biggest and gayest of the local festivals. The job was usually done by late afternoon. By the early 1970's road repair had ceased to be a hamlet function at all. The town government has assumed responsibility for the upkeep of the roads, most of which in the Kurusu area have been paved in recent years. Because it was tied closely to the fall festival of Hachiman, the disappearance of the communal road repair has somewhat diminished the corporate implications of the larger event.

The Women's Association

The women of Kurusu and those of two adjacent hamlets formerly belonged to a branch of the Yasuhara Village Women's Association (*fujin kai*). It had been very active during World War II, making up gift packages for servicemen and conducting classes in cooking and home-making designed to teach women how to compensate for the disappearance of many food and consumer items from the market.

After the war they undertook several programs, but the group's meetings drew only modest attendance, for this was the period of the greatest hardship for rural people, and the women were far too preoccupied with their own work to care much about its activities. The association attempted to promote the simplification of weddings and funerals so as to reduce the great financial burden they imposed on many families, and it used the very interesting argument that much of the money was spent on meeting traditional requirements which had lost most of their meaning anyway. It helped secure contracts for the women engaged in household industries, sharing such work among its members, and tried to assist widows who were having a difficult time financially.

The Kurusu Women's Association, to which all women of the hamlet formerly belonged, has been moribund since some time in the late 1960's. Its fate is an excellent illustration of the kinds of friction that have developed in Kurusu over the years. Some people attribute its demise to the fact that the many women who are employed full-time have no time to participate in its activities. Others say that the companies for which women work sponsor their own clubs and activities, rendering the association superfluous.

On the face of it, both explanations are plausible enough, but the collapse actually began a few years before women entered the job market in significant numbers. Here is one version of the story:

I'll tell you what happened. It all started with that ill-fated plan for a trip to the hot-springs in the mid-1960's. We had asked for some money from the hamlet treasury and every member was putting a small amount of money in the club treasury to supplement the budget for the trip. When the time came, some of the women who had jobs could not go. The club officers went ahead with the plan, and told everyone that they would use only the hamlet funds and the contributions of those who actually went on the excursion, but the ones who didn't go claimed that the others had used their money, too. There was a lot of bad feeling, and although the club kept meeting for a while, fewer and fewer women came.

Finally, the head of the Kurusu Women's Association asked the head of the Yasuhara area association for permission to suspend her duties temporarily. Her request was approved. She explained that she had not wanted simply to resign her office because she did not want people to be angry. No one thinks that the association will be reactivated.

The Kurusu Irrigation Union (Kurusu Yōsui Kumiai)

If there is a single feature of wet-rice agriculture calculated to insure the continuation of cooperative and collaborative enterprise under even the most trying circumstances it is the irrigation system. The rice producer has no choice but to work in concert with others who cultivate land within the same small piece of the mosaic of the river-valley system in which his village lies. He cannot make arbitrary decisions, nor can he decide independently of his neighbors when to take in water, raise or lower the levels in his fields, and when to drain them. Thus, while Japanese agricultural communities, like such communities everywhere, may be disintegrating in other ways, there remains in every hamlet in Japan a powerful organized body that requires the participation of every eligible family (Yoden 1970:63).

Kagawa Prefecture's mild, dry climate has plagued its farmers for centuries. The rainy season from mid-June to mid-July accounts for almost one-fourth of the prefecture's sparse annual precipitation. There is an apt local saying, "Kōchi floods, Kagawa droughts." The heavy rains fall on the Kōchi side of the mountain divide, while there are severe droughts in Kagawa. The worst of these in modern times occurred in 1916, 1929, 1934, and 1939, but the one of 1934 was particularly cruel—a parched August was followed in September by the worst recorded typhoon of the prewar years—and agricultural production declined by 56 percent from the previous year (Yabe 1949:39).

As a consequence of this continuing serious problem, the various levels of government have over the years attempted to stabilize the supply of water for irrigation through the building of agricultural catchment ponds and major reservoirs. In this respect Kurusu has always occupied a rather fortunate position. About 95 percent of its water is taken from the Kōtō River by gravity flow, obviating the need for irrigation pumps. Moreover, the system was greatly improved in 1943 and 1944 when the government subsidized the construction of small dams and channels in the riverbed in an effort to raise production of grain by providing a more stable supply of irrigation water. Indeed, the last serious flooding of the Kōtō River that affected Kurusu directly occurred in 1918, and the small feeder stream that runs through the hamlet has never posed a serious threat to the fields.

Nonetheless, of all the activities that involve most but not all the households of the hamlet, the most important by far is the Kurusu Irrigation Union, established in roughly its present form in 1948. In the early years its budget ran between ¥20,000 and ¥25,000, and in 1951 it counted as its members all twenty-nine resident and non-resident households who cultivated land in Kurusu.

The position of union head was always held by a Kurusu man. Before 1948, the affairs relating to irrigation water were managed by a respected and trusted individual who was known as *ide-oya*, a term whose two characters mean literally "well" or by extension "water," and "parent" or "father." It was his duty to organize inspection of the entire irrigation system that serves the paddy fields of Kurusu and to preside over discussions and make decisions about maintenance and repairs. At times of drought and flood he exercised unquestioned authority over the disposition and distribution of the water. Before the construction of the reservoir at the Naiba Dam in Shionoe and various other improvements to the system, when there were flash floods and water shortages along the river, the *ide-oya* occupied a crucial position. People in their sixties today remember watching him set up an incense stick at the sluice gate and light it. These sticks were designed to burn just long enough for the irrigation of one *tan* of paddy field; when it burned down, the gate was closed and the next one opened and the process repeated.

In 1951 the old system had given way to the new, and the head of the irrigation union was elected annually, to what was universally regarded as an onerous and demanding job. Every member household was assessed annual dues, which were calculated on the basis of total estimated cost of all the work to be undertaken in a twelve-month period by the union, apportioned on the basis of the amount of land each member household cultivated in Kurusu. The assessment could be paid in cash, in kind, or in labor, or any combination of these. Thus a family could send a member to work at the fixed rate of ¥150 per day or it could sell the union straw mats of the kind used in shoring up earthen banks and channels. The value of these contributions in labor and materials was deducted from the assessment and the balance paid in cash. In 1951, only one member household paid more than half of its assessment in cash, which was scarce then. The assessment that year was ¥440 per *tan* of paddy-field land cultivated within the area under the jurisdiction of the union.

At the end of the year, if the planning had been well carried out and if no emergencies had arisen, all the funds in the union's treasury would be exhausted. Also at year's end, the group threw a party for all of its members. This affair, held at one of the larger houses in the hamlet, was usually attended by the heads of all member households, for in addition to eating and drinking, there was the business of launching the coming year's operation by electing the new head after the incumbent had read his financial report. For some years the man who had been *ide-oya* before the war was repeatedly returned to office in the elections because of his experience and high standing in the eyes of his fellows.

In 1975 the Kurusu Irrigation Union had a membership of twenty households—twelve from Kurusu, five from neighboring Chūtoku, and three from other nearby hamlets. Membership remains compulsory for all who cultivate paddy fields in Kurusu. The head still keeps the record book and arranges discussions of proposed work on the irrigation system for the year in which he will hold office. The cost of repairs and general maintenance is still apportioned among all the households on the basis of the amount of land they cultivate in the hamlet.

Every spring two people from every household in the Kurusu Irrigation Union go up to the place in the river, about two kilometers upstream, to check on the condition of the diversion channel that carries the water to Kurusu. They do whatever cleaning and maintenance are required well before transplanting time. About the end of May, all the irrigation channels within the hamlet must be weeded and cleared of silt. In the old days, even the children turned out to help, bringing straw mats and old clothing to use in shoring up the channel banks, but today all the channels are concrete and the weeds along them can be cut in very short order with the new motorized portable cutters.

Nevertheless, things can go wrong, and when one household has a problem and wants to suggest repairs, the members of the union are called to come and survey the situation. They decide whether or not they want to undertake them, but it is clearly in the interest of the member households to keep the assessments, and therefore the number and scale of jobs to which they commit themselves, as low as possible. Only routine maintenance and clearly major threats to the whole system provoke quick approval of corrective action. There is, for example, one spot in Kurusu where an irrigation channel that leads past the house-yard of one dwelling into the paddy of another farmer regularly overflows. The union attempted to remedy this situation one year, but without success. When asked by both parties to try again, the membership refused to do so on the grounds that the small likelihood of correcting the problem did not justify the expense.

If for any reason a paddy field in Kurusu is not being cultivated—an inconceivable case in 1951, but one which did occur with a very large field in 1975—its owner or renter will not be assessed at all. This obvi-

ously means that the shares of all other members will be proportion-
ately greater, but no one objects in the rare event that a field is left
to lie fallow, on the ground that only for very good reason would a
farmer make such an extraordinary decision.

Members still have the option of paying cash or working off their
assessments by supplying labor and materials. In 1973, when the assessment was ¥2,600 per ten ares, the daily rate for work for the union
was ¥1,200 for men and ¥1,000 for women. Since many people make
a great deal more at their regular jobs, it is hardly surprising that most
elected to pay cash rather than to take the time to work off part of
their assessment.

As an example of how the system worked in 1973, let us consider
the case of one household with just under four *tan*, assessed a total of
¥8,160. Rather than pay out so much cash, they contributed labor,
some straw mats, and a few other items used in repairs, valued at a
total of ¥5,560. They paid the balance in cash. Depending on a family's circumstances in a given year, its members may contribute so
much labor that it will receive money from the union rather than paying any out. As in the past, the treasury is supposed to be completely
empty on December 31, and on January 1 the new head takes over. It
has been many years since the year-end party has been held. Thus
shorn of virtually all of its social importance, the matter of irrigation
management on the technical level nonetheless remains the bastion of
communal activity. In other communities where new kinds of large-
scale irrigation systems have been built, even this has been swept away
(Shimpo 1974:489).

Much of the material presented in this chapter is representative of
what has happened to agricultural communities throughout Japan, for
all have been exposed to the same processes that have so greatly
weakened hamlet ties. But Kurusu has gone through an experience
which, while by no means rare, so severely strained relations among its
residents that for a time it appeared to them that the hamlet's corporate character would be lost forever. That experience is the subject of
the next chapter.

CHAPTER EIGHT

The Decline of Hamlet Solidarity

THROUGHOUT THE early weeks of our return visit, collection of the obvious kinds of material went very smoothly, both in the Town Office and in the community. People were eager to tell me about many things that had happened since 1952, and I became reacquainted with grandfathers and grandmothers who, when I had first known them, were vigorous heads of families, and met the children of young men and women who had themselves been boys and girls in 1952. My wife and I visited the houses where we found anyone at home, looked through the family photograph albums, and lighted incense at the ancestral altars on behalf of the spirits of people I had known who had since died. We talked about old times, and about those who had moved away to the cities, and reminisced about festivals and weddings and all of the community activities that had changed so much in character or disappeared altogether.

It was all very pleasant and occasionally poignant. What, then, could possibly account for the vague feeling of unease that finally was crystallized for me when, after one particularly long day of making our rounds, my wife asked, "Are Kagawa farmers always so guarded and reserved?" I had never thought them reserved, but because she had not known them before, the question struck me with special force. Something was wrong.

And then one day it all came out. We were sitting one afternoon with an older woman and her small granddaughter, watching a televi-

Some of the material in this chapter and the Epilogue appeared in slightly different form in the *Journal of Japanese Studies* (R. Smith 1976). I am grateful to the editors for granting permission to adapt portions of that article for inclusion here.

sion program. Without preamble, she said, "All those things they are saying about us are lies!" We were stunned, for no one had said anything to us about her or her family. We assured her that she was mistaken and that we had no idea what she meant. But she was not to be deterred, and launched into a rambling, disconnected account of a series of events that had occurred in Kurusu more than two years before. The events she described were disturbing enough, but what was genuinely shocking was the obvious depth of her bitterness and anger.

As she talked, it slowly dawned on me that there had been one very peculiar circumstance attending all of our calls at houses in the community: we had never found other visitors there. The significance of that new pattern of behavior was brought home to me as we listened to the woman's story. For the three weeks that we had been there, the people of Kurusu had been concealing what they regarded as a shameful episode in the life of their community. Two years before, the place had been torn apart by something called the Clover affair. Whatever that was, it had left its mark to such an extent that people had stopped dropping in to visit one another. As the old woman went on with her story the television screen flickered with images of Japan's feudal past. Her granddaughter dozed off. We were transfixed.

This is the substance of what she told us. Just after New Year's in 1973 a subsidiary of a large corporation had approached the Town Office about the possibility of acquiring some land on which to build a factory. They had scouted the area and had tentatively selected a site not far from the mushroom nursery and the storage facility for human waste, a spot on a good paved road and near a small stream. The Town Office had asked the Kurusu Jichikai to meet on the issue, because all of the traffic generated by the plant would pass through the community and the discharge from it would enter part of Kurusu's irrigation system. The council met, and after lengthy discussion unanimously approved the project, she said, and delegated four representatives to negotiate with the company and the Town Office. The land was acquired by the town and the paperwork completed when without warning a group of Kurusu families demanded that the contract be canceled. They claimed that the Jichikai had not approved the project at all, but had only instructed its representatives to find out more about it. The representatives in turn said that they had done just as they were told, and denied any wrongdoing.

Charge and countercharge were hurled; some people had stopped speaking to others; playmates had been separated and forbidden to associate even at school; houses had been stoned and windows broken; denunciatory placards had been posted, and there was even a public demonstration against the project—"It was held right in front of the Town Office," she said, "for all the world to see." Forewarned, the newspapers and a television station had their people there, and the story broke in Takamatsu the following day. The upshot was that the project was killed, and the town government was still trying to find another place to locate the factory. Kurusu as a community was gone, she said, and to their shame all the world knew about it.*

Something was very wrong indeed. Thinking to avoid letting others know what we had heard, we sought further information about this extraordinary story from a local man of affairs, the sort of person who makes it his business to keep abreast of doings in the Yasuhara area. This man, who has since died, gave an outsider's account that was surprisingly critical of most of the parties to the dispute. From two long conversations with him, we have assembled an only slightly edited version of what he told us:

Although the town government had been trying for years to attract small-scale industry, this was not the case with Clover. They're a broiler-processing outfit, and had originally planned to put up the plant somewhere else, but the local authorities there had rejected it. The spot in Kurusu on the small stream that runs through its paddy fields must have seemed just what they were looking for. It's an excellent location because of the bridge that crosses the river from the highway at the entrance to Kurusu. Moreover, the rather small area that would be needed for the plant could be put together from four contiguous fields, one of which belonged to a Kurusu family. It must have seemed a simple

---

* It was originally my intention to write about Kurusu without dealing at all with the events that I have called the Clover affair. I did not want to embarrass anyone and it seemed best to let the matter rest. As work on the manuscript progressed, however, I became increasingly convinced that what I was doing would result in a serious distortion of the record, a kind of falsification by omission. Earlier drafts made it painfully obvious that the decision to avoid the Clover affair had forced me to ignore a development to which the people of Kurusu themselves assigned great importance, and for very good reasons. Nevertheless, had there been no sign at all of the restoration of broken ties or any indication of a continuing vendetta, I would have suppressed the story. It is precisely because I found that many people were making tentative efforts to reaffirm valued relationships and return to established patterns of interaction that I abandoned my plan to write about Kurusu as though the Clover affair had never happened. Instead, I have tried to show how resilient the hamlet has proved in the face of a grave internal threat to its survival.

enough matter for the Town Office to help the Clover company to obtain the land and the approval of the people of Kurusu.

On January 5, 1973, the company agent met with the Kurusu Jichikai to lay out the plans and to answer questions about how many people would be employed, how much additional traffic there would be, and how the plant's wastes would be disposed of. I've heard that he passed out a slick brochure depicting the operation of a similar plant. Right then and there the Jichikai selected four persons to act as its representatives, but later there was sharp disagreement as to exactly what instructions they were given. Anyway, they met with officials of the company and the town government and signed an agreement giving the project the go-ahead.

Absolutely no one was prepared for what happened next. All of a sudden several families announced that they were strongly opposed to the building of the plant. The opposition formed swiftly and organized a petition drive calling for cancellation of the contract. They delivered it to the Town Office and posted placards denouncing Clover as a polluter of the environment. As far as I know, the posters carried no personal attacks on anyone in Kurusu, but there was certainly a lot of nasty talk. Some people were saying that the representatives had been authorized only to discuss the matter further before reporting back to the Jichikai, but the representatives insisted that they had followed their instructions to the letter. Some people say that the origin of the trouble was political, and others that the company had offered insufficient compensatory payment to the community for the disruption the truck traffic would cause. Whatever the truth of the matter, very grave accusations were made by both sides and tempers flared.

Apparently some people went to extremes, and I am sure that they all regret having done so. It's not like people up here in these hills to go public on anything. They always try to cover up internal disputes. Why, one small delegation went so far as to go to Takamatsu to the prefectural office and talk to the assemblyman from the district. When the Town Office got wind of that, they sent a man down right away to explain the situation to the governor in hopes of salvaging the project. I think they talked to the Clover people, too, but unfortunately the press got hold of the story and the whole deal was finally called off. Everyone looked bad.

What do I think happened? Well, my guess is that a lot of the trouble stems from the way decisions are made in the Kurusu Jichikai. It's not very different from all the hamlet councils up here. As you know, people don't usually speak their minds in such a group, especially when there's an outsider like the Clover agent present. I doubt if anyone could really tell you exactly what happened at that meeting, although everyone is quite sure that he remembers it accurately. There is often honest disagreement over what was decided because so much is left unsaid. At least one thing is clear to me; if anyone had serious reservations about the plan he did not speak out against it at the Jichikai meeting. It looks to me as though that's where all the misunderstanding began.

They say that they've started to patch things up in Kurusu, but in my opin- ion it will take a long time before they can restore the kind of unity the place used to be famous for. I wonder if they'll ever recover. You see, what really got people upset was that the whole thing was fought out right in the open. Everyone hates that to happen. Places like Kurusu are a bit like a stage where most of the action goes on with the curtain down. But the Clover affair tore the curtain to shreds, so that everyone could look in and see exactly what was going on.

People do say that the affair is over and best forgotten, but it's unlikely that anyone directly involved will ever forget. And from what people tell me, I'd say it's unlikely that the Town Office will ever try to deal with Kurusu again. There have been many cases in Kagawa of small communities turning down really dirty industries like cement plants, but this was an unusually bad busi- ness because of all the publicity it got.

In the course of his remarks this man had referred to Clover as a polluter of the environment. The grandmother who had first told us of the affair had mentioned neither the sort of plant it was nor the prob- lem of potential pollution. Clearly her concerns lay elsewhere, but we were puzzled by her omission of what seemed to have been the crux of the matter. As it turned out, the next person we talked to had played a role in blocking the Clover project. He was very eager to tell us about it, apparently having concluded that someone in the rival faction must have been talking to us about the scandal:

There is a lot of loose talk about that business with the Clover company, and I want you to know what the real issue was. You've probably heard that one of their men asked to meet with the Jichikai. He was a smooth talker— probably used to dealing with farmers and getting pretty much his own way—but he seriously underestimated us. There were a lot of people there, including some of the young ones, and it was a very long meeting. Anyway, he made his presentation and answered a lot of questions. What they wanted to build was a broiler-processing plant, a place where they kill and dress chick- ens. He said they'd handle about a thousand birds a day. Just before we broke up he handed out a pamphlet with lots of photographs and explanations about one of their plants over on the coast.

I put it in my pocket and when I got home and found my glasses I had a good look at it. You cannot imagine what I saw. I'm not a Buddhist, but I was horrified—all that killing and blood. . . . I was quite relieved that the Jichikai had only agreed to look into the proposition, because I was sure we'd decide against it. Some time passed without any more meetings, and one day when I was over at the Town Office on personal business, I heard someone mention Clover, and found out that the papers had all been signed.

I couldn't imagine what had happened. Upset? I was so angry that I took off from work the next day and went right over to the coast to visit their plant. It was an awful place, even worse than I had thought. It turned out that its capacity was not a thousand birds a day, but forty thousand! There was a terrible stench and the river was badly fouled. Obviously, we'd been lied to. There was no way for Clover to purify the water it would discharge into our irrigation system, and the volume of truck traffic carrying live and dressed chickens and feathers and entrails would be far heavier than we'd been told. Clover would ruin Kurusu's environment and spoil it as a place to live. I went straight home and told some people about it. All the young people were upset. It was a hard job, but at least we got the thing stopped.

We were to hear many other versions of the story in the weeks that followed, each with different emphases and variation in detail. A middle-aged woman who had favored the project had this to say:

At the Jichikai meeting with the man from the Clover company, we all had questions about what the plant would mean for us. I didn't speak—if my husband had not been away, I would not even have been there—but one older man who expressed some doubts was unceremoniously told that since he would not qualify for a job anyway, he should defer to younger people who might find employment with Clover. After a very long discussion, we appointed four people to negotiate the contract. I know what some people say about that, but there is just no question about it—that's what we agreed to.

Of course they acted in good faith and they are right to feel badly about what happened. They were very angry when the contract was canceled, and accused the opposition of distorting the facts. It seems to me they did the right thing and I don't think they deserved any of the trouble they got for their pains. What kind of trouble? Well, I'd rather not say much more about it. They certainly lost face. The whole thing should have been handled differently. Personally, I wish that Clover had come in here. We need all the local jobs we can bring in. You know, it's a funny thing about the jobs. As I see it, the young people were originally all for the project just for that reason. Then they did an about-face and kept Clover out even though it meant humiliating the Jichikai representatives. I've always wondered why they shifted ground so suddenly. Anyway, I can't see that anybody gained, the way it turned out.

At last we had the story of the Clover affair, given us in several different versions by people who were parties to the events and those who had only heard about them. In the following commentary on it, we have limited ourselves to what many outsiders already know and what appeared in the newspapers, for there are some issues that need not be raised outside the confines of Kurusu. We are unsure of some details and have no corroboration of certain allegations; where we are in doubt we have remained silent.

Of some things, however, there can be no doubt. In part, the fight was between the families who had owned some farmland before the reform, on the one hand, and the former tenant families and newly emerging local entrepreneurs, on the other. The former had not been landlords, for as we have seen, landlordism here before the end of World War II was minuscule in scale. Nevertheless, the reform did precipitate a long downward slide of the families who had once rented out some of their fields and cultivated the rest themselves. As a result of the confrontation over the Clover plant, these families have hit bottom in terms of community influence, for they were on the losing side. It may well be, as more than one person suggested to us, that among the former tenants were some who seized the chance to complete the ruin of the former landowners at whatever cost.

Yet this formula is too neat. While the Clover affair did involve most of the fifteen old families and their newly appended branches, a few remained neutral, as did all of the new families in Kurusu. On the face of it, it is odd that anyone could have refused to take sides in a dispute that is alleged to involve the very future of the environment of the hamlet's residents. All of those who favored the building of the plant were ex-landowners, to be sure, but those in opposition to it were a much more heterogeneous group of ex-tenants, families that were never more than marginally involved in agriculture, and one or two who have tried entrepreneurial responses to the new rural scene of the postwar period. Like its membership, the motives of the opposition seem to have been mixed. In any event, they successfully blocked the construction of the plant.

The nature of the alignment is curious in another important respect. Ordinarily, one would expect that rural industrial development would be opposed by the former landowners, who are generally charged with being a conservative if not reactionary drag on the forces of change in the countryside. Only where they stand to profit from the direct sale of land, it is claimed, will they support such developments. Such was not the case here. On the other hand, those with little land or only marginally engaged in agriculture usually favor local industries for the additional jobs they create for the very kinds of people who need them in order to hang on at all. The reversal of roles here suggests how tangled the relationships were between the contending parties, and how mixed their motives.

The disagreement between them was fundamental, yet there is ample evidence to support the claims of both groups that they felt they were acting in the best interests of the community. It is something of a tribute to the durability of the routines that help sustain the solidary spirit of Kurusu that shortly after the demonstrators had posted the placards denouncing the Clover company, the head of the Jichikai actually made the rounds of every house in the hamlet to collect money from each family to defray the cost of the poster paper. It had been, after all, a community response, and whether one was for or against the plant, he argued, everyone was obligated to chip in. At least one person we talked to still shook with rage when he recalled that visit and his own refusal to pay.

The universal stance of those who opposed the plant is that they waged a righteous campaign to prevent irreparable damage to the environment. They claim victory over forces that would have exploited the gullibility of those who had favored the project, who for their part insist that it is quite clear that everyone lost. There is no plant and there are no new jobs. Each bitterly assails the other for the harm done to interpersonal and community relations and for the destruction of Kurusu's reputation. The place, all agree, will never be the same.

Because they think so, it never will. At one juncture in the upheaval, the head of the Jichikai called a meeting to which he did not invite four families. Such a thing had never happened before, and one man walked out when he realized why the four family heads were not there, vowing never to attend another meeting of the hamlet council. Public threats of ostracism were made in the heat of the debate. This most serious of all sanctions had not been imposed on a Kurusu family for more than forty years, and the shock was felt throughout the community (R. Smith 1961).

In an earlier day the situation would never have been allowed to go so far. Some third party from outside would have been sought out or have decided on his own to intervene. Typically such conciliatory roles were taken by former landlords, officials of local government, or other respected senior males credited with having a sense of the character of

the community and a gift for securing compromise of conflicting interests. In this case no such help was sought and none was offered. With
no restraining force at hand, most people say that everyone went too
far. All up and down the river, the residents of other hamlets know
what happened in Kurusu. None thinks the place will ever be the same,
even though tempers had cooled by the summer of 1975. As one person put it: "The wounds in old communities like this may seem to have
healed, but they break open in an instant at the first sign of stress."

Were it not for the emotional intensity of the accounts given us by
the principal figures in it, we might be prepared to argue that they
exaggerate the apocalyptic character of the Clover affair. Not one person treated the matter lightly, however, and for many it had clearly
been a devastating experience. Yet, as we have been at pains to show,
Kurusu is still a functioning community despite its trauma. Why, then,
do its residents attach such importance to the dispute?

We must remember that, for the most part, the heads of Kurusu
families have lived there all their lives, and that their spouses have
spent most of their adulthood in the community. They have attended
each other's weddings, carried their dead to the cremation ground together, helped to tide one another over in emergencies, and seen and
talked to each other on a daily basis for years. The dispute over the
Clover plant was waged with the peculiar vehemence of which only
people who have known each other for a long time are capable. It is
also likely that the very ideology of hamlet solidarity, to which the
residents of Kurusu had long publicly subscribed, proved in the event
to compound their difficulties. As Dore (1959:343) has observed:
"Competition within a group which is in theory harmoniously united
tends to become fiercer and more emotionally involved than in one
where competition is accepted as normal. As such it leaves scars after
the event in the resentful humiliation of the defeated."

There can be no secrets in such a place, nor is there room for the
development of permanent enmity. More than one person remarked
on how threatening the turn of events had seemed: "I never dreamed
that people could say such things. We'd always been close and only a
few months before we'd been discussing plans for going into growing
vegetables together. We were so upset that we actually talked about
moving away."

A younger person expressed shock at what had gone on, and while he felt that in the long run the members of his generation would be able to put the thing behind them, he was quite critical of his elders:

Those old timers are a stiff-necked lot. I'll tell you why the whole business turned into such a mess—there were a few people on both sides who decided to settle some old scores. It could have been avoided, but I doubt if anyone saw what was coming in time to head it off. Who's to blame? My feeling is that the whole problem ought to have been settled by the Town Office, but they didn't really try to do anything after they canceled the contract. I don't know why, but there's been a lot of talk.

Quite naturally others lay the blame elsewhere. One man, who assured us that he had stayed out of the affair because he thought both sides in the wrong, said:

As you know very well, we've had our troubles before, but this is the first time that Kurusu was ever so bitterly divided over an issue. I really don't know how the sides formed, but it seems to me that in the end the more vocal young people won because they are so clever with words—a lot more so than we were when we were young—and they say exactly what they think.

And one man, attempting to sum it all up, unwittingly echoed the sentiments expressed by those in the rival faction as well:

They realize now they were in the wrong, even if they won't admit it. How do I know? I can tell because just recently they have started to return my greetings when we meet on the road. Of course, I never stopped speaking to them, even when things were bad, but they used to look the other way. Why, you'd never do that even to a total stranger. It was so bad here that when my wife went to the funeral of an old woman who died during the worst of it, she was actually snubbed by people she had known for decades. It was a terrible time.

They say it's all over now and best forgotten. I'm trying to forget, but I'll never forgive them for what they did. Still, as they say, after the rains the ground hardens (*ame fureba ji katamaru*).

He used an old proverb that expresses the optimistic view that after a time of troubles, unity can be achieved once more.

A woman confessed that she was at a loss to explain how things had turned out so badly. She said: "It's hard to figure out why people didn't just sit down and discuss the pros and cons calmly and decide as a group what we ought to do. That's how we'd always done it before." She, too, thought that things had begun to improve only recently.

About two years after the Clover agent first met with the Jichikai, the head of one of the families who had favored the building of the plant had sent his daughter to ask her to come to help out at a wedding, the first since the blowup. She went, but reported that it was an unusually subdued gathering. When the married women of Kurusu assembled to meet the bride, she said, everyone was very uneasy and stiffly formal, because they were not at all sure what might happen. They carried off the occasion, but left right away rather than linger to talk after the bride had withdrawn. She added that there have been no funerals in Kurusu for the past six years, and said that no one knows what would have happened had the *dōgyō* been called on to discharge its obligations to the bereaved family during the crisis.

In July of 1975, while we were still there, the head of a family asked a man from the opposing group to come to lend a hand with some work he was doing. He went, for the first close interaction between them in more than two years, and reported that everything had gone well. Nonetheless, most people said that the Jichikai meetings are sparsely attended and the meetinghouse little used because everyone is wary of some unpleasant development.

We found that many people had given a great deal of thought to analyzing their situation, seeking explanations for what had happened. They tended to single out one factor, especially if they could see in it a specific difference between the Kurusu of an earlier day and the community now. One explanation, for example, holds that there was so much trouble because there are so few senior males, and it is true that only two men over seventy live in the hamlet. The implication is that they would have been able to effect some kind of resolution of the Clover affair before it reached the stage of confrontation and denunciation. Alternatively, it is held that these men could have called on outside arbiters to settle the matter, while maintaining the all-important appearance of unity and solidarity vis-à-vis the outside world that their generation so prized.

Another explanation, offered by some of the older men and women, is that there are simply too many adopted husbands who, being outsiders, neither know Kurusu customs well nor have any particular feeling for the place. To be sure, there have always been adopted husbands, but without the restraining presence of older Kurusu-born men, they are alleged to have pushed things to lethal extremes. A related charge is that the middle-aged residents of the hamlet are an unusually hard lot, who are far more interested in money than in preserving the sense of community.

None of these is a very satisfactory explanation, but all of them reflect interesting and instructive perceptions of the nature of the hamlet and the character of its people. Older males of probity and influence who could have moved to prevent schism, adopted husbands who as outsiders do not share in the orientations of old-time residents, and the intermediate generation of those employed full-time outside Kurusu who are charged with valuing money more than human relations—all are community residents. It was not larger forces and systemic considerations that are thought to have precipitated the clash within Kurusu. The failure, they feel, was their own, reflecting an inability to activate the safeguards that had served them so well in the past.

In part, they are right to assume the major responsibility for having let the situation get out of hand. Nonetheless, places like Kurusu do confront larger forces and systemic threats to their continued existence today, and it would be less than just to ignore their role in the Clover affair. At the heart of the matter lies the conception of community and common interest that once defined the Japanese agricultural hamlet and bound its residents to one another, and the heavy inroads that have been made into its corporate character over the past century or more. The hamlet is viewed by some of its harsher critics primarily as a feudal vestige of a discredited social system, a vestige whose demise is as desirable as it is inevitable. Others, more favorably inclined, hold that the hamlet is indeed a survival from the traditional past, and that its many good features ought to be strengthened while there is yet time. Neither position does justice to a subtle and complex form of corporate community. There are serious shortcomings to the widespread notions that the hamlet somehow embodies a mystical spirit of community and harmony and, conversely, that its members are the hapless victims of the oppressive control exercised over them by the wealthy and powerful. Both views ignore the importance of competition within the hamlet, on the one hand, and its members' willingness to mobilize to defend community interests against external threats, including those posed by the duly constituted authorities of local government, on the other.

In either event, our understanding of Kurusu's recent history will not be much advanced by romanticizing the place or, alternatively, by excoriating it for its repressive character. On balance, it seems to us that such communities as this may well have a future in rural Japan, and we are inclined to agree that "Whatever the future of the hamlet might be, its continued existence will depend on its utility to those who live in it. Moral judgments will probably not affect the hamlet's continuing existence one iota" (Johnson 1967:183).

It is this theme of utility that another observer stressed when he wrote of the period immediately following the land reform:

The democratization of the hamlet very rarely went so far as to destroy the sense of community discipline, since this would have threatened both agricultural production and the very livelihood of the farmers. The community-like nature of the hamlet served in fact as a means of alleviating, temporarily at least, the anomalies produced by the minute scale of farming operations. Without this solidarity, owner-cultivation on such a small scale was not a practical proposition [Tahara 1966:59].

But things were soon to change, particularly as the labor market expanded in the 1960's. The farmer who sought employment outside the community came to place less emphasis on solidary behavior, for the community was less and less crucial to the well-being of himself and his family. Rather, it became the place where he could grow enough rice for his own consumption while holding down a full-time job (Tahara 1966:62).

The shift in the economic base of farm-family livelihood was not the only factor leading to a decline in hamlet solidarity, for there were massive shifts in government policy toward local communities as well. The 1953 law that brought about the consolidation of the villages and towns into larger administrative units reduced the political importance of the hamlet more than any single action since the establishment of the local government system in 1889.

The chief consequence of this policy has been substantially to undermine the power of the hamlet to defend itself against outside incursions. At the same time, although it hardly seems possible, national control through the local offices of the Agricultural Cooperative has been increased. They have long handled government subsidy payments for grains and a variety of incentive grants, but in recent years many additional kinds of financial assistance to farmers have been channeled through them and they retain their stranglehold on the marketing of produce. Legally, the cooperatives deal with families or individuals, but like the governments of towns and villages themselves, they have not entirely abandoned the convenient habit of dealing directly with "the hamlet as a natural unit" (Tahara 1966:65).

The words "natural unit" are calculated to rouse the suspicions of the wary. There are, after all, natural units and natural units, and it would be a grave mistake to overlook the manifold ways in which the hamlet has been defined and redefined at the convenience of the authorities at many levels and in many contexts. For example, although the hamlet disappeared as a legally recognized entity shortly after the end of World War II, it retained much of its former importance for a very good reason:

These postwar years have been characterized by relative economic and social chaos in Japan and have, at the Occupation's behest, given rise to a peculiarly bifurcated and partially contradictory attempt to decentralize radically the structure and operations of government and, at the same time, to put into effect nationwide economic and financial programs of the complexity and dimensions of rationing and crop-requisitioning systems. The *buraku* have constituted the rural administrative termini of both these latter systems and have been most useful to the harassed village officials. Connections of this sort make up the chief administrative relationship between *buraku* and village [Ward 1951:1033–34].

We have already seen how the central government attempted to consolidate the hamlet-level Shinto shrines into a single village-wide focus of loyalty and reverence, but we have not commented on the ways in which the hamlets were repeatedly manipulated by the central government during the 1930's and 1940's. During part of that period, Kurusu and an adjacent hamlet of about the same size were merged into a single "neighborhood group" (*tonari-gumi*) in line with a national and later empire-wide effort to organize the smallest units of society into more efficient and more easily supervised units. In connection with the war effort, the 37 hamlets of Yasuhara Village were transformed into 25 units called *jōkai* without regard to traditional social boundaries. At the same time Kurusu was divided into three work-groups (*kumi*), which promptly ceased to function with the repeal of the legislation that had created them. By 1951 all of this was a memory and Kurusu had resumed its earlier dimensions.

Over the years, then, the hamlet has continued to be used administratively by local government and by the local office of the Agricultural Cooperative. But there are many occasions on which the hamlet, self-defined as an interest group, takes action as a unit. This happens most frequently in the context of disputes within the village and town councils. These are, for the most part, "conflicts of hamlet interest—over the location of a school, over the expenditure of village funds on road or irrigation works that might benefit one hamlet more than another, and so on. Issues which might divide the rich from the poor, the radicals from the conservatives, are not decided in Village Councils, but in the National Diet" (Dore 1959:341). Thus in village politics, class interests usually seem to be subordinated to hamlet interests. Indeed, it has been argued that the very requirements of life in the hamlet tend to reduce the occurrence of conflict based on class identification (Yoshida 1964).

By what mechanism are class interests subordinated to those of the hamlet? Many commentators have seen outright repression, but there is substantial disagreement on this point. It is well to remember that there can be egalitarian as well as authoritarian solidarity, and that "in part thanks to a sense of hamlet loyalty, leaders exercise authority by real and rationally given consent, not by virtue of their lineage or superior economic power, and exercise it with a sense of responsibility, and with more regard for the welfare of the poorer members of the community than one finds in most societies" (Dore 1967:xiii).

Even those who see more repression than rationally given consent do not deny that the hamlet possesses common properties and facilities, and that its members do participate in communal activities.

[Communal activities] provide the basis for an integrated hamlet life. They are looked on as property or facilities which belong to the *whole* hamlet, and communal activities are looked on as activities in which the *whole* population of the hamlet should participate. Consequently, despite differences between farming and non-farming households, or among farming households between the bigger and the lesser farmers, between the full-time and the part-time, the hamlet is nevertheless a united body [that] exercises strong restraining social pressures on every inhabitant [Fukutake 1967:93–94].

Writing some years later, this same author attempted to pinpoint the essential character of the agricultural hamlet and the origins of some of its current difficulties:

The farm settlement of the past had a design. It centered around the landlords and a class of prominent people next to them who managed production and the life of the settlement as a whole. The breakup of the landlord system, however, has made the formation of common goals difficult in a settlement whose members are divided between those engaged solely in agriculture and the promotion of farm production and those who earn additional income in other industries, farming only for their own food supply and for security in retirement. (A young or middle-aged man will plan to carry on farming after retirement from the other occupation; in the meantime, the farm work will be done by women and old people.) Also, because many nonfarm families now live in farm villages and commute to work simply because they cannot have houses in the town or city, it is difficult to unite all the inhabitants into a community within the framework of the village [Fukutake 1974:55–56].

Therefore, it is obvious that "The era when the members of a village, regardless of occupation, formed a single community and cooperated in all aspects of life, when the village itself controlled and regulated its inhabitants—that era is a thing of the past" (Fukutake 1974:57). Nevertheless, there remains the necessity for the exercise of community control over irrigation water (Eyre 1955, Shimpo 1976, Yoden 1970), and a continued emphasis on the duty of every family to share the burden of expenses by contributing equal amounts of labor, kind, or cash in support of some communal tasks. Despite the heterogeneity of the population, then, "the old-time 'village spirit' survives: the attitudes that made solidarity and tranquillity the goals of village society and that gave priority to the common interests of those living in it. Thus the village continues to emphasize communal interests over class interest" (Fukutake 1974:8).

Yet it would be foolish to maintain that every hamlet has retained its spirit, or that all of those that have come apart have been restored: "In some it is beyond restoring—particularly in large hamlets and in the central commercial hamlets of villages, or hamlets astride main lines of communication whose members have widely ramifying ties outside the hamlet. Even some Japanese are egoists, moreover, and rival factions led by irreconcilable leaders are sometimes found" (Dore 1959:342).

In the preceding chapter we discussed several issues on which the residents of Kurusu have disagreed in the past, and we have seen how community cohesion has declined in many areas of life. What made the Clover affair stand out, then, was not the dispute over a course of action but the public show of conflict resulting from that dispute. By and large, it had been the case that the residents of a hamlet would make every effort to prevent a situation from reaching the point where one faction clearly emerged victorious over another; after all, they would have to continue living with one another, and the strains engendered by such a decisive outcome would be too much for both winners and losers to bear. Furthermore, as Dore has pointed out (1959:379), "Unlike the farmers of many peasant societies, Japanese villagers are not given to feuding as a pastime. Life has to go on and compromises are reached."

And in fact, when we returned to Kurusu in 1975 just such a process was already under way, and compromises were being reached. One person told us: "You are lucky not to have come back here two years ago. I doubt that you could have dealt with the place as it was then. You'd surely have been forced to take sides." But we were not forced to take sides, for harmony or the appearance of harmony is still highly valued. People are ashamed when word gets out that the place where they live cannot manage its affairs with enough discretion to conceal disagreements from outsiders. Most of them still resent those who take what they see as essentially community problems to an outside agency for resolution, whether it be the police or some other authority, and they have not hesitated to ostracize member households who have violated the norm in this regard.

Why is harmony so highly valued? Among other pragmatic considerations, the experience of older people suggests that in a solidary community even the weak are comparatively secure, for pseudo-kinship ties serve to supplement the pool of those on whom they can call for support. When neighbors turn against one another, who can feel safe? The horizontal ties of a voluntary character are as important to those people as the vertical ties of superordination-subordination, which are so heavily emphasized in the literature on the corporate community in Japan. Of course, the former tenants were subordinate to their erstwhile landlords, but it was primarily the strength of voluntaristic, essentially egalitarian relationships that made it possible for the hamlet to withstand so many blows to its integrity for so long a period. People are sufficiently aware of the practical benefits of these relationships to be persuaded that, unless they are prepared to make the final break and move away, it is well worth nurturing them carefully and restoring those that have been ruptured.

In the case of the Clover affair, because no effort was made to mediate a settlement that might have blurred the stark clarity of the outcome, it has fallen to the people of Kurusu themselves to restore relationships as best they can. Some have tried; others take the position that the only practical response in the circumstances is to withdraw from all but the mandatory community functions. Only one thing is certain: no one wants a continuation of hostilities in this small war. It is significant, nonetheless, that not one of these proud people has ever offered an apology to another for any action taken or word spoken in anger. They have, however, begun to take up the threads of long-established relationships that still bind them firmly to one another. After all, every hamlet resident who became embroiled in the Clover affair still lives in Kurusu, and they still meet almost daily as they go about their business. Weddings and funerals are still *dōgyō* affairs as they have always been, and there are certain obligatory tasks in which all who remain in agriculture must participate. The boundaries of the community, then, define at least a minimal community of interest. And yet the older people say that they do not feel the same about their hamlet as they once did. The young, for their part, have no long history to regret, or to forget.

As much as many people regret the decline of hamlet solidarity, it is difficult to see what might happen or could be done now to alter the present situation in Kurusu. It is unlikely that Takamatsu's urban sprawl will soon reach so far into the countryside, but as its suburbs overwhelm adjacent agricultural areas Kurusu farmers will undoubtedly turn increasingly to raising vegetables, flowers, and nursery stock. Land prices probably will not rise high enough to persuade many more people to sell out, but distaste for farming—or lack of interest in it—in the next generation may well produce the same result. The town government will keep trying to stem the outflow of population, and some people are bound to return; but it is hard to imagine why anyone would stay in the remoter, more isolated areas of Shionoe Town. There will continue to be considerable interest in increasing the number of jobs available to young people locally, but not even the managers of the factories see much hope for significant new developments or expansion of current enterprises in an area such as this.

Kurusu is not alone in its fate, of course. The pressures on the small farmer in industrial societies are in many ways the same around the world. The echoes of Kurusu's situation in the following account of two Basque agricultural communities, for example, cannot be missed: "The emerging pattern appears to be of a very special nature, a kind of suburb without a city. [These are not bedroom communities but a] blend of part-time agriculture, commuter industrial employment, occasional emigration, and tourism. The resulting life style . . . is found throughout many former peasant areas of Western Europe" (Douglass 1975:191).

Yet, widespread as the problems may be, it is nonetheless tempting to ask why Kurusu in particular has given up so much. Few other hamlets up and down the river have fallen into such disarray, and in some places there have even been overt attempts to reassert hamlet solidarity and to reaffirm loyalties that had nearly been abandoned completely. But Kurusu has seen no such organized efforts; even though its people are painfully aware that they have let something slip through their hands, they seem paralyzed in the face of forces that are diluting their commitment to the continuity of community. One woman in her mid-fifties said of the situation: "And to think that I married into an agricultural hamlet with the idea that it would be a quiet and peaceful place even if the work were hard. How wrong I was!"

Was it unreasonable of her to hold such expectations, so clearly crushed by events? It was, if one takes the view that this small place simply represents the working out of great historic forces that have sealed the fate of the traditional Japanese corporate community. As farmers increasingly seek outside employment, their horizons broaden and their interest in the hamlet wanes. No longer so dependent on the goodwill and good opinion of their neighbors, and forced to mechanize their marginal operations to keep going at all in the face of a severely depleted labor force, they come increasingly to think of Kurusu as a place only to live in or to leave. The constraints of a hamlet-centered life have little appeal to the young, and their elders seem powerless to communicate to them their own sense of its value and its promise. Indeed, by their own example they have placed its most fundamental principles in jeopardy. Perhaps what has happened is that the villagers at two extremes—those who found the older system most repressive, and those who found it most rewarding—have managed to escape it entirely, leaving behind only those who lack the energy or capacity either to resurrect the system or to destroy it completely.

It seems certain that by the end of this century there will be more houses and more families, and correspondingly fewer fields, in Kurusu. Yet the further attenuation or even disappearance of the form of community that has been our central concern in this book will most likely be lamented by few. Whether the residents of Kurusu will be happier then, after another generation is gone, we cannot say; but if most of them should feel fortunate in their gains, it will be because the passing years will have dimmed their appreciation of all they have lost.

Epilogue

TRAUMATIC AS THE Clover affair was, its aftermath—including the attempt to keep me from learning about it—was in some ways heartening. Kurusu had come out of it diminished but not irrevocably divided. That outcome testifies both to the continuing utility of the community to its residents and to the continuing strength of the old affective bonds.

If we suppose for a moment that they had managed to conceal the Clover affair from me successfully, it is clear that much of what I observed and heard would have been very difficult to interpret. Would I not have assumed that the light turnout at hamlet council meetings was simply a consequence of a long-term decline of involvement with community affairs on the part of more and more people? I doubtless would have seen in the lack of visiting among certain families who were once on quite intimate terms evidence of a progressive growing apart as the labor market drew people out of the hamlet by day. Without knowledge of the conflict, I would in all probability have invented a picture of gradual decline, slow erosion, and stagnation over a generation—a period of extended decline in corporate sentiment and community spirit.

There had been decline, erosion, stagnation; the Clover affair would not have been carried to such extremes otherwise. But the severity of the fragmentation that followed was disproportionate to the gravity of the issue, with no compelling reason in the logic of things that dictated the outcome and no parallel in nearby communities. By the time of our visit, Kurusu's community spirit either had sufficiently recovered or had never eroded so far as to be beyond reviving for a special occasion, as we learned on the day we left.

On the previous day, the head of the hamlet council, one of those who had opposed the building of the Clover plant, came to invite us to a farewell party. He apologized for any possible inconvenience the invitation might cause, but was so oddly insistent that we come that we readily agreed. When we arrived at the meetinghouse on the following morning, we found to our astonishment that one adult from every family was there, except for the three new households.

We ate and drank and talked at length about the good old days, and how young we had been then, and about how much easier life is now even though everyone is so busy. We reminisced about the old work-groups, compared the vanished draft-cows favorably with the cultivating machines, lamented the eclipse of community festivals, talked about the big party that always ended the day when the hamlet households all turned out to repair the roads and paths, and once more remembered the young who had moved away and the old who had died. For a few hours it was as if Kurusu was still alive as its older residents like to remember it, and as its young people will never have the chance to know it now.

Reference Matter

Bibliography

Restudies often take a different form from the one chosen for this book. Some consist of an addendum to a reprinting of the original publication, with varying degrees of emendation in the original text; a well-known example is that of the town of Peyrane (Wylie 1957, 1964). Other restudies are entirely new works by the authors of the originals; notable examples are those describing "Middletown" (Lynd & Lynd 1929, 1937), Chan Kom (Redfield & Villa Rojas 1937; Redfield 1950), the South Indian villages studied by Epstein (1962, 1973), the two reports on the Iravas of Kerala State by Aiyappan (1943, 1965), and the Japanese community of Takashima reported on by Norbeck (1954, 1977, 1978). Sometimes the two accounts are by different authors, as in the studies of "Plainville" (West 1945; Gallaher 1961), Tepoztlan (Redfield 1930; Lewis 1951), Cunha (Willems 1947; Shirley 1971), Panajachel (Tax 1953; Hinshaw 1975), and the west of Ireland (Arensberg & Kimball 1968, Brody 1973, and the review by Gibbon 1973). This last category also includes the Japanese agricultural community of Suye Mura, which may well be the most intensively restudied village in the world. The initial account is Embree's (1939). Suye was also one of the thirteen communities included in a survey conducted during the American occupation just after World War II (Raper et al. 1950), and is the subject of an unpublished doctoral dissertation and a brief article by Yoshino (1955, 1956) and an unpublished master's dissertation (Ushijima 1958). The latter formed the basis for continuing research that led to the publication of a book-length restudy by Ushijima in 1971.

Over the years I have reported on various aspects of life in Kurusu. The most extensive treatment is *Kurusu: A Changing Japanese Agricultural Community*, my doctoral dissertation (Cornell University, 1953). A severely abridged version appears in John B. Cornell and Robert J. Smith, *Two Japanese Villages* (1956), reprinted by the Greenwood Press in 1969. The many articles in which Kurusu has figured will be found under my name be-

low. The community was also the subject of an Encyclopaedia Britannica
filmstrip, Number 8883, which utilized photographs taken in January 1958.

Aiyappan, A. 1943. Iravas and Culture Change. *Madras Museum Bulletin,*
New Series, General Section 5 (1).
―――. 1965. Social Revolution in a Kerala Village: A Study in Culture
Change. New York: Asia Publishing House.
Anonymous. 1972. Agricultural Policy in Japan. *Oriental Economist* 40
(738):8–14.
―――. 1975. White Paper on Agricultural Trends. *Japan Report* 21
(13):1–5.
―――. 1976a. White Paper Charts Changes in Society. *Japan Report* 22
(8):4–6.
―――. 1976b. More than Half Want to Work After Retirement. *Japan Report* 22 (15):8.
―――. 1976c. Planning for Food Supply Security. *Oriental Economist* 44
(788):12–14.
―――. 1976d. Farm Population Older. *Japan Report* 22 (23):5.
―――. 1977. Average Income of Company Employees Rises. *Japan Report*
23 (1):8.
Arensberg, Conrad, and Solon T. Kimball. 1968. Family and Community in
Ireland. 2d ed. Cambridge: Harvard University Press.
Armstrong, Robert C. 1912. Just Before the Dawn: The Life and Work of
Ninomiya Sontoku. New York: Macmillan.
Beardsley, Richard K., John W. Hall, and Robert E. Ward. 1959. Village Ja-
pan. Chicago: University of Chicago Press.
Befu, Harumi. 1962. Corporate Emphasis and Patterns of Descent in the
Japanese Family. In Robert J. Smith and Richard K. Beardsley, eds.,
Japanese Culture: Its Development and Characteristics. Chicago: Aldine
Publishing Company.
Bernstein, Gail L. 1976. Women in Rural Japan. In Joyce Lebra, Joy Paulson,
and Elizabeth Powers, eds., *Women in Changing Japan.* Boulder, Colorado:
Westview Press.
Brody, Hugh. 1973. Inishkillane: Change and Decay in the West of Ireland.
London: Allen Lane, The Penguin Press.
Bureau of Statistics. 1975. Japan Statistical Yearbook. Tokyo: Office of the
Prime Minister, Government of Japan.
Chang, Kenne H-K. 1970. The Inkyo System in Southwestern Japan: Its Func-
tional Utility in the Household Setting. *Ethnology* 9 (4):342–57.
Cornell, John B., and Robert J. Smith. 1956. Two Japanese Villages. Ann
Arbor: University of Michigan Press. (Center for Japanese Studies, Occa-
sional Papers, Number 5.) Reprinted 1969 by the Greenwood Press.
Donnelly, Michael W. 1977. Setting the Price of Rice: A Study in Political

Decisionmaking. In T. J. Pempel, ed., *Policymaking in Contemporary Japan*. Ithaca, N.Y.: Cornell University Press.

Dore, Ronald P. 1959. Land Reform in Japan. London: Oxford University Press.

———. 1967. Translator's Introduction. In Tadashi Fukutake, Japanese Rural Society. London: Oxford University Press.

Douglass, William A. 1975. Echalar and Murelaga: Opportunity and Rural Exodus in Two Spanish Basque Villages. New York: St. Martin's Press.

Economic Planning Agency. 1973. Whitepaper on National Life, 1973: The Life and Its Quality in Japan. Tokyo: Government of Japan.

Embree, John F. 1939. Suye Mura: A Japanese Village. Chicago: University of Chicago Press.

Epstein, T. Scarlett. 1962. Economic Development and Social Change in South India. Manchester: Manchester University Press.

———. 1973. South India: Yesterday, Today and Tomorrow. New York: Holmes and Meier.

Eyre, John D. 1955. Water Control in a Japanese Irrigation System. *The Geographical Review* 45 (2):197–216.

Friddell, Wilbur M. 1973. Japanese Shrine Mergers, 1906–12. Tokyo: Sophia University Press.

Fukutake, Tadashi. 1967. Japanese Rural Society. London: Oxford University Press.

———. 1974. Japanese Society Today. Tokyo: University of Tokyo Press.

Gallaher, Arthur. 1961. Plainville Fifteen Years Later. New York: Columbia University Press.

Gibbon, Peter. 1973. Arensberg and Kimball Revisited. *Economy and Society* 2 (4):479–98.

Goode, William J. 1963. World Revolution and Family Patterns. New York: The Free Press of Glencoe.

Grad, Andrew J. 1952. Land and Peasant in Japan: An Introductory Survey. New York: Institute of Pacific Relations.

Halloran, Richard. 1976. The Fear Is That Hard Times in Japan Will Be Permanent. *New York Times*, February 8.

Hinshaw, Robert E. 1975. Panajachel: A Guatemalan Town in Thirty-Year Perspective. Pittsburgh: University of Pittsburgh Press.

Iinuma, Jirō. 1974. The Curious Crisis in Japanese Agriculture. *Japan Quarterly* 21 (4):341–48.

———. 1976. Unfit for Human Consumption. *Japan Interpreter* 11 (2):213–15.

Ishida, Takeshi. 1971. Japanese Society. New York: Random House.

Ishiguro, Tadaatsu, ed. 1955. Ninomiya Sontoku: His Life and "Evening Talks." Tokyo: Kenkyusha.

Ishino, Iwao. 1962. Social and Technological Change in Rural Japan: Continuities and Discontinuities. In Robert J. Smith and Richard K. Beardsley, eds., *Japanese Culture: Its Development and Characteristics*. Chicago: Aldine Publishing Company.

Johnson, Erwin H. 1967. Status Changes in Hamlet Structure Accompanying Modernization. In Ronald P. Dore, ed., *Aspects of Social Change in Modern Japan*. Princeton: Princeton University Press.

Kagawa ken chō (Kagawa Prefectural Office). 1951. Kagawa-ken tōkei nenkan 1951 (Kagawa Prefectural Statistical Yearbook 1951). Takamatsu.

―――. 1952. Kagawa-ken tōkei nenkan 1952 (Kagawa Prefectural Statistical Yearbook 1952). Takamatsu.

Kato, Tsuyoshi. 1971. Generational Differences in Values and Attitudes Between Japanese College Students and Their Fathers, with Some Implications for Historical Change of Values. *Monumenta Nipponica* 26 (3/4):415–29.

Kawano, Shigeto. 1969. Effects of the Land Reform on Consumption and Investment of Farmers. In Kazushi Ohkawa, Bruce F. Johnston, and Hiromitsu Kaneda, eds., *Agriculture and Economic Growth: Japan's Experience*. Tokyo: University of Tokyo Press.

―――. 1973. Impeding Factors in the Adjustment of Japan's Agriculture. *Developing Economies* 11 (1):3–22.

Kawashima, Takeyoshi, and Kurt Steiner. 1960. Modernization and Divorce Rate Trends in Japan. *Economic Development and Cultural Change* 9 (1, Pt. 2):213–39.

Koyama, Takashi. 1962. Changing Family Structure in Japan. In Robert J. Smith and Richard K. Beardsley, eds., *Japanese Culture: Its Development and Characteristics*. Chicago: Aldine Publishing Company.

Kunimoto, Yoshirō. 1970. Rural Communities of Northeastern Japan. *Japan Quarterly* 17 (4):443–50.

―――. 1973. Deserted Mountain Villages of Western Japan. *Japan Quarterly* 22 (1):87–96.

Lebra, Takie Sugiyama. 1974. Intergenerational Continuity and Discontinuity in Moral Values Among Japanese: A Preliminary Report. In William P. Lebra, ed., *Youth, Socialization, and Mental Health*. Honolulu: University Press of Hawaii.

Lewis, Oscar. 1951. Life in a Mexican Village. Urbana: University of Illinois Press.

Lynd, Robert S., and Helen Merrell Lynd. 1929. Middletown: A Study in American Culture. New York: Harcourt, Brace and Company.

―――. 1937. Middletown in Transition: A Study in Cultural Conflicts. New York: Harcourt, Brace and Company.

Matsumoto, Y. Scott. 1962. Notes on Primogeniture in Postwar Japan. In Robert J. Smith and Richard K. Beardsley, eds., *Japanese Culture: Its Development and Characteristics*. Chicago: Aldine Publishing Company.

Misawa, Takeo. 1969. An Analysis of Part-time Farming in the Postwar Period. In Kazushi Ohkawa, Bruce F. Johnston, and Hiromitsu Kaneda, eds.,

Agriculture and Economic Growth: Japan's Experience. Tokyo: University of Tokyo Press.

Morioka, Kiyomi. 1967. Life Cycle Patterns in Japan, China, and the United States. *Journal of Marriage and the Family* 29 (3):595–606.

Morris, V. Dixon. 1973. The Idioms of Contemporary Japan, IV: *Kin no tamago. Japan Interpreter* 8 (1):124–27.

Nōgyō hakusho 1975 (White Paper on Agriculture 1975). 1976. Tokyo: Ministry of Agriculture and Forestry, Government of Japan.

Norbeck, Edward. 1954. Takashima: A Japanese Fishing Community. Salt Lake City: University of Utah Press.

————. 1961. Postwar Cultural Change and Continuity in Northeastern Japan. *American Anthropologist* 63 (2):297–321.

————. 1977. Changing Associations in a Recently Industrialized Japanese Community. *Urban Anthropology* 6 (1):45–64.

————. 1978. Country to City: The Urbanization of a Japanese Hamlet. Salt Lake City: University of Utah Press.

Ogura, Takekazu. 1967. Agrarian Problems and Agricultural Policy in Japan. Tokyo: Institute of Asian Economic Affairs, Occasional Papers Series Number 1.

Ohkawa, Kazushi. 1966. Agriculture and the Turning-Points in Economic Growth. In Seiichi Tōbata, ed., *The Modernization of Japan*, Vol. I. Tokyo: Institute of Asian Economic Affairs.

Oriental Economist. 1976. Japan Economic Yearbook 1976–77. Tokyo.

Plath, David W. 1977. Bourbon in the Tea: Dilemmas of an Aging *Senzenha. Japan Interpreter* 11 (3):362–383.

Raffles, Sir Stamford (edited by M. Paske-Smith). 1971. Report on Japan to the Secret Committee of the English East India Company by Sir Stamford Raffles, 1812–1816. New York: Barnes and Noble.

Raper, Arthur F., et al. 1950. The Japanese Village in Transition. Tokyo: General Headquarters, Supreme Commander for the Allied Powers, Natural Resources Section, Report Number 136.

Redfield, Robert. 1930. Tepoztlan: A Mexican Village. Chicago: University of Chicago Press.

————, and Alfonso Villa Rojas. 1934. Chan Kom: A Maya Village. Washington, D.C.: Carnegie Institution of Washington.

————. 1950. A Village That Chose Progress: Chan Kom Revisited. Chicago: University of Chicago Press.

Rustin, Bayard. 1976. No Growth Has to Mean Less Is Less. *New York Times Magazine*, May 2.

Sawada, Shūjirō. 1969. Technological Change in Japanese Agriculture: A Long-term Analysis. In Kazushi Ohkawa, Bruce F. Johnston, and Hiromitsu Kaneda, eds., *Agriculture and Economic Growth: Japan's Experience.* Tokyo: University of Tokyo Press.

Shikoku chihō keizai fukkō kaihatsu iinkai. 1950. Shikoku chihō ni okeru sangyō no genkyō to sono yusōryō no bunseki (Analysis of the Import-Export Situation of the Industries of Shikoku). Takamatsu: Shikoku Chihō Kaihatsu Chōsa Jisseki.

―――. 1951. Shiō shokuryoku sakumotsu tōkei chōsa jisseki (Results of a Statistical Survey of Staple Food and Major Crop Production). Takamatsu: Shikoku Chihō Kaihatsu Chōsa Sho.

Shimpo, Mitsuru. 1974. Social Change in Rural Japan. *Asian Profile* 2 (5):483–91.

―――. 1976. Three Decades in Shiwa: Economic Development and Social Change in a Japanese Farming Community. Vancouver, B.C.: University of British Columbia Press.

Shionoe-chō shi henshū iinkai, 1970. Shionoe-chō shi (History of Shionoe Town). Tokyo: Shionoe-chō Shi Henshū Iinkai.

Shirley, Robert. 1971. The End of a Tradition: Culture Change and Development in the Municipio of Cunha, São Paulo, Brazil. New York: Columbia University Press.

Smith, Robert J. 1952. Cooperative Forms in a Japanese Agricultural Community. University of Michigan Center for Japanese Studies, Occasional Paper Number 3:59–70.

―――. 1953. Kurusu: A Changing Japanese Agricultural Community. Unpublished doctoral dissertation, Cornell University, Ithaca, New York.

―――. 1956. Kurusu: A Japanese Agricultural Community. In John B. Cornell and Robert J. Smith, *Two Japanese Villages*. Ann Arbor: University of Michigan Center for Japanese Studies, Occasional Papers Number 5:1–112.

―――, and Eudaldo P. Reyes. 1957. Community Interrelations with the Outside World: The Case of a Japanese Agricultural Community. *American Anthropologist* 59 (3):463–72.

―――. 1961. The Japanese Rural Community: Norms, Sanctions and Ostracism. *American Anthropologist* 63 (3):522–33.

―――. 1974. Ancestor Worship in Contemporary Japan. Stanford: Stanford University Press.

―――. 1976. A Japanese Community and Its Anthropologist, 1951–1975. *Journal of Japanese Studies* 2 (2):209–23.

Smith, Thomas C. 1969. Farm Family By-Employment in Preindustrial Japan. *Journal of Economic History* 29 (4):687–715.

Suenari, Michio. 1972. Yearly Rituals Within the Household: A Case Study from a Hamlet in Northeastern Japan. *East Asian Cultural Studies* 11 (1–4):77–82.

Sugiyama, Koichi. 1972. Changing Agrarian Rites in a Rice-Growing Village in Northeast Japan. *East Asian Cultural Studies* 11 (1–4):58–76.

Tahara, Otoyori. 1966. Class Differentiation of Farmers and Social Structure of Farming Communities in Postwar Japan. In Paul Halmos, ed., *Japanese Sociological Studies. The Sociological Review*, Monograph No. 10:45–67.

Takane, Matsuo. 1957. Rice Culture in Japan. Tokyo: Yokendo.

———. 1961. Rice and Rice Cultivation in Japan. Tokyo: Institute of Asian Economic Affairs.

Tax, Sol. 1953. Penny Capitalism: A Guatemalan Economy. Washington, D.C.: Smithsonian Institution, Institute of Social Anthropology, 16.

Trezise, Philip H., and Yukio Suzuki. 1976. Politics, Government, and Economic Growth in Japan. In Hugh Patrick and Henry Rosovsky, eds., *Asia's New Giant: How the Japanese Economy Works*. Washington: The Brookings Institution.

Tsuchiya, Keizō. 1969. Economics of Mechanization in Small-scale Agriculture. In Kazushi Ohkawa, Bruce F. Johnston, and Hiromitsu Kaneda, eds., *Agriculture and Economic Growth: Japan's Experience*. Tokyo: University of Tokyo Press.

Ushijima, Morimitsu. 1958. Suye Mura in Transition. Unpublished master's dissertation, Atlanta University, Atlanta, Ga.

———. 1971. Henbō suru Suye mura (Suye Mura in Transition: A Fundamental Study of Socioeconomic Change). Kyoto: Minerva Shobo.

Ward, Robert E. 1951. The Socio-political Role of the Buraku (Hamlet) in Japan. *American Political Science Review* 45 (4): 1025–40.

West, James. 1945. Plainville, U.S.A. New York: Columbia University Press.

Willems, Emilio. 1947. Cunha: Tradição e Transição em uma Cultura Rural do Brasil. São Paulo: Secretaria da Agricultura. (Reprinted as *Uma Vila Brasileira: Tradição e Transição*. São Paulo: Difusão Européia do Livro, 1961.)

Wylie, Laurence. 1957. Village in the Vaucluse. Cambridge. Harvard University Press.

———. 1964. Peyrane Ten Years Later. In *Village in the Vaucluse*. Revised ed. New York: Harper and Row.

Yabe, Kazuyoshi. 1949. Kagawa no sugata (Conditions in Kagawa Prefecture). Takamatsu.

Yamamura, Kozo, and Susan B. Hanley. 1975. Ichi hime, ni Tarō: Educational Aspirations and the Decline in Fertility in Postwar Japan. *Journal of Japanese Studies* 2 (1): 83–125.

Yamane, Tsuneo, and Hisaya Nonoyama. 1967. Isolation of the Nuclear Family and Kinship Organization in Japan: A Hypothetical Approach to the Relationships between the Family and Society. *Journal of Marriage and the Family* 29 (4): 783–96.

Yoden, Hiromichi. 1970. The Village Community in Japan: The Irrigation System and the Village Community. *Kwansei Gakuin University Annual Studies* 19: 55–65.

Yoneyama, Toshinao. 1967. Kaminosho: A Farm Village Suburban to Osaka in South Central Japan. In Julian H. Steward, ed., *Contemporary Change in Traditional Societies*, Vol. II: *Asian Rural Societies*. Urbana: University of Illinois Press.

Yoshida, Teigo. 1964. Social Conflict and Cohesion in a Japanese Rural Community. *Ethnology* 3 (3):219–31.

Yoshimoto, Tadasu. 1912. A Peasant Sage of Japan. London: Longmans, Green and Company.

Yoshino, I. Roger. 1955. Selected Social Changes in a Japanese Village, 1935–1953. Unpublished doctoral dissertation, University of Southern California.

———. 1956. A Re-study of Suye Mura: An Investigation of Social Change. *Research Studies, State College of Washington* 24 (2):182.

Index

Abortion and birth control, 21, 41
Absentee landlords, 54, 73–74, 110f
Adopted husbands, 42, 55–59 *passim*,
  187, 212; and Clover affair, 239–40
Age at death, *see* Demography
Age distribution, *see* Demography
Agricultural Cooperative, 13, 64, 71–72,
  80–88 *passim*, 92–93, 99–109 *passim*,
  209, 243; and tea-processing factory,
  126; Women's Section of, 210; increasing power of, 241–42
Agricultural equipment (traditional),
  79–80, 88–93 *passim*, 108
Agricultural Experiment Station, 93
Agricultural households: ratios of full-
  time and part-time, 67–73 *passim*, 117;
  income of, 2–6 *passim*, 16–20 *passim*,
  58, 71–72, 81, 95–117
Agricultural land, 73–75; restrictions on
  disposition of, 54–55, 100–111; rental
  of, 95, 100–112; sales of, 73–79 *passim*, 189; size of fields, 74f; changes in
  use of, 38, 76–78 *passim*, 109, 133,
  246–47; consolidation of, 6, 74–75,
  83, 111; paddy and dry fields compared, 6, 77ff, 88, 109; prices for, 78,
  109–10, 246–47; abandonment of, 88,
  120; technical reasons for cultivating,
  111–12, 227–28
Agricultural Land Law, 110f
Agricultural machines, 35, 58–63 *passim*,
  71, 109, 116, 122, 134, 168f, 203;
  rotary weeders, 79; binders, 79, 84–
  86 *passim*, 90; rice transplanters, 79–90
  passim; engines and motors, 80ff, 93;
  hullers, 80–87 *passim*, 93; threshers,
  80f, 86, 93; polishers, 80, 136; tractors,

combines and reapers, 82f, 89; dryers,
  82–88 *passim*; sprayers, 82–86
  passim, 92; tillers, 82, 86–92 *passim*,
  173; brush cutters, 84–86 *passim*, 227;
  cultivators, 84–87 *passim*; straw cutters, 84–86 *passim*
Agricultural organizations, 98f
Agricultural policies, 2–3, 76, 97–102
  passim
Agricultural practices representative
  (hamlet officer), 13, 207–9 *passim*
Agricultural products: marketing of, 19,
  102–5 *passim*, 148. *See also* Barley and
  wheat; Cash crops; Crops; Rice
Agricultural roads, 18f, 127–28
Agriculture: decline of, 67–93; mechanization of, 5ff, 74–93 *passim*, 107, 112,
  129, 187–89 *passim*, 197; women and
  the elderly in, 68, 107–11 *passim*, 188,
  200; and size of farms, 69ff, 74f; capital
  investment in, 79–93; labor requirements in, 80f; subsidy programs for, 96,
  101–4; attitudes toward, 7, 108,
  187–90 *passim*; population in, 117,
  191
Ainslee, D., 13
Air conditioning, 123ff, 147f
Air travel, 8–11 *passim*, 59, 214
Alcoholic beverages: beer, 36, 58, 142–45
  passim; sake, 35, 142–45 *passim*, 157,
  220f
Alcoholism, 32
Almanac, 141–42, 155, 185–86, 214, 220
Amaterasu-ō-mikami (Sun Goddess), 153,
  178
American communities, *see under* Comparisons

American Occupation, 56, 175, 190, 242; and Shinto, 153; and educational reform, 177–78
Amphetamine abuse, 32
Ancestors, 7, 16, 29, 45–46, 111, 189; worship of, 152–65; role in weddings, 213–14. *See also* Buddhism; Graves; *O-bon*; Religion; Ritual
Ancestral altars, 136f, 153–54, 163, 229
Anthropologist: involvement with community, 1–5 *passim*, 207–8, 229–34, 250
Apartments, 61, 136–38
Armstrong, Robert C., 180
Asahi Shimbun (newspaper), 96, 108, 116ff, 149, 179, 191
Ato-tori, see Succession
Automobiles, 5–11 *passim*, 31–37 *passim*, 75, 114–16, 129–34 *passim*, 138, 147–51, 158, 165, 194–99 *passim*, 217. *See also* Commuting

Barley and wheat, 71, 99, 168f; yields and sales of, 96–100 *passim*, 131, 219–22 *passim*. *See also* Diet; Food
Basque communities, 247
Beardsley, Richard K., 151, 202
Befu, Harumi, 57, 190
Beggars, 155
Bernstein, Gail L., 187, 200
Bicycles, 26, 148f, 215
Birth, *see under* Hamlet association
Black market, 4–5, 62, 95–98 *passim*
Bowling alleys, 195
Branch family, 44f
Broadcast relay system, 17, 93, 138, 209
Buddhism, 152–65, 233; and education, 27, 155; priests, 119, 152–57 *passim*, 162–63; temple affiliation, 154; pilgrims, 155, 205; prayer groups, 203–4; funerals, 216–17. *See also* Ancestors; Graves; Jizō; Shingon; Shinshū
Buraku, see Hamlet
Buraku chō, see Hamlet association, head of
Burma, 175
Bus service, 26, 30–36 *passim*, 147–51 *passim*, 183, 197, 214
Butsudan, see Ancestral altars

Calendar, 151, 155–56, 185–86
Caloric intake, *see* Diet
Carnation greenhouse complex (*Carnation-danchi*), 19, 127ff

Carpenters, 60, 116, 120, 140ff
Cash, 95f, 116, 189, 203, 208f, 222–28 *passim*
Cash crops, 97–105, 154; fruit, 16f, 101–5 *passim*; nursery stock, 16–19 *passim*, 104–6 *passim*, 246; tea, 16f, 126; chestnuts, 17–20 *passim*, 71, 101; mushrooms, 17–19 *passim*, 71, 75f, 173; flowers, 19, 104–6 *passim*, 246; bamboo shoots, 71; tobacco, 71f, 101, 134; vegetables, 71, 102–6 *passim*, 246; cotton, 97, 101; rush for tatami mats, 101; rape seed, 101; sorghum, 101; soy beans, 101
Cemeteries, 43, 74, 158–62 *passim*. *See also* Funerals; Graves
Chamber of Commerce, 14
Chang, Kenne H-K., 140
Charcoal, 17ff, 76, 135
Chickens, 105f, 134, 157
Children's Club, 182
China, 175, 184
Chūtoku (hamlet near Kurusu), 74, 128, 133, 149, 157–60 *passim*; shops in, 14, 136, 144, 148
Civil Code, 45–46, 53–55
Clothing, 96, 116, 131, 143, 158, 170–74 *passim*, 196
Clover affair, 5, 23, 230–40; role of town office in, 230–33 *passim*, 238; recovery from, 231–38 *passim*, 246–49 *passim*
Clover broiler-processing plant, 20, 84, 250; and potential local employment, 234–36
Coffins, 216f. *See also* Funerals
Communal propery, *see under* Hamlet association
Community restudies, 1, 253–54
Community spirit, 204, 244, 249–50
Commuting, 19–24 *passim*, 36, 58–69 *passim*, 119–20, 129, 150–51, 190, 198, 211, 247
Comparisons: of Kurusu and other Japanese communities, 5–6, 81, 104–10, 137, 151, 202, 228, 244; of Japanese and British and American working classes, 11, 33–34; of American communities and Kurusu, 165; of Japan and Western Europe, 247
Conflict, 93, 98, 128, 207–11 *passim*, 224, 228–31 *passim*. *See also* Clover affair; Factions; Government, relations with Kurusu; Ostracism
Confucianism, 177–81 *passim*. *See also*

Shionoe Hot Springs Hotel, 34–37, 186, 213
Shionoe Town, 13–37; budget, 14; schools in, 26–28; agricultural households in, 71–72
Shokuba kekkon, see Work-place marriage
Shōwa period (1926 to present), 176
Smith, Robert J., 83–85 *passim,* 92, 150–54 *passim,* 178, 192, 202–4 *passim,* 229, 236
Smith, Thomas C., 68
Social class, 94–95, 111, 243f. *See also* Comparisons
Sōka Gakkai (New Religion), 152
South Pacific, 175
Standard of living, 3, 7–12 *passim,* 43–44, 113–14, 144, 197; and recreation, 33–34; immediate postwar decline in, 10–11, 58, 147–48, 184–85
Staple Foods Control Act, 100
Steiner, Kurt, 46
Stem family, *see* Family, types of
Succession, 45, 54ff, 59–65 *passim,* 81, 90, 106–9 *passim,* 153, 178, 187–90 *passim,* 200–201; and inheritance, 33, 54–55, 106, 188; housing for successor, 62–63, 139–43, 198; form of wedding for successor, 213. *See also* Intergenerational relations; Living arrangements
Suenari, Michio, 5, 162
Sugiyama, Koichi, 151
Sunday: as recreational day, 150–51, 199; as ceremonial day, 151–58 *passim,* 210–12 passim; as agricultural work day, 83–85 *passim,* 92, 188–90 *passim*
Superstitions, 160, 185–86
Suye (village in Kyushu), 151, 203

Tahara, Otoyori, 241f
Taishō period (1912–1926), 176
Taiwan, 44, 84, 148, 175
Takamatsu (capital of Kagawa Prefecture), 8, 18, 23ff, 31ff, 57, 71, 142f, 150, 163, 178, 188, 232, 246; employment in, 62–65 *passim,* 113, 120ff, 187–90 *passim,* 215; as market, 101f, 127; suburbs of, 112–13, 133, 211, 246; facilities available in, 147, 194–95, 212–13
Takane, Matsuo, 79f
Tatami (floor mats), 27, 35f, 65, 101, 134

Tax collection agent (hamlet officer), 13, 207ff
Taxes, 14, 95f, 112, 116, 121. *See also* Tax collection agent
Tea-processing factory, 26, 126
Teachers, 27–30, 178–83 *passim*
Telephone, 18, 30, 116, 138–39, 215–18 *passim*
Television, 5ff, 36, 116, 130, 135–38 *passim,* 143, 147, 165, 194, 201, 209, 229–30
Temagae, see Labor exchange
Tenri-kyō (New Religion), 152
Tenshō-daijin, *see* Amaterasu-ō-mikami
Three-Legged Race, *see* Ninomiya, Sontoku
Tochi narikin (nouveaux riches), 113–14
Tōgumi, see Shinto, sponsorship of shrine festivals
Tōishi (hamlet in Shionoe Town), 26f
Tokushima Prefecture, 34f, 42, 65, 126, 141, 147
Tokyo, 118, 158–61 *passim,* 179, 196–97
Tonari-gumi, see Neighborhood groups
Tottori Prefecture, 123
Tradition, 17, 58, 134, 141, 185–86, 192, 213, 223
Transportation, *see* Automobiles; Bicycles; Bus service; Gasoline-powered railway; Highway; Motorcycles
Tourism, 7, 17–20 *passim,* 128–29, 164, 247
Tōya, see Shinto, sponsorship of shrine festivals
Tsuchiya, Keizō, 90f
Tutelary deity, *see* Jichin-san

Undertakers, 216–17. *See also* Funerals
Unemployment, 116–17, 195
Uno (town on Honshu), 8
Ushi-gami-sama, *see* Jichin-san
Uxorilocal marriage, *see* Adopted husbands

Values, 11, 176–85 *passim,* 196–97, 245–48. *See also* Education, *dōtoku* (moral education); Intergenerational relations
Violence, 4

Wages and salaries, 33–34, 87, 97–100 *passim,* 108–9, 113–21 *passim,* 129, 149, 179, 228; bonus, 113–19 *passim,*